Creative PROFESSIONALS PRESS™

ADOBE PAGEMILL 3

f/x and design

DANIEL GRAY

Adobe PageMill 3 f/x and design

Limits of Liability and Disclaimer of Warranty

Trademarks

The Coriolis Group, Inc.
An International Thomson Publishing Company
14455 N. Hayden Road, Suite 220
Scottsdale, Arizona 85260

602/483-0192
FAX 602/483-0193
http://www.coriolis.com

Library of Congress Cataloging-In-Publication Data
Gray, Daniel, 1961-
   Adobe PageMill 3 f/x and design/by Daniel Gray.
      p.   cm
   Includes index.
   ISBN 1-57610-214-9
   1. Adobe PageMill.   2. Web sites--Design.   I. Title.
TK5105.8885.P34G73   1998
005.7'2--dc21   98-6834
                                              CIP

Printed in the United States of America
10 9 8 7 6 5 4 3 2 1

Publisher

Keith Weiskamp

Acquisitions

Stephanie Wall

Project Editor

Michelle Stroup

Production Coordinator

Jon Gabriel

Cover Design

Anthony Stock

Layout Design

April Nielsen

CD-ROM Development

Robert Clarfield

an International Thomson Publishing company

Albany, NY • Belmont, CA • Bonn • Boston • Cincinnati • Detroit • Johannesburg
London • Madrid • Melbourne • Mexico City • New York • Paris • Singapore
Tokyo • Toronto • Washington

ABOUT THE AUTHOR

Daniel Gray is a journeyman designer/author and has written for a number of graphics and Web-related publications. He is the author of *The Photoshop Plug-ins Book* and *Web Publishing With Adobe PageMill 2,* and co-wrote *The Official Palace Tour Guide* and *The Comprehensive Guide to CorelWEB.GRAPHICS Suite* (all by Ventana), among other books in the computer and graphic arts fields. His best-selling *Inside CorelDRAW!* (New Riders), now in its sixth edition, has been translated into Chinese, Greek, Portuguese, Dutch, and Italian.

ADOBE
PAGEMILL 3
F/X AND DESIGN

ADOBE
PAGEMILL 3
F/X AND DESIGN

ACKNOWLEDGMENTS

I'd like to thank everyone involved with this book. There's no better place to start than with the Coriolis Group. I've been blessed with a wonderful crew, including: Keith Weiskamp, Stephanie Wall, Michelle Stroup, Chuck Hutchinson, Jon Gabriel, Robert Clarfield, and all the folks in production and marketing. I've been penning design books for close to a decade, and this one shapes up to be the best-looking of all.

To all the developers that kindly allowed us to include their software on our boffo CD-ROM, in particular: Melissa Worthington at Worthington Software Engineering; Terry Morse at Terry Morse Software; Kevin Bromber, John Halloran, and Gary Cartwright at 3D Planet; Shelly Hayduk at Natrificial Software; Michael Herrick at Matterform Media; Nancy Congdon and Foy Sperring at Interleaf; Mark Craemer at InfoAccess; Shayne Jolie at AutoF/X; and Paul Whitelock at Modern Minds. And to David Adams at Open Market (formerly ICentral) for setting us up with a ShopSite store.

To the folks at Adobe who helped make this possible: Bruce Bullis, Brian Kusler, Kelly Davis, Loni Singer, Roger Spreen, and the entire PageMill engineering, support, and marketing team.

Hats off to the designers whose beautiful work is featured in the "PageMill Sites Done Right!" color gallery: Laura Diemert, Jason Bramer, Bob Staake, Enzo Borri, Douglas Ladendorf, and Julian Matthews. For PageMill help online, be sure to check out the PageMill-Talk email list at http://www.blueworld.com/lists/pagemill-talk/.

To my long-time partner in editorial crime, John Shanley, many thanks for your diligent tech editing efforts.

As always, my family has been wonderfully understanding throughout the process. To Debbie, for those 5:00 a.m. cups of coffee; to Colt, for his expert help in photographing his cool car collection; to Allie for understanding why she had to wait to use the Mac; and heck, even to my Mom (pain in the neck that she is), for teaching me to read at a ridiculously young age.

And to you, my readers, my heartfelt thanks. May this book pay for itself many times over.

Cheers,
Daniel Gray
Somewhere in the swamps of Joisey
April 23, 1998

ADOBE
PageMill 3
F/X AND DESIGN

TABLE OF CONTENTS

ADOBE
PAGEMILL 3
F/X AND DESIGN

INTRODUCTION

Rest assured. You've chosen the right tool (and the right book). Adobe PageMill 3 is your best choice for Web page creation. Whether you're building Web sites for a living, or for your brother-in-law's carpet store, this little program delivers the goods. *Adobe PageMill 3 f/x and design* will enable you to build great Web sites by quickly teaching you the ins and outs of site design and PageMill, alike.

PageMill is a beautiful thing. As powerful as the program is, it's both easy to learn and easy on your budget. With PageMill, you'll quickly create high-quality Web sites in a fraction of the time that it would take to generate the Hyper Text Markup Language (HTML) code by hand.

Of course, PageMill is not the be-all-end-all. There's lots of competition out there. If your design and technical skills progress to a high level, you'll be enticed by tools such as Macromedia DreamWeaver, GoLive CyberStudio, and NetObjects Fusion. Keep in mind, however, that PageMill sells for just a fraction of the cost of these programs and can accomplish most of your Web page needs.

The PageMill 3 box contains the majority of the software that you'll need to build your Web site. Version 3.0, a dramatic improvement over version 2, melds the Web site management tools of Adobe SiteMill into PageMill, and gives you the means to edit images with Adobe Photoshop LE.

A Little PageMill History

PageMill made its first showing at Macworld Boston, in early August 1995. The Macintosh community immediately embraced the product, with none other than Apple Fellow (and perennial pundit) Guy Kawasaki heralding it as "the PageMaker of the Internet." The tiny booth of PageMill's original developer, Ceneca Communications, was constantly packed five and six deep with enthusiastic showgoers.

The attention was well deserved. At long last, there was a product that allowed mere mortals to build classy pages for the World Wide Web. Kawasaki and other Mac mavens were, no doubt, ecstatic that such an application had arrived first on the Macintosh platform. For if 1967 is best remembered for its Summer of Love, some might remember 1995 best for its Summer of Windows 95 Hype. The Macintosh needed a "killer app" and PageMill happened at just the right time.

I'M STILL USING PAGEMILL 2, CAN I USE THIS BOOK?

Absolutely! Adobe PageMill is similar enough from version 2 to version 3. By purchasing this book, you'll get up to speed with PageMill 2 and be ready to rock with PageMill 3.

Adobe Systems was quick to react. The company moved to acquire Ceneca just a month or so after PageMill's triumphant debut. Adobe rushed PageMill 1 to market, releasing it on October 31, 1995. The program was sold and delivered over the Internet, with packaged software following soon afterward. In its first month of release, Adobe reportedly shipped a hefty 30,000 copies, ensuring a rapid return on its wise investment. Adobe never released a Windows version of PageMill 1.

The Macintosh version of PageMill 2 was released in late 1996. The first Windows version followed in the spring of 1997. Although version 2 sold respectably, Microsoft's FrontPage97 quickly grabbed a sizable share of the market for Web design software. With PageMill version 3, however, Adobe has taken off the kid gloves. While PageMill 3 ignores high-end Web trends such as Dynamic Hypertext Markup Language (DHTML) and Cascading Style Sheets (CSS), it gets the job done.

Who Needs This Book

Adobe PageMill 3 f/x and design is intended for the intermediate PageMill user who is not a techie; it has been designed to get users up and running in nothing flat. The potential audience for this book is huge and surely includes:

- Graphics designers

- Multimedia developers

- Technical documentation specialists

- Teachers and students

- Business owners

- Advertising agency folks

- Public relations pros

- Marketeers

- Webmasters (fledgling and otherwise)

...and even hobbyists!

How This Book Is Organized

We start off in Chapter 1, by looking at what you hope to accomplish with your Web site. Planning *before* you publish saves time and heartache. We'll talk about what you want to do before you set out to do it.

Chapters 2 and 3 get you rolling with all of the basics of Web page text and graphic design. These chapters lay the groundwork for the rest of the book.

Chapter 4 launches you into the realm of professional Web page design with multi-column tables. Chapter 5 proves that frames aren't as complicated as you might think (unless you build them that way). Chapter 6 gives you the preparation you need to create forms and interactive pages with the best of them. Chapter 7 shows you how to deliver excitement with time-proven tools, including GIF animation, Java, JavaScript, and Shockwave. Once you've been through these first seven chapters, you'll be able to walk the walk, and talk the talk.

However, once you've built your Web site, your work is only half done. Chapter 8 provides the lowdown on attracting visitors. Chapter 9 clues you into file transfer and site maintenance issues. Chapter 10 is an essential read for Web developers that want to create Web storefronts. You'll learn how ICentral ShopSite Express can be used to deliver up-to-the-minute information via the Web.

Chapter 11 explains how PageMill 3 adds extensibility via application plug-ins (à la Photoshop) and Adobe Acrobat Portable Document Format (PDF) files. For up-to-the-minute information on plug-ins, be sure to check out the *Adobe PageMill 3 f/x and design* Web site at www.geekbooks.com.

Want to see what your peers are up to? The color section delivers a gaggle of great PageMill-created sites from around the world.

SO WHAT'S ON THE CD-ROM?

The CD-ROM features a host of demo software, slick Java applets, and cool graphics, , as well as the files that support the exercises in this book. We've even included some bonus chapters from the predecessor to this book, *Web Publishing With Adobe PageMill 2.0.*

MAC PAGEMILL NOTE

With PageMill 3, Adobe chose to ship the Windows version months before the Mac version. While this is a cross-platform book, it was written using the Windows version of PageMill. Adobe software is typically feature-consistent across platforms. Mac fans should dig this book, regardless of how the screen shots appear. We made a concerted effort to provide pointers, tips, and software for both the Windows and Mac versions. Once again, we'll cover any changes online at www.geekbooks.com.

Dan's Philosophy On How Computer Books Should Work

I'm not yet another swelled head Web author (YASHWA). I'm not a professor, nor a high-priced designer. I'm not some pompous windbag with an agenda. I work in the trenches.

It's my goal to provide a premium experience for my readers. I want each book I write to be the best book on the subject and I strive to provide maximum value. Fun is at the core of my game plan; I have fun writing these books, so that you'll have fun learning from them.

This field is constantly changing. Often, right after we put a book to bed, an important new development crops up. I'm committed to providing online updates to this book via my personal Web site: www.geekbooks.com. The next time you're out clicking around, please stop by our little corner of the Web.

Hardware And Software Requirements

It's even possible to create pages on a machine without an Internet connection. There's no inherent need to be hooked up to a corporate network or even an Internet Service Provider (ISP) while creating pages. Road warriors can create Web pages while on the go, whether they are at a remote site or at cruising altitude. Once your pages are looking good, you can plug in, log on to the Net, and beam 'em up.

And although this book doesn't provide a copy of PageMill, it does include just about everything else you will need to create exciting, effective Web pages.

Fire Up The Mill!

Since its introduction in 1995, PageMill has represented the best Web page creation application for novices and professionals alike. Together with a copy of the program, this book will help you to create awesome, effective Web pages in record time. By the time you finish Chapter 2, you'll be tagging text and hyperlinking like a pro. So without further ado, let's get down to business and fire up the mill!

TAKING THE SITECENTRIC DESIGN APPROACH

1

In this chapter, you'll assess your goals, review resources, and plan the framework of your Web site.

"Sitecentric," you ask, "what does that mean? Is this all just another load of design book hooey?" In a word, nope. Sitecentricity is more than just Web *page* design. It's about designing great Web *sites*.

When you embark on your quest to design a Web site, strive to conceptualize the site as a whole. Envision the entire site by looking first with blurry eyes. After the shimmering outline of the site is in view, you can begin to squint, bringing the specific sections, features, and pages into view.

Think of yourself as an architect. Your clients have invited you to design their dream house on a special lot. You need to assess the lay of the land, determine the needs of your clients and their visitors, and develop a scheme to bring that dream house to reality.

"So what does being an architect have to do with Adobe PageMill 3?" you may ask.

In short, Adobe PageMill 3 provides the means to work with entire sites. This chapter will help you to assess your goals and set realistic expectations, and will provide a solid footing for you to build your Web site. As you progress through this book, you'll gain a thorough understanding of how PageMill fits into the Web site design, production, and maintenance cycle.

PageMill is only a tool, a means to an end. The most powerful tools are those that become transparent—those that provide a harmonious expression of the designer's vision.

What Do You Hope To Accomplish?

The first general question to ask yourself is "What do I expect this Web site to do?" You should consider this from two points of view: that of the folks who "own" the Web site and that of the visitors.

Who Are Your Clients?

Identify your clients. Learn what they do, how they do it, and why they do it. Their Web site's success is dependent on your understanding their specific goals and general philosophy.

Professional Web site designers deal with either *internal* or *external* clients. Internal clients are entities within a designer's organization. External clients are people or organizations that have hired the designer as an independent contractor or service provider.

Small-business owners often design their own Web sites. Acting as both the client and the designer, these people have a tough but rewarding job. Objectivity can be one of the most difficult aspects of these dual responsibilities, although complete control can be fulfilling.

Who Are You Trying To Attract?

In a commercial Web site, the main audience typically consists of either *consumers*, *business-to-business customers*, *channel partners*, or *employees*. A big corporate site might encompass all these audiences:

- *Consumers*—Marketing your wares to Joe Public? Keep your message simple, but make sure that it's engaging.

- *Business-to-business customers*—Does your company concentrate on direct business-to-business sales? Provide the information your customers need on which to base their purchase decisions.

- *Channel partners*—Does your company sell through channels? Make sure your marketing materials and contact information are available online.

- *Employees*—Have you thought about providing information on a corporate intranet? Using the Web is an ideal way to provide human resources support, such as benefit forms and other materials.

Plan for that audience. Give them information that they need, without delivering an extraneous message. You also should accommodate the needs of the press and investors (if your clients are publicly traded entities).

What Should The Site Provide?

When you're deciding what your site should provide, you really need to think from the visitors' perspective. What would get them interested in coming to your site? Is it just information? Is it some kind of trinket, whether real or virtual? Take the time to make a list of what you think your visitors are looking for. Have your clients do the same. Then ask a handful of actual customers.

What Are Your Resources?

Be honest with yourself as to what you can accomplish. If you want a cutting-edge design but lack the talent to devise or execute that design, you'll need to allocate the appropriate resources. The three general types of resources are *copy*, *design*, and *mechanics*.

INTRANET

An *intranet* provides internal Web resources within an organization. These resources are not open to the world at large. Controlled access from outside the company network may be provided through a password-protected gateway.

- *Copy*—Are you a wordsmith? If you don't have the proper writing skills, find someone who does.

- *Design*—Can't design your way out of a paper bag? Hook up with an artist who can.

- *Mechanics*—Dreaming of Java goodies and CGI scripts? If you have the experience or time to learn, that's cool. If not, team up with a pro.

Are You Experienced?

Something can be said for time in the saddle. Whether you're riding a horse, building a house, or designing a Web site, experience matters greatly. I'm not saying that you can't design a great Web site without having designed 10 great Web sites before. The time you take to research and tweak your site design will benefit the end result.

Who Can You Drag Into The Fray?

If you can't hack it alone, bring in some help. A division of labor between the right individuals will yield wonderful results. If you have the right people in your organization or have other buddies you can rely on, you're ahead of the game. If not, you should look outward for help. Compile a list of resources on which you can draw.

Who Rules The Land?

The manner in which your site grows depends on your vision and vigilance. Will you plan for your site to grow in a centrally planned manner, like Walt Disney World, or in a helter-skelter manner, like Las Vegas? The manner in which the site grows is controlled by many factors, including these:

- How much control do you have? Will you have final say?

- Does your site have a guiding force, or are there multiple agendas?

- Will the site be subject to the whims of the market? If the site needs to change at the drop of a hat, you'll need to plan for that flexibility.

It's My Site And I'll Do What I Want To

Where do you fit into the hierarchy of control? If the site *belongs* to you, you're in the clear. You can make the decisions; success or failure depends entirely on your actions. This responsibility can bring great rewards. No matter what happens, you are responsible. If the site succeeds, you're the hero. If the site fails, you take the blame.

A solo flight can provide a wonderful sense of achievement. It can also be a harrowing journey through a storm-filled night.

Team Up

On larger sites, a team-based approach makes great sense. Breaking down a site into tasks and responsibilities can build on the strengths of the individual members.

The right person using a strong yet flexible leadership can effect a more cohesive unit. An overly committee-driven approach can lead to dilution and disarray. Of course, if the *wrong* person takes the strong hand, you may not be able to vote the mayor out of office.

The person in charge should understand not only the purpose and goals of the site, but also the mechanics. This knowledge is not gained overnight. You can't say to your boss, "Go read blah blah's book on Web design," and expect your boss to come away from the experience wiser for reading that book.

Budgeting Time And Resources

Have you ever done any home improvement work? If so, you've probably learned to be honest with your estimates. Take a solid assessment and add 50 percent (or so) for a margin of error. Building a Web site always seems to take longer and cost more than what you initially expect. Just like renovating a house!

Plan *Before* You Publish

What if you've already started building your site? Take a drive out of town. Stop to get an ice cream cone. Then, turn around and look at your skyline. If you need to bring in the demolition crew, doing so may be easier *before* the entire site is built.

Target Your Audience

Effective Web site designers understand the wants and needs of their audience. First, you capture the interest of your audience. Then you must deliver what they need (which isn't always, for your purposes, exactly what they *think* they want) in an engaging and orderly manner. Balancing the needs of the audience and the site sponsor can be tricky. After all, Web sites, for the most part, are not altruistic endeavors—no matter how warm and fuzzy they make the visitor feel.

Content Is King

One Web site design principle you'll hear over and over is that *content is king.* People come to your site in search of the information it provides, not for its great design. They might come back to an attractive but empty site once to show a friend how cool it looks, but they will return to an informative site repeatedly. In the Web world, as throughout the entire Internet, steak matters far more than sizzle.

Your first task is to determine what information your audience is looking for. You must look coldly at your site from your visitors' perspective. Then you must take stock of the resources at your disposal and figure how you can use them to provide the content your audience demands.

Your organization—large corporation or small hobby group—possesses a lot of information. This information may be on paper, on computer disks, on videotape, or only in the minds of you and your cohorts. Supply and demand both dictate the information that will be available on your site. If the information your audience demands exists in another form, repackage it. If the needed information doesn't exist in usable form, create it. If you can't create it for whatever reason, set up a hyperlink (as you'll learn in Chapter 2) to another Web site that has it.

When you embark on your site-building journey, try not to start with a predetermined design in mind. Stay focused on the information your audience needs, not on how you think your site should look. I don't mean to say that design is irrelevant to the success of your site. On the contrary, design has a great deal to do with its success. A clear, concise design enables visitors to get at the good stuff with just a few clicks of a mouse. A complex, dense design can boggle the users' minds and lead to frustration. Like the best designs of any type, the form of your Web site should follow its function.

Design Your Site Around Its Content

Keep in mind that your responsibility as a Web site designer is akin to that of an architect. You must design the overall layout of your Web site so that visitors can find what they need quickly. When visitors land at your front door, you want to greet them warmly and provide a floor plan of your site. Don't let the first doors your visitors encounter be those leading to closets, basements, or boiler rooms.

If your most important content is in the kitchen, make sure all visitors can get there immediately from your front door. You must not expect your Web site guests to click happily away until they find what they're looking for. Because many cyberspace explorers aren't sure what they're looking for, you must provide a place where they can find *everything*.

Think about the grand old department stores. (If you've never had the pleasure of experiencing one, check out the movies *Miracle on 34th Street* or the Marx Brothers' *Big Store*.) At the elevator entrance, a friendly operator greeted shoppers and announced what they would find on each floor. Your Web site should have a central lobby, with self-service escalators to specific departments for the folks who already know where they're headed. You also should design an elevator with a friendly attendant to help other visitors quickly locate what they seek.

Planning The Framework

Let's think about the home-building metaphor again. If Web sites are houses, Web pages are the individual rooms. Planning carefully during the "blueprint" phase is important, and PageMill 3 enables you to knock out prototypes easily. Sketch out some floor plans. Build some rough test pages. Get a feel for the flow—don't get involved with minute design issues at this point. See what it's like to move from room to room. Optimize the interaction between pages.

What's The Navigational Orientation?

The *navigational orientation* of your Web site greatly influences the *shape* of your Web pages. The three basic types of navigational orientation are *top*, *side*, and *bottom*. These schemes can be implemented with either text or graphics links and in either framed or unframed windows. Figures 1.1, 1.2, and 1.3 demonstrate these basic navigational schemes.

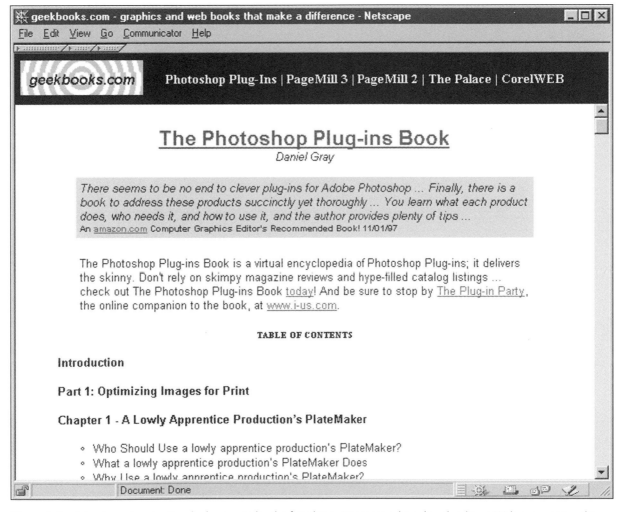

Figure 1.1 A top-based navigational scheme can be the first thing visitors see when downloading a Web page. Using this scheme, visitors can quickly and easily jump to another page.

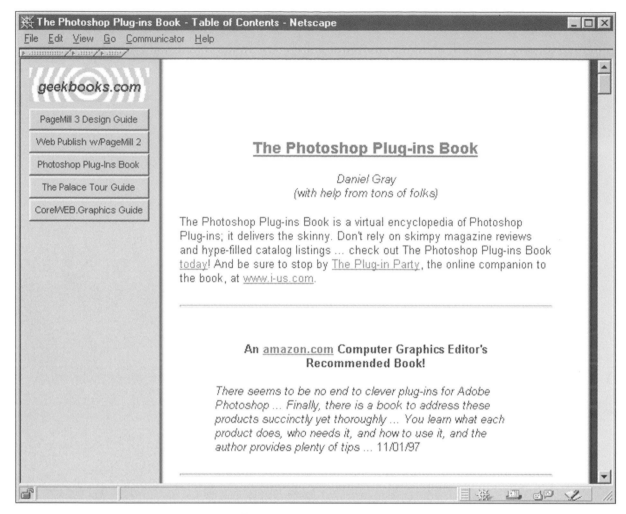

Figure 1.2   A side-based navigational scheme forces you into creating a table-constrained page layout. We'll cover tables in depth in Chapter 4.

Framed layouts have a distinct advantage over unframed layouts, in that the navigational elements are persistent. In a well-constructed framed layout, the navigation never scrolls out of view. Frames also make combining navigational schemes practical. We'll discuss the pros and cons, the where-tos, the what-fors, and the how-tos of creating a framed layout in Chapter 5.

Provide A Site Map

An effective *site map* provides the same level of assistance as a friendly elevator attendant. A good site map enables viewers to find the information they seek at a glance.

Developing a site map is a good way to optimize the effectiveness of your Web site. You can follow several approaches to displaying a site

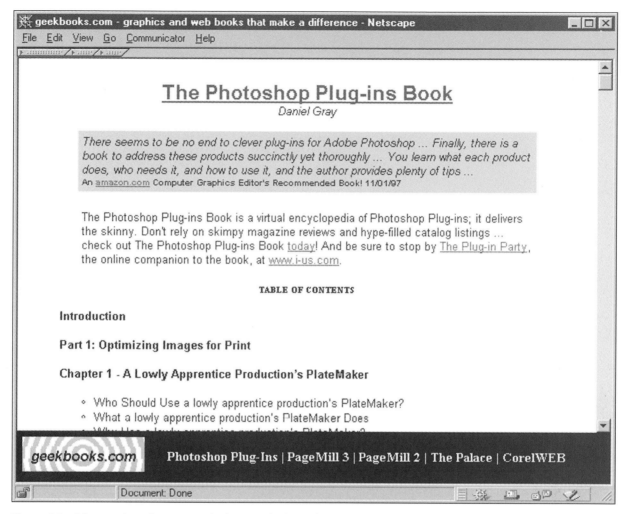

Figure 1.3   A bottom-based navigational scheme is the least obtrusive, although it forces the visitors to scroll all the way through a long page (unless you've put the navigation into a bottom frame, as shown here). Bottom-based text navigational schemes are often used in conjunction with top- or side-based graphic navigational schemes.

map, but one key is to provide both graphics and text routes through your site. Figures 1.4 and 1.5 show routes to allow fast site access for both high- and low-bandwidth browsers. Those lucky folks who can download the elevator panel image map quickly over a corporate network or speedy cable modem will enjoy the playful graphics. And those with slow modem connections should be satisfied with the slim and trim linear text directory. If this description all sounds a little confusing, don't worry. We'll delve further into the concepts of browsers and bandwidth later in this chapter.

As you design your Web site, you should aim to move folks through so that they see what you want them to see and do what you want them to do. Your Web site has a purpose, be it commercial or fun. Make sure

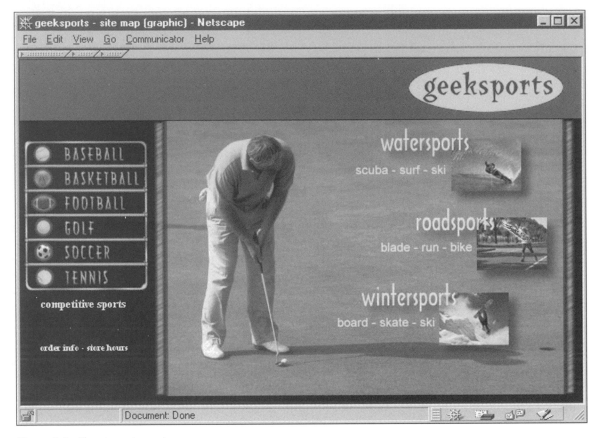

Figure 1.4   Elevator going up!

that the value you receive and the value your visitors receive are equal. The following are some ideas to help you achieve that goal:

- If your goal is to build a mailing list and qualify sales leads, give visitors a compelling reason to offer their names, addresses, and other pertinent demographic information.

- If your goal is to sell products online, make sure the mechanisms to do so are in place and your products are presented in the best possible manner.

- If all you intend to do is build brand identity, your job is easier. Your primary purpose probably is not to have visitors give you anything but to have them feel good about you and your product.

Keep It Simple And To The Point

If you must err in your Web site design process, you should always err in favor of simplicity. A complex design—besides being harder for the visitors to deal with—is usually harder to create and maintain. A simple, elegant design lets the content shine without getting lost in a

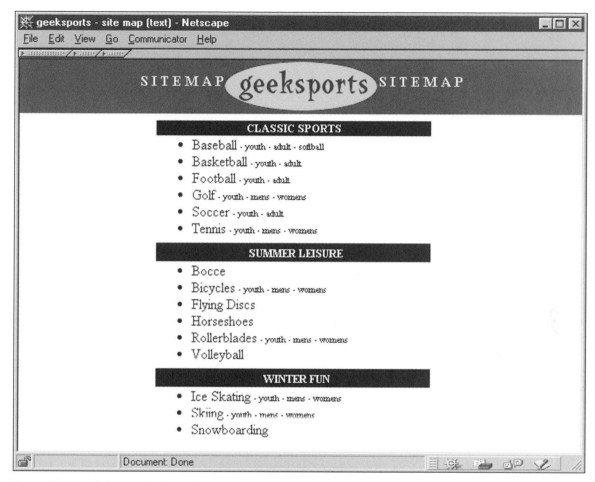

Figure 1.5 Text links provide the quickest way to navigate through a Web site.

hackneyed presentation. Speed and readability should always be paramount. Keep these points in mind:

- Use consistent, limited-palette color schemes for backgrounds, graphics, icons, and buttons.

- In general, use solid color backgrounds or skinny background tiles. Save those wild seamless tiles for special pages.

- Don't use more than one or two animated images per page. Avoid the carnival midway look.

Streamline Navigation

When the Beach Boys' Brian Wilson wrote "I Get Around," back in the early sixties, never in his wildest dreams could he have imagined that the song would become a Web surfing mantra. The whole idea of using the Web is to get quickly from one place to the next without "getting bugged driving up and down the same old strip." If you fail to

TINY TEXT
NAVIGATION BARS

If you set your text navigation bars with the Smallest Heading format, you'll get a nice, unobtrusive look that you can easily implement across your Web site.

provide a smooth navigational interface, your visitors are likely to go off in search of a whole new Web site where the pages are hip.

When you design your navigational features, you should keep them consistent throughout the Web site to the greatest extent possible. Take a gander at "the electronic feedbag" example. Figures 1.6 and 1.7 demonstrate two different ways to implement a horizontally oriented navigational scheme. Figure 1.6 was built from five separate (yet gawky) GIF buttons, with one button swapping out each time visitors hit a new page (to convey a "dimmed" appearance for that page's button). Figure 1.7, on the other hand, uses only two GIF images for the entire Web site. The pointer bounces around as the visitors move from page to page.

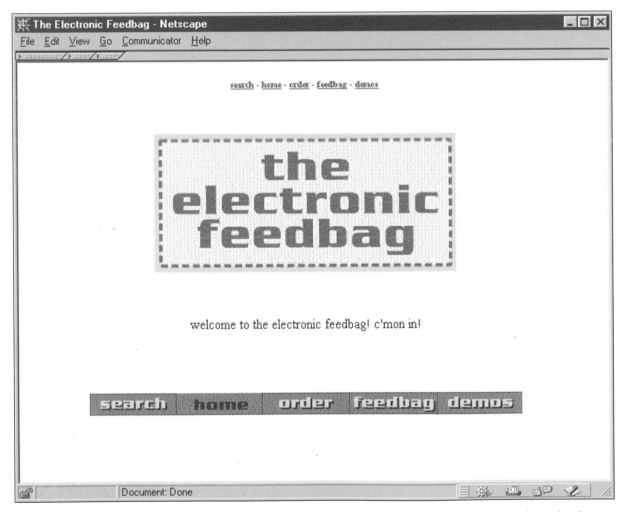

Figure 1.6 This approach uses five GIF images on each page, for a total of 10K. In addition, a new button has to be downloaded with each page.

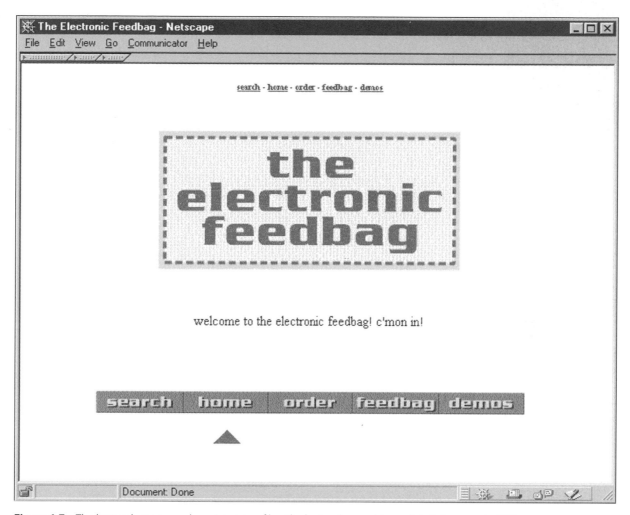

Figure 1.7   The button bar approach uses just two files (the button bar and the pointer), for a total of 8K.

Although these two examples may look similar, using the second method poses a definite advantage. The composite button bar and pointer download only once. This scheme should be incrementally faster for the visitors when downloading the first and subsequent pages. The fewer the connections that the browser and server have to negotiate, the faster the download. The pointer moves from position to position through the use of fixed-width tables. Reusing navigational graphics is a great (and free) way to speed up your site.

The following are some tried-and-true ways to help ensure that your Web site visitors find their way around your cyberplace with ease:

- *Use a consistent navigational interface.* Don't throw your visitors any curveballs. After they've plowed through several of your pages, they've established a pattern in their minds. You don't want to

NAME YOUR DOMAIN

A named domain, such as *mycompanynamehere.com*, helps to set your Web site apart. You can register the name yourself, or your Internet Service Provider (ISP) can register your name for you. Check out http://rs.internic.net/faq/index.htm for the InterNIC FAQ.

undo it. Establish a consistent navigational interface and maintain continuity. Avoid changing your icons midstream, and don't mix your graphical metaphors.

- *Always use a text navigation bar.* Use this navigation bar in addition to a graphic navigational interface. Some folks like to cruise the Web at high speed, with the graphics turned off. If your site has only image map or other graphic navigation, you'll invoke the wrath of these visitors.

- *Stay simple, straightforward, and obvious.* Don't be seduced by way-cool, overly complicated schemes. Navigation has to be instantly comprehensible. Your visitors shouldn't have to figure out how to cruise your site.

Location, Location, Location

No doubt you've heard the tired adage about the three most important factors in purchasing real estate: "Location, location, location." It works pretty much the same way on the Web. For maximum value, you should name your site succinctly and make sure that everyone who needs to find it can find it.

What Will You Name Your Site?

The name of your Web site is important. It should be both definitive and memorable. The site name should be repeated on every page, within the title field. Page titles are a primary means of search engine indexing. If you take a lax or inconsistent approach to titling your pages, you will shortchange your Web site listings. In the next chapter, you'll learn how easily you can add a title heading.

Where Will Your Site Reside?

Is your Web site going to be hosted on someone else's server, or will it be hosted internally, within your organization? Both scenarios present pros and cons. Generally, an external server will consume the least amount of resources (both human and monetary), whereas an internal server will allow for the most control.

Setting Up A Virtual Domain

Putting your Web site on someone else's server is the most painless way to go. In fact, the vast majority of Web sites run on Internet Service Provider (ISP) servers. The best service providers use high-powered Unix servers with network technicians on hand 24 hours a day, 7 days a week (24/7); they'll also have multiple T3 connections to the Internet.

A good ISP can get your server ready within a day's time. Many ISPs offer the convenience of online registration forms. You'll typically pay a setup fee of $50 or so to start the account, along with the first month's (or months') charge, up front. The ISP should submit your domain name registration to Network Solutions (the company that administers domain names in the United States) for you. Network Solutions will bill you separately for $100, to cover the first two years' worth of domain name registration.

Registering your domain name will take a few days to a week (in some cases, it could take even longer). In that time, you can usually access your server via its numeric IP address (for example, 000.000.000.000). After your domain name is registered, *propagating* it across the Internet's domain name servers (DNS) can take a while. The DNS maps *yourdomainnamehere.com* to their numeric IP addresses; so, when someone enters "yourdomainnamehere.com" into their browser, the DNS will point them at your server.

Be wary of ISPs that boast outrageously low prices. You'll get exactly what you pay for.

Running Your Own Server

Do you have a great MIS department and an Internet connection at your disposal? If so, you may be considering running your own Internet Web server. Or perhaps you're planning an intranet site. Either way, you'll need to find the right software.

The subject of running a server goes way beyond the scope of this book. Nonetheless, here's a list of some of the most popular server software solutions:

- Apache HTTP Server: Unix, Windows NT, and Windows 95
  http://www.apache.org/

- Apple Personal Web Sharing: Macintosh
  http://www.apple.com

- Microsoft Internet Information Server: Windows NT
  http://www.microsoft.com

- Netscape FastTrack Server: Netware, Unix, Windows 95, and Windows NT
  Netscape Enterprise Server: Netware, Unix, and Windows NT
  http://www.netscape.com

WHAT'S THE DIFFERENCE...

What's the difference between a domain and a virtual domain? A domain such as *yourdomainnamehere.com* can either run on a computer all by itself, or it can run on a computer that hosts many domains. A domain that runs on a computer that is hosting more than one domain is often referred to as a virtual domain.

- OR&A WebSite Professional: Windows NT and Windows 95
  http://software.ora.com/

- StarNine WebStar: Macintosh
  http://www.starnine.com/

The Importance Of Directory Structure

Want to keep yourself from going nuts in the Web site design and production process? Create a special folder (directory) for each Web site. Be sure to put all your Web site's files into that folder *before* you start making links and inserting images. Otherwise, the situation will get out of hand when you upload your site to the Web server; links will get broken, images will be missing, and you'll have a miserable time.

The Web site management tools built into Adobe PageMill 3 are very powerful. After you understand how they work, and you begin to work *with* them, you will be amply rewarded. Chapter 8 goes into site management in depth.

And A Word On File Names

Creating errant file names is one of the most common problems encountered by Web site designers using PageMill. Fortunately, you can easily avoid this faux pas. Avoiding errant file names might take a little discipline, but it will cut down on your gray hairs and work wonders with your worry lines. Here are a few pointers:

- Name your files consistently. This can be especially important if you're going to use uppercase and lowercase letters in your file names.

- Choose either the HTM or HTML file name extension and stick with it.

- If you have a problem with the Web server truncating your file names, use the tried-and-trusted 8.3 file-naming convention.

Moving On

This first chapter should have you primed to start designing great Web sites with Adobe PageMill 3. By following the principles and pointers laid out here, you can assure yourself a smooth trip. In the following chapters, you'll learn how to implement all of PageMill's powerful features. We'll start with the basics of text and graphics and quickly move into intricate layouts using tables and frames.

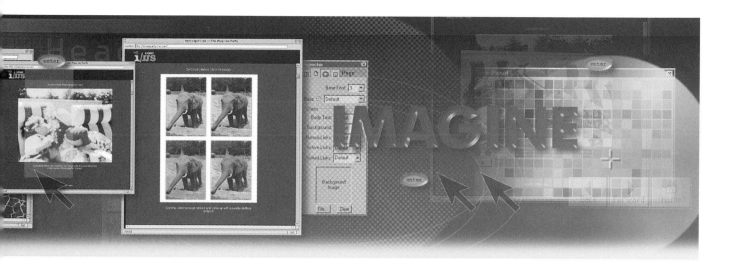

COVERING THE
TEXT BASICS
2

This chapter provides an introduction to the PageMill environment and covers HTML paragraph formats, character styles, hyperlinks, anchors, colors, and fonts.

PageMill 3 makes Web page creation a breeze by hiding the arduous task of Hypertext Markup Language (HTML) coding. This benevolent approach is at the core of the program's continued success. Whether you like it or not, HTML coding lies beneath every Web page, and creating it is never a treat. Writing HTML code by hand is akin to crafting a little program. The beauty of PageMill is that you never have to deal with HTML code if you really don't want to. Rest assured, though, you can still tinker with the code if you're so inclined. Although the first version of PageMill hid the HTML source code entirely, version 2 added the capability for you to "hack it out by hand" with its integrated ASCII text editor, and version 3 improves on that capability.

What This Chapter Covers

This chapter will help you learn how to produce text pages with PageMill. Before long, you'll be churning out Web pages like a pro—pages that include such basic text features as heading and body styles, alignment, type sizes, and linking. (Advanced text features such as tables and frames are covered in Chapters 4 and 5.) As this chapter progresses, you'll learn a bit about the HTML code that underlies every Web page.

Why get into the code? Your effectiveness in building Web pages will be limited if you can't deal with some raw HTML once in a while. It's strong medicine, but it's inherently palatable—once you've acquired a taste for it. To this end, we're sneaking in a touch of code so that you learn through doing (and possibly through osmosis). We'll begin with an overview of the PageMill environment and then cover a bit of HTML gobbledygook before finishing up the chapter with a quick exercise. The second half of the chapter is devoted to creating your own text-based page, in a step-by-step drill.

Working In The PageMill Environment

The PageMill environment is uncluttered and free from "featuritis." The program allows you to have many Web page windows open at one time, and in fact, this multiple document interface is key to its operation. With more than one Web page open, you can easily drag and drop images, text, and links between pages. Although (for some) the act of dragging and dropping can take a bit of adjustment, it ultimately saves time and keystrokes.

If you've grown weary of bloated word processing programs with bewildering interfaces, you're in for a treat. PageMill's streamlined interface consists of a toggling main window along with three basic floating palettes and a Java Console. (You'll also find an "out-of-place" image editing window, but we'll delve into it in the next chapter.)

The Main Window

PageMill's main window has three personalities. Clicking on the large button at the top right-hand corner toggles the window between *Edit* and *Preview modes*. (The pen and paper icon denotes Edit mode; the world icon represents Preview mode.) You'll spend most of your time in Edit mode while developing Web pages. Figure 2.1 shows the Edit window. PageMill is a polite program. If you forget the function of a button, you don't need to dig out the manuals. As you move the cursor over each button, a definition will conveniently pop up. (The first few chapters of this book explain each section of the Edit window in detail.)

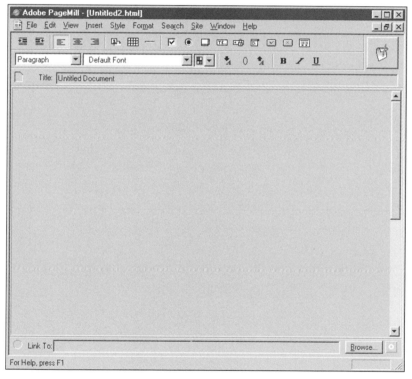

Figure 2.1   When the PageMill window is in Edit mode (as shown by the pen and paper icon), clicking on the big button at the top right switches to Preview mode (denoted by the world icon).

The Preview mode mimics how a Web page looks when viewed in a Web browser, such as Netscape Navigator or Microsoft Internet Explorer. In this handy Preview mode, you can even click on (and check) links before pages are published to your Web server. Keep in mind that a Web page will look much the same when viewed in either Preview

INTERNET EXPLORER PREVIEW MODE

PageMill 3 provides an optional Microsoft Internet Explorer (MSIE) Preview mode. If you have Internet Explorer 3 (or later) installed on your system, you can preview features that aren't supported by PageMill's built-in preview. To select the Internet Explorer preview mode, summon the Edit|Preferences dialog box. Then, click the General tab and choose Internet Explorer under the Preview Mode. The changes will take effect once PageMill has restarted.

Don't be lulled into settling for MSIE previews only. You would be wise to preview your pages in Netscape Navigator, and if you're really serious about your design, in the Opera browser as well. You can add these additional browsers by choosing Edit|Preferences and then choosing the correct options in the Switch To tab of the dialog box.

mode or Edit mode. The difference is akin to turning a pair of trousers inside out. In Edit mode, you can see some of the seams (such as table marquees) that hold the page together.

HTML Source mode allows you to edit the HTML source code by hand. Select View|Source Mode or use the Cmd+H (Macintosh) or Ctrl+H (Windows) keyboard shortcuts to switch to HTML Source mode. (You must be in Edit mode—not Preview mode—before you can switch to Source mode.)

The Inspector

The Inspector is a context-sensitive floating palette, which you can summon from the View menu, or by using the Cmd+; (Mac) or F8 (Windows) keyboard shortcuts. Its four-tabbed appearance changes depending on what's selected in the main window. The first three tabs display the attributes of any currently selected frame, page, or form, respectively. The fourth tab is variable; it displays object attributes for images, tables, or media (such as Java applets, Acrobat PDFs, or sounds). When you start working on a new Web page, the first tab chosen in the Inspector is likely to be the Page tab (see Figure 2.2). On this tab, the base font size, base target, color, and background image attributes are assigned.

PageMill delivers total control over color, on both a page and a character basis. This capability allows you to assign a basic color scheme that can be overridden in special circumstances. The Inspector provides the means to set the *global color characteristics* for the following:

• Body text

• Background

• Normal links (places visitors haven't been)

• Active links (the color that flashes as visitors click on a link)

• Visited links (places visitors have been)

Figure 2.2 The Page tab is generally the first tab you see in the Inspector.

WHAT IS...?

Acrobat PDF—Adobe's Acrobat Portable Document Format files are platform independent. They look almost exactly like the printed document and can be viewed on and printed from any computer equipped with the Adobe Acrobat Viewer.

ActiveX—Microsoft's alternative to Java. Just ask why.

Java applet—A little downloadable program, written in Sun's Java language. Java applets run the gamut from cute animations to full-blown programs.

JavaScript—The *de facto* standard Web page scripting language, supported by the most popular Web browsers (since Netscape Navigator 2.0).

Sounds—Recordings in AU, WAV, and other formats.

You can change the color of a page attribute by using one of three methods. The first method is to merely pick a color from the drop-down menu next to each item. If you want a different color (other than those offered on the menu), you won't have to get out your scientific calculator. Although HTML specifies color in cryptic hexadecimal codes like "ffd303," PageMill eliminates the need to mess with hex. Instead, you can define colors by selecting them from a visual color picker. Select Custom from the drop-down menu next to each item to open the color picker. From there, it's a point-and-shoot procedure. You can also drag and drop colors from the Color Panel directly onto a drop-down menu to make an instant color assignment.

The large square well at the bottom of the Inspector provides a preview of the background image (if any). Background images override background color. You can drag and drop GIF and JPEG image files from the desktop into the background image

well. You can also assign background images, via a dialog box, by
clicking on the File button at the lower left of the Inspector window.
Clicking on the Clear button removes the background image from the
page. We'll cover the topic of background files in depth in Chapter 3.

The Page tab provides two additional controls, the Base Font and the
Base Target. The Base Font setting governs a page's overall text size. The
Base Target setting sets the general target destination of any hyperlinks;
you'll use this control most often when creating framed page layouts.
Both of these controls can be overridden on a case-by-case basis.

You can preset PageMill's page attributes by selecting Edit|Preferences
and then choosing the appropriate options on the Page tab of the
dialog box. The controls include color settings for body text, background, normal links, active links, and visited links as well as the
background image. If you use one set of standard colors in your Web
pages, presetting the page attributes will save you the trouble of reset-
ting them each time you sit down to create a new page.

The Color Panel

Get ready for a kindergarten flashback! PageMill's convenient Color
Panel (as shown on the left in Figure 2.3), which looks just like your
first watercolor palette, can hold 16 different colors. You access the
Color Panel via the View menu or by using the Cmd+' (Macintosh) or
F5 (Windows) keyboard shortcuts. You can drag and drop colors from
the Color Panel onto selected text as well as onto page attributes.
PageMill allows only one Color Panel at a time. The last group of colors you used in a PageMill session will be the same group of colors
loaded the next time you launch the program.

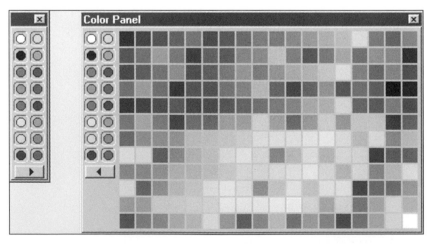

Figure 2.3 In its collapsed mode, the Color Panel provides quick access to 16 user-
defined colors. Expanding the Color Panel provides access to all 216 Web-safe colors.

PageMill 3 added an enhanced Color Panel. Clicking on the button at the bottom of the panel opens the 216 Web-safe Color Panel (as shown on the right in Figure 2.3). Drag and drop these colors to create a custom palette.

Color selection can be a thorny issue. Colors other than those chosen from the Web-safe Color Picker may not accurately convert to nondithered (or pure) browser colors. You'll find more information on color palettes and dithering in Chapter 3.

The Pasteboard

The Pasteboard is a handy holding area that uses a notebook metaphor (see Figure 2.4). You can access the Pasteboard via the View menu. You can drag and drop text and graphics to and from the Pasteboard. The Pasteboard's five pages are useful for holding repetitive graphics, such as site navigation bars, ID graphics, icons, buttons, and horizontal bars, as well as anchors, links, and other recurrent objects.

The following are a few hints for working with the Pasteboard:

- To copy objects from the Pasteboard, hold down the Option key (Macintosh) or Ctrl key (Windows) while dragging.

- To flip between pages, click on the tabs at the bottom of the Pasteboard.

- To resize the Pasteboard, click and drag on a corner.

Figure 2.4 The Pasteboard provides a convenient holding tank for text, links, and images.

ROLL 'EM UP!

In the Macintosh version of PageMill, the Inspector, Color Panel, and Pasteboard are all *roll-up palettes*. Using these handy features, you can temporarily hide (or roll up) each palette to cut down on screen clutter. Roll-up palettes are especially handy when you're using a computer with a smaller monitor. Unfortunately, the Windows version of PageMill does not include this roll-up feature.

The Sad Truth About HTML Text

If you've worked with page layout packages such as QuarkXPress or Adobe PageMaker, you're probably accustomed to having rather extensive control over text. The current crop of word processors do quite an impressive job as well. Most of these programs provide a high level of control over typeface selection, type size, letter spacing, and line spacing.

The sad truth about working with Web page text, however, is that you have practically no control over how your text will be viewed. Almost everything is browser dependent. The HTML specification allows the browser to set individual preferences for typeface and size on a style-by-style basis. When you specify text on the Web pages that you create, you're taking a leap of faith. What looks right and works well on your screen may appear totally different when it reaches your audience. However, HTML *does* provide a sufficient range of text styles for most situations.

Specifying Fonts

That said, PageMill 3 allows you to specify fonts by using a drop-down menu on the menu bar. This capability is kind of groovy, but consider this huge caveat: When you specify a single font using this method, you're betting that your visitors will have that *exact* font loaded on their computers.

If you are going to specify fonts, you should add a couple of alternative fonts to the <FONT FACE> attribute. Instead of just <FONT FACE="Arial">, you might want to add something like <FONT FACE="Arial, Helvetica, Sans-Serif">. To do so, you have to switch to HTML Source mode.

Nonetheless, you would be wise not to drive yourself crazy making all these changes by hand, while in the midst of designing pages. Instead, you can run a Search and Replace on the entire site. We'll cover searching and replacing in Chapter 9.

What About Cascading Style Sheets And Embedded Fonts?

If you've been reading about the latest developments in Web page design, you're probably asking yourself that very question. The Cascading Style Sheets (CSS) and embedded font technology found in the latest versions of Microsoft Internet Explorer and Netscape Navigator are very cool, indeed. Unfortunately, they are not supported by PageMill 3, as it shipped.

This book's support Web site (www.geekbooks.com/pm3dg.html) will provide information on PageMill, CSS, and embedded fonts, as it becomes available.

Paragraph Formats Vs. Character Styles

HTML uses both *paragraph formats* and *character styles.* The difference between the two is that a character style affects selected characters only. A paragraph format, on the other hand, affects an entire paragraph. Character styles are used within a paragraph to bring emphasis to a particular word or phrase, as when the title of a book, such as *Adobe PageMill 3 f/x and design,* is set in italics.

There are three basic types of paragraph formats:

- *Heading* formats

- *Body text* formats

- *List* formats

A properly structured Web page should make efficient use of the various formats. Now, let's examine these formats from the top (of the page).

Heading Formats

HTML provides six logical heading formats. PageMill allows you to assign each format by using a keyboard shortcut, choosing from the Change Format pop-up menu, or selecting Format|Heading. Figure 2.5 illustrates the half dozen heading style choices, and Table 2.1 shows the HTML equivalents and keyboard shortcuts.

Because heading commands are paragraph formats, they affect everything in a text block, from one paragraph return until the next. Therefore, you cannot assign a heading style to selected words within a paragraph. When you're assigning a heading format, just place the cursor somewhere within the text block. When you choose the style, it will be assigned to the whole enchilada.

Table 2.1 Heading formats and their equivalents.

PageMill	Mac Shortcut	Windows Shortcut	HTML Code
Largest	Cmd+Opt+1	Ctrl+Shift+1	<H1>...</H1>
Larger	Cmd+Opt+2	Ctrl+Shift+2	<H2>...</H2>
Large	Cmd+Opt+3	Ctrl+Shift+3	<H3>...</H3>
Small	Cmd+Opt+4	Ctrl+Shift+4	<H4>...</H4>
Smaller	Cmd+Opt+5	Ctrl+Shift+5	<H5>...</H5>
Smallest	Cmd+Opt+6	Ctrl+Shift+6	<H6>...</H6>

Try typing a few lines of text now, separating the lines with a return. Then, go ahead and assign different heading styles to the text. Did you notice that headings 5 and 6 are actually smaller than the body text style? Although this formatting may seem odd, you can use these tiny heading styles to great effect.

Paragraph Formats

HTML's default paragraph format uses nonindented text, set in a plain roman font. In practice, you'll use the paragraph format for most of the text on your Web pages, although you may apply different charac-

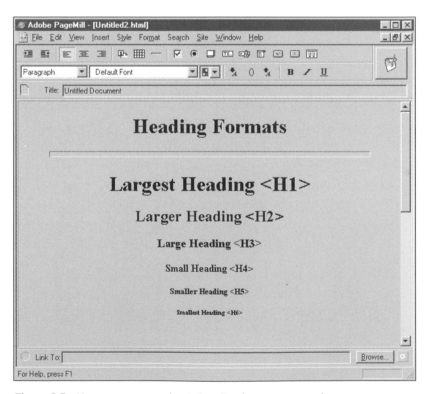

Figure 2.5 Here, you can see the six heading formats on parade.

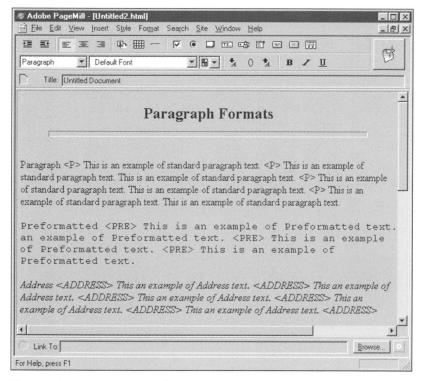

Figure 2.6 Here, you can see the paragraph formats on parade.

ter styles and type sizes. In addition to the default paragraph style, two special types of body text are available.

The preformatted text format is handy for displaying large blocks of text in a monospaced typeface. It's often used to create crude tabular text without using the table commands. The address text format is used to denote "mailto" address lines—for the purpose of soliciting visitor feedback via an email link—which usually appear in an italic typeface. Paragraph formats can be assigned by using a keyboard shortcut, choosing from the Change Format pop-up menu (on the button bar), or selecting from the Format menu. Figure 2.6 displays the three different paragraph formats, and Table 2.2 shows the HTML equivalents and keyboard shortcuts.

Table 2.2 Paragraph formats and their equivalents.

PageMill	Mac Shortcut (PM2)	Windows Shortcut (PM3)	HTML Code
Paragraph	Cmd+Opt+P	Ctrl+Shift+P	<P>...</P>
Preformatted	Cmd+Opt+F		<PRE>...</PRE>
Address	Cmd+Opt+A		<ADDRESS>...</ADDRESS >

List Formats

Several list formats are available for use in various situations. The formats include:

- *Bullet*—Indented and bulleted.

- *Directory*—Indented and bulleted.

- *Menu*—Indented and bulleted.

- *Numbered*—Indented and numbered. (Numbers appear only in the browser. PageMill displays the # sign.)

- *Term*—Used together with the definition format. Set on the left margin.

- *Definition*—Indented text, used together with the term format.

Although the first three formats appear to be identical, the difference between them has to do with the theoretical structure of the document. In practice, however, you'll probably just use the bulleted list format.

Figure 2.7 shows the list formats, and Table 2.3 contains the HTML equivalents.

Table 2.3 List formats and their equivalents.

PageMill	HTML
Bullet	<UL><LI>...</UL>
Directory	<DIR><LI>...</DIR>
Menu	<MENU>...</MENU>
Numbered	<OL><LI>...</OL>
Definition	<DL><DD>...</DL>
Term	<DL><DT>...</DL>

To create nested outlines, use the Indent Left and Indent Right buttons.

Physical Character Styles Vs. Logical Character Styles

Character styles can be either *physical* or *logical*. A physical style tags specific words with specific font attributes, such as bold or italic. Logical styles tell the browser what the intent of the text is rather than define a particular type style. Physical styles appear in the browser as the Web page designer intends for them to appear. If you assign a bold style to a chunk of text, you can rest assured that it will be bold when it appears in your visitors' browsers. In contrast, text assigned a logical style can

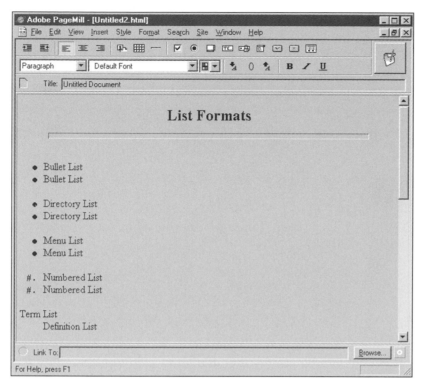

Figure 2.7   Here, you can see the list formats on parade.

vary in appearance from browser to browser, depending on how the browser's preferences are set.

If you're confused by all this, you're not alone. Suffice it to say, you can play it safe by assigning physical styles rather than logical styles. If you want some text to appear in bold, make sure that you use the bold style. Don't leave your typographical decisions to the whims of the browser.

Physical Character Styles

You can use five physical character styles. To assign them, you can use a keyboard shortcut, choose from the button bar, or select from the Style menu. Applying the plain paragraph style clears all the other paragraph formatting. Table 2.4 lists the physical character styles and their HTML equivalents.

Teletype is an interesting style. It uses a monospaced (as opposed to proportionally spaced) font, such as Courier. Every character in a monospaced font takes up the same width, as opposed to a proportionally spaced font, in which the *I* is much thinner than the *W*, and so on. This characteristic enables you to create quick and dirty tables—as if on an old typewriter—simply by using the spacebar to line up columns.

Table 2.4   Physical character styles and their equivalents.

PageMill	Mac Shortcut	Windows Shortcut	HTML
Plain	Cmd+Shift+P	Ctrl+Shift+P	<P>...</P>
Bold	Cmd+B	Ctrl+B	<B>...</B>
Italic	Cmd+I	Ctrl+I	<I>...</I>
Teletype	Cmd+Shift+T	Ctrl+Shift+T	<TT>...</TT>
Underline	Cmd+U	Ctrl+U	<U> ... </U>

Logical Character Styles

Because of the many logical character styles, note a fair amount of overkill with regard to the limited set of typefaces. Some of the character styles share the same kind of typeface, as you can see here:

- *Strong*—Usually a bold typeface.
- *Emphasis*—Usually an italic typeface.
- *Citation*—Usually an italic typeface.
- *Sample*—Usually a typewriter typeface.
- *Keyboard*—Usually a typewriter typeface.
- *Code*—Usually a typewriter typeface.
- *Variable*—Usually an italic typeface.

Figure 2.8 displays the seven logical character styles, and Table 2.5 lists them with their HTML equivalents.

Additional Text Controls

A highly designed Web page calls for enhanced control over text attributes. PageMill provides the means for you to manipulate a variety

Table 2.5   Physical character styles and their equivalents.

PageMill	HTML
Strong	<STRONG>...</STRONG>
Emphasis	<EM>...</EM>
Citation	<CITE>...</CITE>
Sample	<SAMP>...</SAMP>
Keyboard	<KBD>...</KBD>
Code	<CODE>...</CODE>
Variable	<VAR>...</VAR>

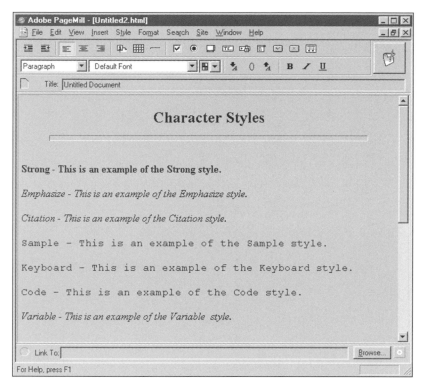

Figure 2.8   Here, you can see the logical character styles on parade.

of text attributes other than those you manage using the paragraph formats and character styles. These additional text controls, including the following, allow you to define your Web page designs more precisely:

- Text alignment
- Text indent
- Text size
- Text color

Text Alignment

Web page text can be left aligned, right aligned, or centered. (HTML does not support full justification.) Text is set left aligned by default. To center a block of text, click within the paragraph and click on the Center Align button at the top of the toolbar. To set the text back to a left alignment, just click the Left Align button. Follow the same procedure to right align text. PageMill also provides control over text alignment as it relates to inline graphics as well as text wrapping (where text appears to flow around a graphic). You will use these controls in the exercise in Chapter 3.

Text Indent

Text indents are implemented through a basic interface. The Indent Left and Indent Right buttons move the indents in and out, respectively. The indents push the text around by predetermined increments, as shown in Figure 2.9. Unfortunately, you have no control over the amount of indent provided by each click of the indent button. When you use the indents to alter any list with bullets, notice that the bullets change when viewed in Preview mode. Normal bullets are solid black. First indents get an open circle bullet, and second indents and beyond get open square bullets. The manner in which they appear is browser dependent, however. For example, Netscape Navigator follows PageMill's solid/open/square pattern, whereas Internet Explorer and the Opera browser display all of them as solid round bullets.

Text Size

You don't need to assign a heading style if you just want to change the type size of a selected block of text (and especially if you don't want the text to be bold). PageMill's button bar affords a convenient way to change the relative font size. Relative to what, you ask? Text size choices are relative to the base font set in the Inspector. HTML allows

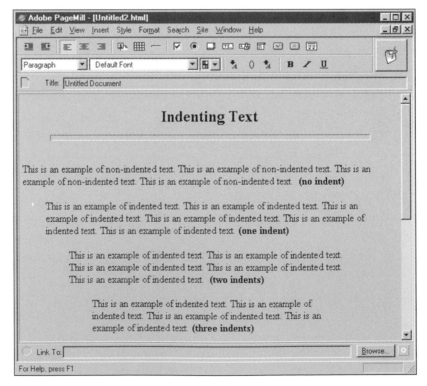

Figure 2.9 Indenting sets off passages of text.

only seven type sizes. As such, the higher the base font is set, the fewer the choices you get when you try to increase the size of a chunk of text. PageMill uses HTML's <FONT SIZE=X>...</FONT> command to control the text size.

Clicking on the up arrow (Increase Relative Font Size) button increases the font size, whereas clicking on the down arrow (Decrease Relative Font Size) button decreases the font size. You can also set font size by choosing a specific size (click on the Change Relative Font Size button, between the arrow buttons) or by using keyboard shortcuts, which are shown in Table 2.6.

Assigning a larger type size to a block of text within a paragraph will alter the line spacing (or leading) for the lines on which the text appears. This change results in a noticeably uneven look, as you can see in Figure 2.10.

Text Color

Although the Inspector provides full control over text color attributes on a per-page basis, you can easily assign colors to specific text as well. To change the color of a selected block of text, you can either drag and drop a color from the floating Color Panel or use the Text Color button on the button bar.

Hyperlinks

Hyperlinks (or more simply, *links*) are at the core of the Web's allure. Some people may even say that hyperlinks are the medium's entire reason for being. Links allow folks to jump from one spot to the next— be it from page to page or from server to server—in a single mouse click. The three basic types of links are *internal, external,* and *anchored.*

Links can be attached to text or to graphics. In the following pages, you'll learn how to create text links between your pages, as well as to other Web sites. Graphic links and image maps are covered in the next chapter.

Like most things "PageMillian," hyperlinks can be created with drag-and-drop ease or through direct text entry. Look at the page icon at the top of the main PageMill window (just below the indent buttons near

Table 2.6   Keyboard shortcuts for changing font size.

PageMill	Mac Shortcut	Windows Shortcut
Increase	Cmd+Shift+>	Ctrl+Shift+>
Decrease	Cmd+Shift+<	Ctrl+Shift+<

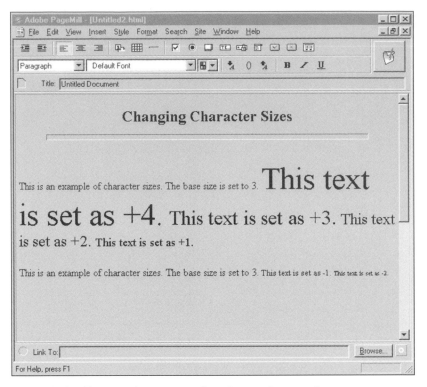

Figure 2.10   Changing the type size affects line spacing as well.

the top-left corner and to the left of the Title line). The page icon is a crucial part of the program's integral drag-and-drop page-linking scheme. Here's a rundown on the three basic types of hyperlinks:

- *Internal* links are hyperlinks to other Web pages within your Web site.

- *External* links are hyperlinks to other Web sites.

- *Anchored* links are hyperlinks to specific places on a Web page and are often used to link to different locations within a page.

Creating Internal Links

To link two internal pages via drag and drop, start by opening both pages. Highlight the linking text; then, drag and drop the document page icon (from the page you want to link to) onto the highlighted text. Bingo! The pages are linked. You can also drag and drop existing links from page to page. In practice, positioning both pages on your monitor can be a bit tricky if you have a small screen or are running at a low resolution (such as 640×480).

To link internal pages via direct text entry, begin by highlighting the linking text (the text from which you want to link). Then, click in the Link To bar at the bottom left of the PageMill window, type the URL (address) of the page you want to link to, and press the Enter key. Alternatively, you can cut and paste (or drag and drop) the URL from the browser window or from the Pasteboard.

Creating External Links

External links are most commonly entered in the Link To bar. The Link To bar uses an "assisted URL entry" feature to help speed the tedious process of typing URLs from scratch. As you type the first letter of the protocol—most typically the *h* in *http*—PageMill will fill in the rest if you simply press the right arrow key. Type the first *w* in *www*, press the right arrow key again, and PageMill will fill in the second and third *w*'s. Type the domain name (followed by a period), press the right arrow key again, and PageMill will cycle through domain type (such as .com or .net). Don't forget to press the Enter (or Return) key after the entire URL appears in the Link To bar; otherwise, it will not be committed.

PageMill also allows you to drag and drop links from Web pages that have been opened in Netscape Navigator or from Navigator's Bookmarks folder, as well as from Microsoft Internet Explorer. These links can be dropped either on the selected text or in the Link To bar. If you drop the link onto the Link To bar, be sure to press the Enter (or Return) key afterward to implement the link.

Dropping Anchors

HTML provides the means to link to specific places within a Web page by using *anchors*. You can think of these handy devices as akin to house numbers. After the anchors have been dropped in the proper places, your links can deliver visitors to the exact doorstep (that is, location within a Web page) where the information is housed. By using the Insert menu, you can place anchors, which are visible only in PageMill's Edit mode. When an anchor is placed, PageMill assigns an arbitrary anchor name, such as "anchor245189." Clicking on a placed anchor enables you to specify a meaningful anchor name on the Inspector's Object tab.

PROJECT 1 Virtual Shore Realty

Your first hands-on project will be to create a text-only page for Virtual Shore Realty, a mythical real estate company on Long Beach Island. Virtual Shore caters to well-heeled beach lovers. This realty company's first tentative foray into Internet advertising is a single-page affair, sans graphics. Even

NEED TO CREATE A TABLE OF CONTENTS?

A table of contents (TOC) comes in handy on long Web pages. Anchored links make this a snap. The Virtual Shore Realty Project uses a short TOC at the top of the page to facilitate quick navigation.

FIRST POSITION "LINK TO" SHORTCUTS

Don't worry, you don't have to know what all these cryptic acronyms stand for! Most often, all you'll need to use are *h*, *ft*, and *m*.

The following are the first position "Link To" shortcuts:

- h = http://

- f = file://

- ft = ftp://

- g = gopher://

- m = mailto:

- n = news:

- r = rlogin://

- s = shttp://

- t = telnet://

- w = wais://

though the page will not feature any images, it will have a distinctive look through the judicious use of text and background colors.

As you work through the exercise, notice that it repeats the basics covered earlier in this chapter.

Bringing Text Into PageMill

To begin the exercise, you will need to have PageMill running on your PC or Macintosh. Open the ASCII text file lbi.txt in the CHAP-2 directory on this book's CD-ROM. You can use any of the following methods to bring text files into PageMill:

- Open the file with any text editor, such as Simple Text (Macintosh) or Notepad (Windows). Then, copy all the text and paste it into PageMill. Try this method first.

- Open the file with a text editor that supports drag and drop. Then, drag and drop the text into PageMill.

- Select File|Open. In the Open dialog box, select Convertible Files in the Files of type: list, select the file, and click on Open.

Selecting Text

PageMill follows conventional text selection procedures. The program allows you to choose text by using these methods:

- Clicking once selects an insertion point.

- Double-clicking selects a word.

- Triple-clicking selects an entire line.

- Clicking and dragging selects a range of text.

PageMill goes to work the instant the text is brought into the program by assigning HTML coding to imported text. If you opened the file in a text editor and then cut and pasted it into PageMill, you'll notice that the text looks pretty good when it's imported into PageMill (as shown in Figure 2.11). PageMill

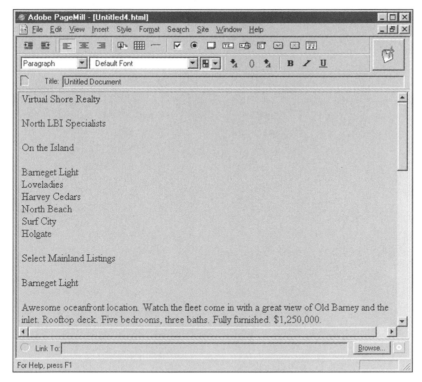

Figure 2.11 When text is cut and pasted into PageMill, it automatically inserts <P> paragraph commands.

automatically senses blank lines and places <P>...</P> paragraph commands around each paragraph return encountered.

When you first open a file, PageMill presents it in Preview mode. Before you start editing the file, PageMill must be in Edit mode (showing the pen and paper icon). Change modes by clicking on the large button at the top right of the window.

Assigning Heading Formats

Now, you're ready to assign some heading formats. Because heading formats work on a paragraph basis, you don't need to select the entire block of text—you can just click somewhere within the block. Let's try this approach on the first three lines of text. Use the Paragraph drop-down menu (on the button bar) to assign styles, as follows:

1. Click on *Virtual Shore Realty*, and select Largest Heading from the Change Text Format drop-down menu.

2. Click on *North LBI Specialists*, and select Larger Heading from the Change Text Format drop-down menu.

IMPORT TARIFFS

The method you use to import the text into PageMill can have an effect on how it is interpreted. Cutting and pasting text into PageMill will cause the text to come in assigned with the plain old <P> Paragraph style. Using the File | Open method will assign the Teletype style and place <BR> codes between paragraphs.

DOMAIN TYPES

Domains in other countries typically end with abbreviations of the name of the country. Half a dozen domain types are common in the United States, as shown in the following list:

- .com—Commercial
- .edu—Educational
- .gov—Government
- .mil—Military
- .net—Network
- .org—Organization

3. Click on *On the Island*, and select Large Heading from the Change Text Format drop-down menu.

4. Save the file.

Skip the next six lines (*Barneget Light* through *Holgate*) right now; you'll come back to them in a moment. Go through the rest of the text, and assign Large Heading to *Select Mainland Listings* and each of the subsequent town names (the first town name, *Barneget Light*, is shown in Figure 2.12).

Assigning A List Format

The six town names between *On the Island* and *Select Mainland Listings* will form a bulleted internal jumplist for the page. The Bullet List is undoubtedly the most popular of HTML's six list formats. In fact, the Bullet List, the Directory List, and the Menu List look pretty much the same.

The method used to assign a list format differs a bit from the method you used to assign the heading styles in the preceding section. When assigning a list style, you should select all the lines of text in the list (instead of just clicking an insertion point). You do so by clicking and dragging over the block of text. Let's give it a whirl.

Now, click and drag from the *B* in *Barneget Light* (under *On the Island*) through the *e* in *Holgate*. Select Directory List from the Change Text Format drop-down menu. You may notice that PageMill placed a bullet only at the beginning of the first line. If you get only one bullet, place the cursor at the end of each line, press Delete, and then press Return (Macintosh) or Enter (Windows). By using this approach, you will remove the <BR> command that PageMill *thought* you wanted at the end of each of those lines.

The text should appear as shown in Figure 2.13. When it looks right, save the file. Try experimenting with the different lists to see whether you

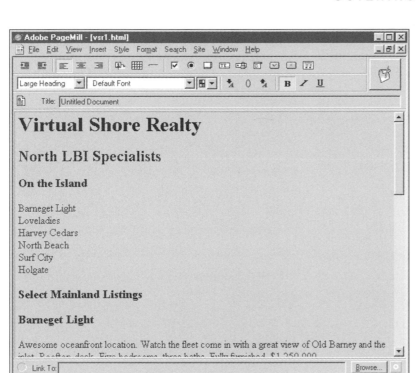

Figure 2.12   Heading styles help define a text hierarchy.

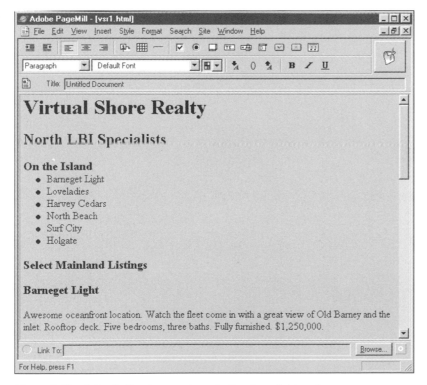

Figure 2.13   Using bullets is a great way to tie a jumplist together.

notice any difference in appearance. You'll definitely be able to see a difference after you've completed the next section. And further on, you'll turn this bullet list into a jumplist by assigning links.

Assigning Indents

PageMill provides basic control over indents through the progressive use of HTML's <BLOCKQUOTE> command. Each time you click on the Indent Right button, text and other page elements are indented equally on both margins. Clicking on the Indent Left button pushes the text back out toward the full margin. It's not complicated, but it is effective.

When you indent a bulleted list, however, PageMill uses successive indent commands (such as <UL> for an unordered list) rather than the <BLOCKQUOTE> command.

Indent the jumplist now to give it the appearance of being centered on the page. Click and drag from the *B* in *Barneget Light* through the *e* in *Holgate*. Click on the Indent Right button four times. Watch how the level of indent affects the bullet style. Your list should appear as shown in Figure 2.14. If it looks okay, save the file.

Aligning Text

As you learned previously in this chapter, HTML allows for three types of text alignment: left, right, and center. Text alignment works on a per-paragraph basis. To change the alignment of a single paragraph, click within the paragraph and then click on the appropriate alignment button. To change the alignment of a number of consecutive paragraphs, highlight the paragraphs and click on an alignment button.

Select *Virtual Shore Realty* and *North LBI Specialists* by clicking and dragging. Next, click on the Center Alignment button. Then, click on *On the Island* and click on the Center Alignment button. Repeat this process for *Select Mainland Listings* (see Figure 2.15). When you're done, save the file.

Adding Text

Our copywriter has apparently left out a crucial tag line at the top of the Virtual Shore Realty page. Click an insertion point directly after the last *s* in *North LBI Specialists* and press Return (Macintosh) or Enter (Windows). Type "LBI: One of the True Gems of the Jersey Shore", highlight the line, and assign the basic paragraph format (by clicking a button on the button bar or by selecting Format|Paragraph). Then,

ALWAYS START WITH A ROOT FOLDER!

Save yourself some heartache. When you save the first file in your Web site, be sure to save it in the Web site's root folder. If you haven't created a root folder, you can do so as you are saving the file. If you will be using existing files in your Web site, make sure that you've copied them into the root folder *before* you use them in PageMill. Web site file management is covered in Chapter 9.

assign the Emphasis style (from the Style menu). Press the right arrow key once to deselect the text and press Return. Finally, save the file.

Adding Horizontal Rules

Now, you can set the heading off from the rest of the page by adding a pair of horizontal rules. The cursor should be in exactly the right place to add the first rule (on the blank line, between *LBI: One of the True Gems of the Jersey Shore* and *On the Island*). Click on the Insert Horizontal Rule button on the button bar to set the first rule. Then, click after the last *s* in *Select Mainland Listings*, press Return (Macintosh) or Enter (Windows) again, and click on the Insert Horizontal Rule button again to set the second rule. The results should resemble Figure 2.16.

Through the Inspector, you can set horizontal rules to a specific width and size (or weight). The width can be defined as a percentage of the browser window or by an exact pixel width. You can also choose between a shaded (embossed) or no shade (solid) style.

Changing Text Size

Because the body text looks too small, let's bump up the base font size by one level. On the Inspector's Page tab, change the base font to 4 (the default is 3). Notice that the change will affect the body text only (not the headings). Experiment with different base font sizes to see how they affect the look of the page. When you have the page looking just right, be sure to save the file.

Assigning Physical Character Styles

Now, you can run through the page to assign some physical character styles. Highlight the opening phrase of each house listing, and apply a bold italic style by clicking on the Bold and Italic buttons. Next, highlight each of the prices and apply

WHAT'S THE DIFFERENCE BETWEEN A HARD AND A SOFT RETURN?

When you press Return (or Enter), you create a *hard return*, which commonly includes an extra line space after the line ending. The hard return uses a <P> (or the current heading) command. Pressing Shift+Return creates a *soft return*, which does not add any extra line space. The soft return uses a <BR> command to "hold the line."

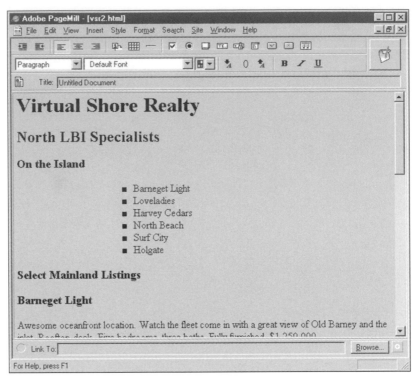

Figure 2.14 Indenting a bulleted list helps to center it visually on the page.

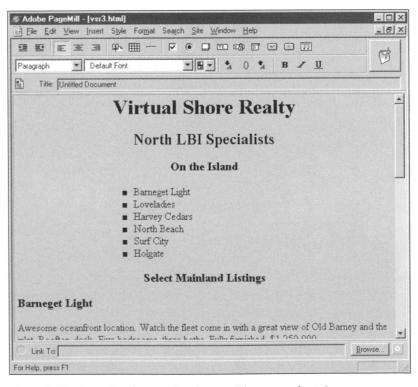

Figure 2.15 Centering the page heading provides a more formal appearance.

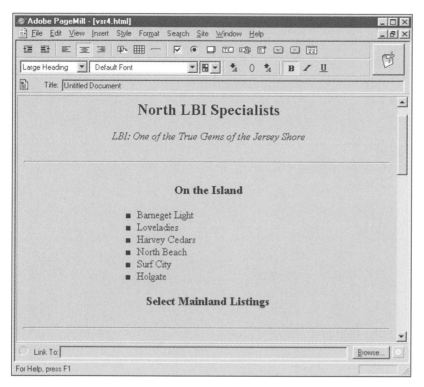

Figure 2.16 Horizontal rules help to differentiate areas of a Web page.

an italic style. When you're done, the text should appear as shown in Figure 2.17.

Copying Text Between Pages

Often, you may want to copy a repetitive passage of text (or a graphic) from page to page. If you have to copy a piece of text only once, doing so is easy. If you have to copy the same piece of text several times, however, you should use the Pasteboard. Next, you'll open an existing Web page and copy text from it onto the main Virtual Shore Realty page:

1. Select File|Open.

2. Navigate to the CHAP-2 directory on this book's CD-ROM. Open the file named about.html.

    You're going to copy the rule and text at the bottom of the About page onto the main Virtual Shore page. To do so, scroll down to the bottom of the main page.

3. Click an insertion point at the end of the main page.

4. Select the About.html window.

5. Highlight the rule and the last line of text (*Copyright, 1998...*).

> **Note:** *If your monitor is large enough to display both pages, you can drag and drop. If you're working on a smaller monitor, you'll have to copy and paste. You may also find it useful to select Window|Tile Horizontally.*

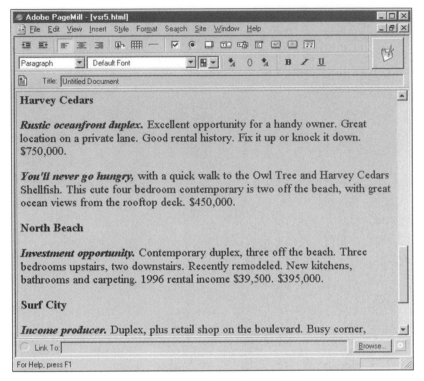

Figure 2.17   Larger text and selected styles help make Web page text more readable.

6. Drag and drop the selected rule and text onto the bottom of the main Virtual Shore Realty page.

7. Save the file.

Linking

At last the time has come to add those crucial links. In the following section, you will create internal, external, and anchored links. You'll begin by creating an internal link between the About page and the main page of the Virtual Shore Realty site. Before you make that first link, however, copy the About.html file into your Web site's root folder.

Dragging And Dropping An Internal Link

After you copy the rule and text, link the words *Virtual Shore (un)Realty* on the main page to the About page by following these steps:

1. On the main page, select the words *Virtual Shore (un)Realty*.

2. Click and drag the document page icon (from the About.html window About page) onto the selected text. The bottom of the main page should appear as shown in Figure 2.18.

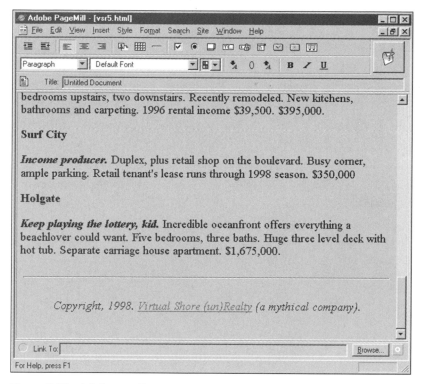

Figure 2.18   A link to an About page is a common internal link.

Typing An External Link

External links exploit the power of the Web by connecting sites around the globe with a single click. Follow these steps to link the acronym *LBI* in the line *LBI: One of the True Gems of the Jersey Shore* with the www.longbeachisland.com Web site:

1. Select the letters *LBI*.

2. At the Link To line at the bottom of the PageMill window, type "http://www.longbeachisland.com". Press Enter, and the link is complete.

3. Save the file.

Alternatively, you can use PageMill's assisted URL entry feature, as described earlier in this chapter.

Creating Anchored Links

Now, you'll create an internal jumplist to link all the town names. To do so, you'll click an insertion point in front of each of the town listings, drop an anchor, and name each accordingly. After the anchors are placed, you'll link them to the jumplist at the top of the page with a drag-and-drop technique, as you can see in the following steps:

1. Click in front of the *Barneget Light* listing (not the jumplist).

2. Select Insert|Anchor. The anchor is placed.

3. Select the new anchor.

4. On the Inspector's Object tab, type "Barneget" under Name and press Enter. The anchor is now properly named.

Repeat these four steps for each of the town listings. When you're done, you can create the jumplist. The act of dragging and dropping the anchored links is a straightforward procedure (as you'll see in the following steps) when both the anchor and the link are visible on the screen. The procedure gets trickier when you have to scroll and drag the anchors.

1. Select the words *Barneget Light* in the jumplist by triple-clicking.

2. Click and drag the anchor from the *Barneget Light* listing onto the selected text. The listing is now linked.

Repeat these two steps for each of the town listings. To make the window scroll, place the cursor just below the window boundary. When you're done, the page should appear as shown in Figure 2.19. Don't forget to save the file after you make all your changes.

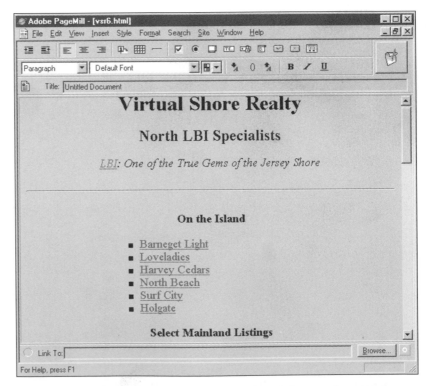

Figure 2.19   Using jumplists is a great way to aid navigation on a long page.

Changing Colors

The Virtual Shore Realty Web page has come a long way in a short time. Even though it doesn't contain any graphics, you've made it a functional page, and you're on your way to giving it a distinctive look as well. In the next section, you'll assign colors on a global page basis, in addition to coloring selected text.

Changing Colors On A Page Basis

To globally change the colors of the Virtual Shore Realty Web page, click on the Page tab in the Inspector. Assign some colors for the Body Text, Background, Normal Links, Active Links, and Visited Links attributes. After you're done fiddling, click and drag the Body Text button down to Custom. The color picker then appears. Use the color picker to assign some suitably beachy colors for the different elements. A light salmon-colored background with dark turquoise body text is a nice place to start.

Changing The Colors Of Individual Words And Characters

To change the color of a character, word, or phrase, begin by highlighting the text you want to change. You then have the choice of dragging predefined colors from the color palette or assigning custom colors by accessing the color picker from the toolbar. Use this technique to change the color of the introductory phrase of each listing.

Changing Fonts

Try assigning some different typefaces. Select the text and choose a font from the drop-down list. To be safe, you should try to stick to the ubiquitous faces, such as Helvetica, Arial, or Times Roman. Expecting all your visitors to have fonts other than these loaded can be a tad presumptuous. Figure 2.20 shows some of these changes.

Adding A Page Title

Remember to add a page title to every Web page you build before posting it on your Web server. The

HSL OR RGB?

If you're determined to build custom colors, you can do so using either HSL (Hue-Saturation-Luminence) or RGB (Red-Green-Blue) modes. Don't sweat the techie-details; the difference between the two is merely the manner in which they specify color.

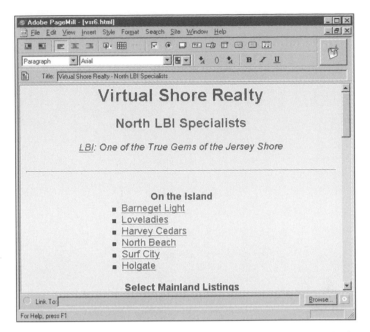

Figure 2.20   With a different font, the Web page takes on a new look.

page title should never be considered as an afterthought. It's a crucial part of the page because it appears in your visitors' history lists and bookmarks (should they choose to bookmark your page). Even more importantly, the page title figures prominently in the search engine listings. Proper listing in the search engines is key to the success of a Web site. (The subject of search engines is covered in Chapter 8.)

To finish this exercise, copy and paste the top two lines of text (*Virtual Shore Realty* and *North LBI Specialists*) into the title bar. Put a hyphen between the words *Realty* and *North,* and remember to press the Return key or the Enter key. Finally, save your file.

Congratulations! You've just created a fully functional Web page by using Adobe PageMill!

Moving On

In this chapter, you built a foundation upon which all your Web pages will grow. You learned how to find your way around the PageMill environment and how to master the basics of HTML text through the program's elegant interface. As you proceed through this book, you'll soon master the medium. The following chapters will delve first into the mysteries of Web page graphics and then into advanced controls, such as tables, frames, and forms.

WORKING WITH GRAPHICS

3

In this chapter, you'll learn the ins and outs of images, as we cover topics such as backgrounds, navigational graphics, and transparency.

A Web page without graphics is a pretty boring sight, and it can lead, quite possibly, to a boring Web site. A text-only page does little to entice readers—although the text content might carry the bulk of the informational value, readers may never absorb the information if it is poorly presented. Pages that are visually pleasing, on the other hand, are sure to attract more attention and, we can hope, allow the readers to achieve a higher level of comprehension. As a Web page designer, you should always strive to provide a balance between the steak and the sizzle.

When you're planning a page, you must make several graphic-related decisions. This chapter will help you get familiar with the different types of graphics and will explain how to implement each form. At the end of the chapter, you will put your new skills to use in a special graphics exercise.

In practice, you can use up to seven general types of graphics when designing your Web pages:

- Backgrounds
- Navigational aids
- Icons
- Dingbats
- Divider bars
- Illustrations
- Photographs

Although Adobe PageMill is not a graphics creation tool, per se, it allows you to work with graphics from a wide variety of sources. PageMill version 3.0 includes Adobe Photoshop LE, which is great for handling most Web graphics chores.

Backgrounds Set The Stage

Custom backgrounds set the mood of a Web page. They provide the designer with the means to banish the boring default gray of the browser window and replace it with a distinctive look (as shown in Figure 3.1). In the exercise at the end of Chapter 2, you assigned various colors to the body text, links, and background. Image backgrounds take those changes one step further by allowing you to use a patterned graphic instead of a solid color background. The right background treatment will set your pages apart from the pack. However, the wrong

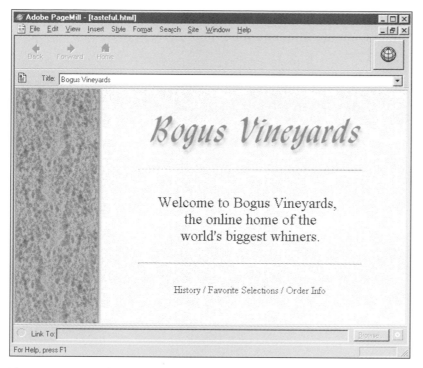

Figure 3.1 A tasteful background sets the proper mood.

background treatment, as illustrated in Figure 3.2, will compromise legibility, reduce effectiveness, and irritate the readers.

Color is one of the first decisions you should make when designing a Web page. You should always try to choose a background color or image that works well with your text colors. Text legibility should be valued above all. Choosing a background color that is too close in hue to a text color will make the text difficult to read. On the other end of the color scale, though, you should avoid using combinations that have too much contrast. Wild color pairings such as screaming yellow type on a plum purple background can contrast and vibrate so hard that they rattle the brain.

Setting (And Removing) Background Images

Setting background images in PageMill is a snap. Just drag the GIF or JPEG image file from the desktop and drop it into the Inspector's background image well. (The Inspector must be in Page mode.) Bingo...instant background image! To remove a background image, click on the Inspector's tiny trash can button (at the lower right). You can also import background images via a dialog box by clicking on the File button at the bottom of the Inspector.

WEB GRAPHICS FORMATS

GIF and JPEG are the most common graphics file formats on the Web. GIF format should be used for solid color graphics, line art, and logos, whereas JPEG format is best used for photographs and continuous tone artwork. PNG is a great new format but, unfortunately, it is not universally supported.

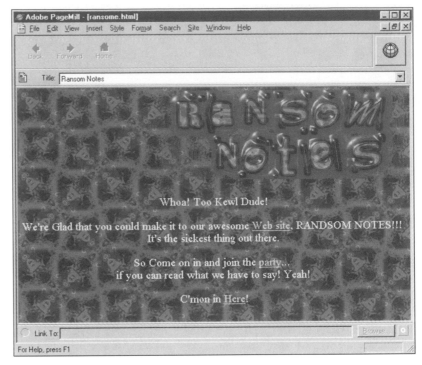

Figure 3.2 Say what? The wrong background treatment will muddy a page.

Background images are often referred to as *tiles* because the browser repeats the image to fill the open window. If the window is resized, the background image is retiled. Look at some patterned wallpaper, fabric, or carpeting, and you'll get the basic idea.

Backgrounds come in different aspect ratios and sizes, although square background images (see Figure 3.3) are among the most common. The browser will automatically tile background images, regardless of aspect ratio (the relationship of width to height). When using background tiles, you don't have to think in square terms. For example, look at the two margin lines running down the page in Figure 3.4. You couldn't achieve this common "yellow-ruled paper" effect with a square texture. Instead, a short and wide rectangular tile (24 pixels high by 1,024 pixels wide) was used.

Because the browser handles the tiling, it will repeat this pattern at the 1,025th pixel (if the browser window is opened that far). The viewers won't notice that the pattern is repeating unless their browser windows are open all the way to the repeating margin rules. You can find many uses for these short-and-wide background tiles. Square tiles work fine when you're using symmetrical seamless textures. If the background design is asymmetrical, however, a tiling scheme similar to the yellow-

WHAT ABOUT PICT AND BMP FILES?

No problemo! PageMill allows you to drag and drop Macintosh PICT and Windows BMP format images (such as screen shots) right from the desktop by performing the conversion to GIF on the fly. For the optimum performance, however, you should use Photoshop to convert the file format.

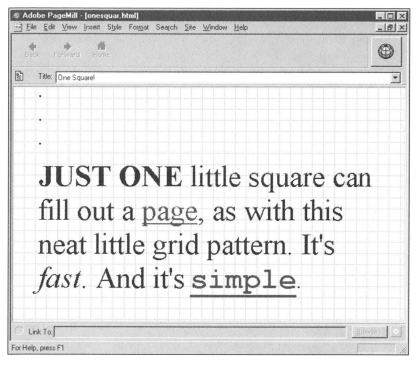

Figure 3.3 One little square tiles to fill out the window.

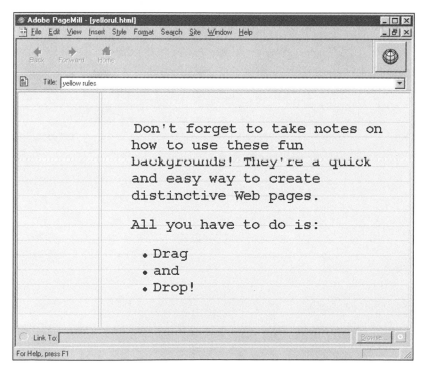

Figure 3.4 Wide patterns can be cool! And best of all, they will download in a flash.

WHAT DOES SEAMLESS MEAN?

A seamless tile is one that tiles smoothly, with no visible edges. Seamless texture tiles first came into vogue with three-dimensional rendering programs. Creating seamless textures is not a trivial undertaking. Achieving a result that does not look forced takes painstaking effort.

ruled paper (as illustrated in Figure 3.4) is the best solution.

You are not limited to using only background tiles; you can use full-page images as backgrounds as well. Full-page images open up your design possibilities. You might use a photograph of your town's skyline or perhaps an image of puffy clouds. A note of caution is in order, however. Although not being limited to tiled backgrounds is nice, full-color, full-page background images can be huge. Use them sparingly and only when their impressive imagery makes waiting for the download well worth the viewers' time.

Learning Where To Find Backgrounds

Background images are everywhere. You can pick them up on the Web for free, you can spend some time creating your own, or you can spring for a CD-ROM filled with commercial images. This book's CD-ROM features more than 3,000 cool (and totally free, if you've already bought this book) textures along with hundreds of patterned backgrounds that you can use on your own Web pages.

If you're thinking about building your own custom backgrounds, you can choose from a handful of programs that are specifically designed to create seamless textures. Xaos Tools Terrazzo and the Seamless Welder (in Kai's Power Tools) are two Photoshop plug-ins that allow you to create seamless textures. The latest versions of the CorelDraw! suite include CorelTEXTURE (which is based on technology from Three D Graphics, which also sells a stand-alone version of its software). MetaCreations TextureScape (formerly Specular TextureScape) is another cool texture generation tool.

The commercial texture choices are burgeoning. It seems as if a new CD-ROM full of textures hits the streets every week. Many of the commercial texture collections on the market are targeted at print designers who need high-resolution files to complete their projects. These high-resolution images contain three to four times more digital information than you need to complete your Web page. Print files are typically from 225 through 300 dpi (dots per inch); Web files don't need to be higher than 72 dpi. Visual Software's (now Micrographx) Textures for Professionals offers scores of seamless textures, including the ever-popular wood grains and marbles (as shown in Figure 3.5).

Don't overlook the print-oriented selections, however. Although they may be more expensive, they're often of higher quality and usually contain low-resolution images in addition to the high-resolution images. You can always downsample high-resolution images in Adobe Photoshop or other paint editors.

Speeding Up Background Images

Because background images are just that—in the *background*—you can use some tricks to speed up loading. The basic rules of graphic loading speeds apply. The smaller an image's file size, the faster it will load. Tiles with just a few colors will load faster than tiles with many colors. The yellow-ruled paper tile shown in Figure 3.4 loads quickly, regardless of its width, because it uses a limited color palette.

When you're dealing with background images, you would be wise to limit the color palette. The amount you limit it to depends on the image; some images will tolerate a tight color palette, and some won't. We'll delve further into the subject of palettes and palette reduction, with a specific focus on what's known as "The Netscape 216 Palette," online at www.geekbooks.com.

Placing Images

After the stage has been set with a background image, you need to think about what types of images to use on top of the background. In the

CHECK OUT THESE BACKGROUND SITES!

- Julianne's Background Textures
  http://www.sfsu.edu/~jtolson/textures/textures.htm

- Pattern Land
  http://www.netcreations.com/patternland/index.html

- Texture Land
  http://www.meat.com/textures/

- The Virtual Background Museum
  http://www.teleport.com/~mtjans/VBM/

- The Texture Chef
  http://www.geekbooks.com/textures/thetexturechef.htm

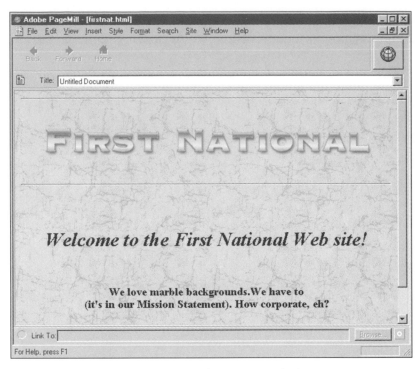

Figure 3.5 A marble background provides a corporate look.

next section, you'll learn how images are manipulated after they've been imported into PageMill. You can place images on your Web pages either by dragging and dropping from the desktop or via a dialog box (which you open by clicking on the Insert Object button on the button bar or by selecting Insert|Object|Image). You can try bringing in a few images now, just to get the hang of this process.

To reposition an image within a page, you can either drag and drop or cut and paste to the new position. If you want to drag the image to a place on the page beyond what's visible in the browser window, drag the image to a point just inside the window border to scroll. (This approach is a little tricky, but you'll soon get the hang of it).

It's important to consider where the actual image files reside, in addition to where you're going to place them on your Web pages. Otherwise, when you move your files to the Web server, you'll end up breaking links and losing files. Chapter 9 goes into depth on creating a working directory structure.

Controlling Images Via The Inspector

After an image has been placed on the page, your work is only half done. The Inspector's Object tab provides precise control over a num-

GENERATE CUSTOM BACKGROUNDS VIA THE WEB!

Check out Vision Thing Design's cool Java Background Network at http://www.vtdesign.com/bgnet/

ber of image characteristics. In practice, you will use this tab for just about every image you place, although you won't alter all the settings for each image. The Object tab controls the following image characteristics (as shown in Figure 3.6):

- Width

- Height

- Alternate (text) Label

- Behavior

- Border

Figure 3.6 Take charge of your images by using the Inspector's Object tab.

Width and *Height* can be set as an exact pixel size or as a percentage relative to the browser window. When an image is imported into PageMill, the width and height default to the actual size of the image. Although you can easily change the size of an image within PageMill, the safest method is to change the actual size of the image in an image editing application such as Adobe Photoshop be-

WHAT ABOUT CONVERTING WINDOWS WALLPAPER?

Although you could easily convert Windows wallpaper (BMP) files to GIF format by using Photoshop, you should consider whether the wallpaper image makes for a suitable Web page background. Many Windows wallpaper files are far too busy or dark to be used effectively as Web page backgrounds.

PUT THEM IN THEIR PLACE!

Always try to copy your images into your Web site's folder before importing them into PageMill.

fore bringing it into PageMill. Otherwise, the image may become distorted in the browser. And even more importantly, scaling down the image in Photoshop will reduce file size and slash download time.

You should specify an *Alternate Label* for every image you place. The Alternate Label is the wording that is shown in the browser window if an image is not displayed (such as when the browser has images turned off or when a page download is stopped in midstream). Naming each image may seem like a tedious task, but doing so is considered good netiquette. If the images have proper labeling, visitors can "see" what each image is without actually downloading it. If they're enticed by the Alternate Label, they can reload the page at will. Figure 3.7 shows a partially loaded page that uses properly labeled images.

Specifying the *Behavior* of an object tells the browser what to expect—a picture, form button, or image map. Images come into PageMill as pictures by default. Forms are covered in Chapter 6, and image maps are described later in this chapter.

Images come into PageMill with a default *Border* of 0 pixels. You can set the border as thick as you could possibly want, but using a border thickness heavier than 1 or 2 pixels becomes awkward. The border color is determined by the object behavior. A picture will use the page's Body

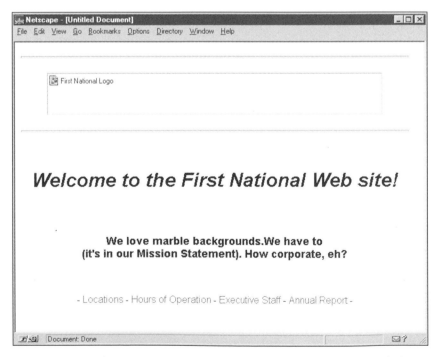

Figure 3.7   Don't leave your viewers guessing. Always specify an Alternate Label.

Text color, and a form button or an image map will use the page's Link colors (normal, active, and visited). Although you wouldn't want to use a border on an irregularly shaped (transparent) graphic image, a border can look great around a rectangular photographic image. Figure 3.8 shows the same photograph with and without a border.

Aligning Images

After you've set your image attributes (or perhaps before), you can position the image on the page. To align the image, you can use one of the aptly illustrated buttons at the top right of the button bar. Just select the image and click away. PageMill provides five options to control how text reacts to an inline image:

- Top Align
- Middle Align
- Bottom Align
- Left Align
- Right Align

The first three choices—top, middle, and bottom—align one line of text with the image and are most appropriately used for short captions.

Figure 3.8 Borders help to "pop" a photograph.

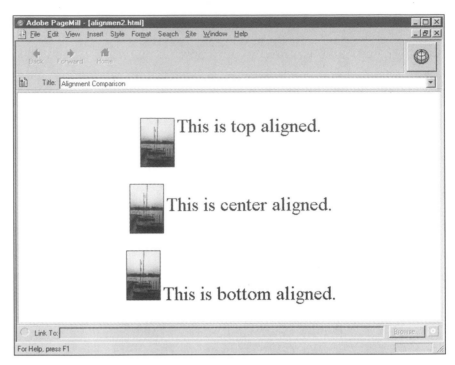

Figure 3.9 Choose top, middle, or bottom alignment when you have a short caption.

You're likely to use either a left or right align (the last two buttons in the group) most frequently. These settings wrap text around the image. Figures 3.9 and 3.10 demonstrate the effect of the five alignment options. More complicated alignment schemes are possible through the use of tables (which will be covered in depth in the next chapter).

Now that you've learned the basics of how to work with placed images, you're ready to look at the various types of graphics you'll use to complete your Web page designs.

Navigational Graphics

Navigational graphics are the road signs of your Web site. They provide the means for your visitors to find their way quickly from place to place. In addition, they are an important part of the overall design scheme, providing much of the look and feel (as well as consistency) of a site. Navigational graphics, which are often called button bars (as shown by Figures 3.11 and 3.12), can come in both horizontal and vertical orientations. When implementing navigational graphics, you have a choice between assigning one URL or multiple URLs to each individual graphic (through the use of image maps).

Your navigational graphics can run either horizontally or vertically, depending on the overall design of your site. Early site designs tended

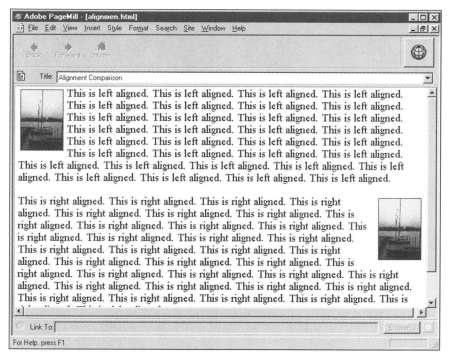

Figure 3.10 Left or right alignment allows text to wrap around an image.

Figure 3.11 A simple three-button horizontal button bar is located near the bottom of this page.

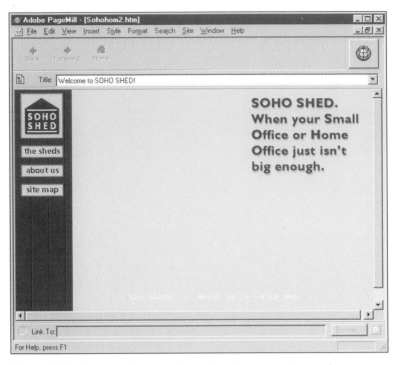

Figure 3.12 Here, a vertical variation, with a discrete text button bar, runs along the left side of the page.

to horizontal schemes (due to the constraints of early versions of HTML—most specifically, the lack of multiple columns); now, however, vertical navigation devices have come into vogue. Regardless of which orientation you choose, you would be wise to provide a text button bar in addition to the navigation graphic. Text links may not look nearly as cool, but they're always faster and straight to the point.

Linking A Single URL To An Image

If you completed the exercise at the end of Chapter 2, you'll already know just about all you need to know about creating simple text hyperlinks. Creating graphic links is just as straightforward because assigning a URL to an image is not unlike assigning a URL to a piece of text. To link a graphic, begin by selecting it. You then can perform one of the following actions:

• Manually enter the link in the Link To bar.

• Drag the page icon from that page onto the selected graphic.

• Drag the URL from Netscape Navigator.

When you first insert an image, PageMill will assign a border of 0 (no border) by default. To override the default, go to the Inspector (as shown in Figure 3.13), type the desired width in the Border field (which will be blank), and press the Return (Macintosh) or Enter (Windows) key. And while you're there, don't forget to add an alternate text label!

Linking To Multiple URLs With Image Maps

Image maps are the coordinates that tell the server which page to deliver, depending on where the visitors click on a navigational graphic. The coordinates provide vertical and horizontal boundaries for each "hotspot" (areas that can be clicked to call up another page). Image maps come in two flavors: server-side and client-side. In general, the difference between the two has to do with where the coordinates reside and how the browser reacts.

Server-side Image Maps

Server-side image maps are separate coordinate mapping files that must reside on the Web server. They require the use of a CGI script (which must also be on the server) to tell the browser which page to fetch. When visitors click on a server-side image map, the browser sends the coordinates to the server, which then runs the CGI and consequently coughs up the appropriate page. Server-side maps are the original method, but these days, they're not the method of choice. They're slower for the visitors, they're more taxing on the server, and they can be a nuisance to maintain. Also, many ISPs require that your page be part of a commercial-level account if you want to use CGI scripting—a real expense if you're just looking to set up a personal page.

If you want to create a server-side image map (for some unknown reason—perhaps you just like the abuse or have too much free time on your hands), you'll have to select Edit|Image|Open Image Window (or press Cmd+D [Macintosh] or Ctrl+D [Windows]) to summon PageMill's Image window. Before you create a server-side map, however, you should consult with your Webmaster to find where to store the map file (and be sure to ask whether the Webmaster would really be happier with a client-side map).

Client-side Image Maps

Client-side image maps reside in the Web page itself. When visitors click on a client-side image map, the browser sends a request for a specific page. Because no CGI script is required, this reduces the load on the server. Because the page URLs are hard-coded into the page, the browser can provide feedback telling where each link leads. For these reasons, client-side image maps are considered the more user-friendly of the two methods.

Figure 3.13 If the Border field is blank, PageMill 3 will not assign a border to linked images.

You can create a client-side image map directly on the page. To access the client-side image map tools, double-click on the image you want to map; the image map tool buttons will replace the table tool buttons on PageMill's button bar (as shown in Figure 3.14). The image map tools provide the following functions:

- *Selector Tool*—This tool allows you to choose an existing hotspot.

- *Rectangle Hotspot*—Using this tool, you can assign rectangular hotspots.

- *Circle Hotspot*—This tool assigns round hotspots; it's great for creating bullets.

- *Polygon Hotspot*—Using this tool, you can assign irregularly shaped hotspots.

- *Shuffle Hotspot*—This tool changes the priority order.

- *Hotspot Color*—These colors are for your convenience; they show only in PageMill's Edit mode, not in the browser.

- *Show Hotspot Label*—These tools toggle on and off, showing only in PageMill's Edit mode, not in Preview mode.

To assign a hotspot, choose the appropriately shaped tool; then drag out a hotspot. You can resize a hotspot after it's placed on the page by

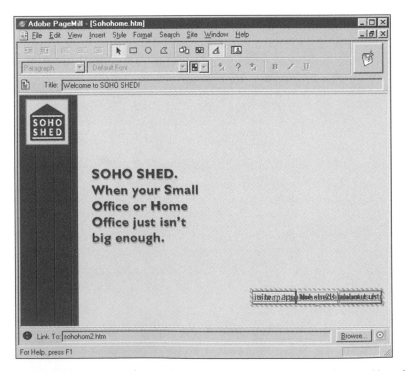

Figure 3.14 Creating client-side image maps using PageMill is a breeze. Note that the hotspot information will obscure the image underneath when viewed in PageMill.

pulling on its handles. Type the URL into the Link To bar, press the Return (Macintosh) or Enter (Windows) key, and you've got a link!

Of course, you can also drag the appropriate page icon onto the hotspot itself. After you've finished assigning hotspots, you can toggle to PageMill's Preview mode to check the links. If you're feeling really brave, you can even look at the HTML created by the image map tool by selecting Edit|HTML Source. The results will look similar to Figure 3.15. The HTML is not very hard to figure out. Each hotspot is defined by an area shape, starting and ending coordinates, and its URL.

Button bars aren't the only type of navigational graphics that you're likely to use in your Web page designs. The possibilities are truly limitless. Chapter 4 demonstrates some more complex navigational designs, and Chapter 7 covers cool Java and JavaScript rollover navigation. In the next section, we'll look at how to use icons, illustrations, and photographs to spice up your pages.

Using Icons, Dingbats, And Dividers

A well-designed Web site uses a carefully crafted aggregate of images to convey its message. So far, we've covered what might be considered the "printing stock" of a site: the background and navigational graphics. These first two image categories form a container into which you'll

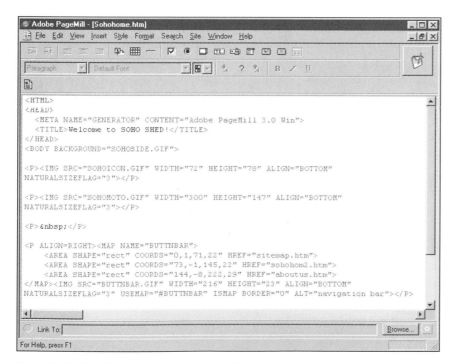

Figure 3.15   Yes! You, too, can make sense of image maps!

pour the good stuff. Now, you're ready to look at the types of images you can use to allow each Web page to stand on its own by enticing and informing its readers.

Icons

Icons are pictographic objects that can convey more information than visitors might glean from a single-word text link (or graphic button). Unfortunately, great icons are not the norm. The responsibility of creating icons is too often left to chance (and a clip art book). The best icons are custom crafted specifically for the application at hand. You must create meaningful images that tell the story properly rather than haphazardly use prebuilt clip art that confuses and frustrates your visitors. The icons used on the mythical Onliner Diner page, shown in Figure 3.16, leave little to chance.

If you decide to use icons as links, you would be wise to include text links to the same URLs also. These text links do not have to be placed physically next to the icons, just as long as they're not buried too deeply on the page. If you're in search of icons, be sure to check out the Appendix. It focuses on online typographical resources and includes URLs for some wonderful sources for icon fonts, such as Émigré and Letraset.

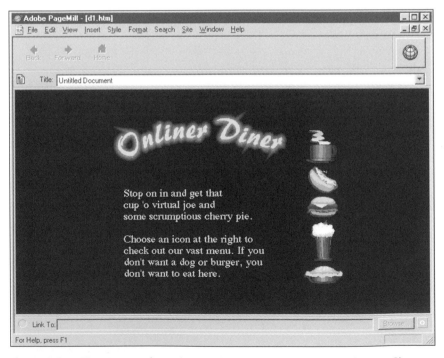

Figure 3.16   There's no confusion here: a dog's a dog and a burger's a burger. Cherry pie with that?

Dingbats

If the only *dingbat* you know is Edith Bunker, you're showing your age. Any desktop publisher worth his or her weight in lead will tell you that dingbats are really just little typographical doodads, falling somewhere between bullets and icons. But the definition can get blurry in both directions. Figures 3.17 and 3.18 display some of the dingbats included with Adobe's Zapf Dingbats and Microsoft's Wingdings fonts. In all likelihood, one or both of these fonts are already installed on your Macintosh or PC.

Dingbats are a wonderful replacement for the dull, boring bullets provided by HTML's list commands. To use a dingbat (from any font) in your PageMill designs, you'll first have to size and rasterize it with your favorite graphics application, such as Adobe Photoshop, Macromedia FreeHand, or CorelDraw! You can use a dingbat in basic black, or you can colorize it to your heart's content.

When you're using images as bullets, pay close attention to how the bullets align with the text. Depending on the bullet shape, you may want to try a top, middle, or bottom alignment. This book's CD-ROM contains basic round and square bullet dingbats in a variety of sizes and 99 "Netscape-safe" colors. These little critters are designed to coordinate with the enclosed vertical striped backgrounds and horizontal divider bars.

Divider Bars

Although HTML provides built-in horizontal rules (complete with control over width and weight), you may find that they do little to jazz up your Web page designs. Standard HTML rules can get a little lost on the page. Graphic horizontal dividers, on the other hand, add a nice touch by breaking pages into clearly defined sections. And to top it off, you can even use animated GIFs as bullets or dividers (should you choose to

Figure 3.17 Adobe's Zapf Dingbats was, perhaps, the most popular dingbat font of all time, until...

Figure 3.18 ...Microsoft rolled out its Wingdings. Both fonts are stuffed full of nifty little doodads.

challenge the barriers of good taste). The appendix lists a number of Web sites where you can find wacky animated bullets and rules.

The horizontal rules on the CD-ROM are available in three convenient widths (based on the widths of the vertical striped background), but they are all two pixels high. You can change the height (or weight) of the rule by typing a new height value in the Inspector (just remember to deselect the Scale to Height and Width options). Try adding a border to the rule for a different effect.

With the graphic appetizers out of the way, let's move on to the main course: tasty illustrations and photographs.

Using Illustrations And Photographs

An expressive illustration or an impeccable photograph can convey more information to visitors in one glance than a Web page chock full of text. The old adage "A picture is worth a thousand words" is true, however, only when it's the *right* picture. Take the time to find or create the right picture, and you will be rewarded. If you use what you have at hand just to fill space, Net users will scoff.

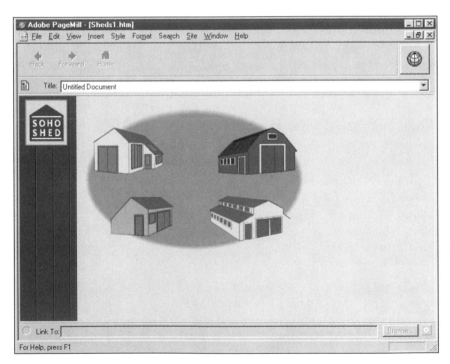

Figure 3.19 Don't look too closely at the perspectives, but these barn illustrations were all created specifically for this Web page.

Finding Illustrations And Illustrators

Illustrations can come in various forms. At the bottom of the list are the commercial clip art collections. Many of these aggregations aim to deliver a huge volume of material at a low price. Although you get thousands and thousands of images for pennies apiece, you may often find that you don't get *exactly* what you need. The illustration that's in your head is rarely found on a commercial disk. If you have the requisite graphics programs and skills, you can try modifying or combining existing artwork, or you can try to create your own art from scratch, like we did for the SOHO SHED page, as shown in Figure 3.19.

The most appropriate and effective artwork is created specifically for the application at hand. That's why it's a prudent business decision to find the right artists and have them render something according to your needs. If you have a budget to spend on real illustration, get your hands on a bunch of artists' sourcebooks or some issues of *Communication Arts* (the *Illustration Annual* is a wonderful resource) to see who's who and who does what. These books will have telephone numbers (and maybe even email addresses) of the artists or the agents who represent them.

Using Photographs

Photographs are among the most compelling Web page graphics. More so than any other type of imagery, photographs quickly tell their story. By conveying a sense of reality, photographs put the viewers right into the picture and leave little to interpretation (unless, of course, the photo is abstract). You can import photographs into the computer in one of four general ways:

- Scanners
- Digital cameras
- Video frame grabs
- PhotoCD

LOOKING FOR AN ILLUSTRATOR?

Professional artists have made their way to the Internet. You can view samples and portfolios online, without ever having to leave your desk chair.

Publishers Depot
http://www.publishersdepot.com/

Zaks Illustrator's Source
http://www.zaks.com/illustrators/

Yahoo

- http://www.yahoo.com/Arts/Graphic_Arts/ Illustration/Artists/

- http://www.yahoo.com/Business_and_Economy/ Companies/Arts_and_Crafts/Illustration/Artists/

- http://www.yahoo.com/Business_and_Economy/ Companies/Arts_and_Crafts/Illustration/Studios/

Scanners convert either reflective or transparent art into digital form. Although basic flatbed reflective scanners—used for digitizing photographic prints, sketches, and the like—start under $200, transparency scanners (which are used for scanning 35mm slides, negatives, and 4×5 transparencies) start at about $1,000 and run up to over a hundred grand for a full-blown commercial drum scanner. For Web page use, however, if you're scanning from 35mm slides, a $1,000 transparency scanner will deliver all the image you need.

Digital cameras capture images directly into digital files. Although the most affordable digital cameras start at just a few hundred dollars, they are not capable of capturing the same quality of image as the combination of a traditional camera and scanner. The most attractive aspect of the less-expensive digital cameras is that they save time by avoiding the steps of photo processing and scanning. High-end digital cameras, however, deliver serious image quality and are a boon to the quality-oriented, time-constrained Web publisher. As with high-end scanners, though, top-notch digital cameras still cost many thousands of dollars, and are out of most people's reach.

Video frame grabs allow you to import still images from a video camcorder or VCR into your Web page designs. The most economical

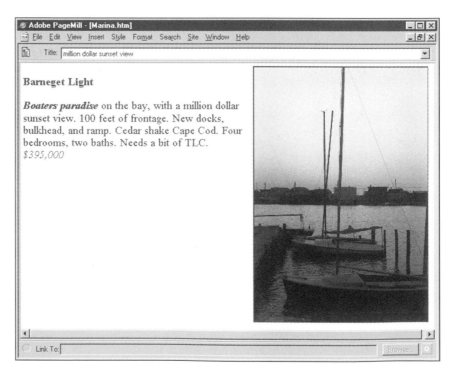

Figure 3.20   Remember the waterfront property in Chapter 1? You can tell your site visitors about the $1 million sunset view, or you can show them.

option is Play Inc.'s Snappy, which plugs into the PC's parallel (printer) port and delivers surprisingly good image quality.

Kodak's *PhotoCD* is a great choice if you've shot conventional photographic film but don't have access to a scanner. A Kodak photo lab can take your negatives and scan them onto PhotoCD media. If you use PhotoCD, you'll need a CD-ROM-equipped computer and software capable of converting from the PhotoCD format.

Regardless of source, photographs should almost always be saved as JPEG format files for Web page use. JPEG provides the highest level of detail and compression, which means that your viewers will get the juiciest shots in the shortest possible time (as shown in Figure 3.20). You can also use digital stock photographs in your Web page designs, in addition to photos you've taken (or had taken) yourself. Just be sure to check those copyright agreements to verify that their use is well within the constraints of the fine print.

In the next section, you'll put PageMill to work as you create a simple pair of pages for SOHO SHED, a mythical purveyor of alternative working environments.

PROJECT 2 SOHO SHED

SOHO SHED has decided to launch its own Web site. SOHO, a unique company, manufactures sheds and small barns for the small office/home office marketplace. When you're working from home and run out of room, give SOHO a call. It can deliver a complete air-conditioned and heated shed in two weeks or less. These beauties are ready to move in, fully wired with Ethernet, an Internet router, phone jacks, and even satellite hookups. Its customers never have to pick up a tool—only the telephone. And now, SOHO is ready to extend its marketing blitz to the Web.

Your task will be to create two sample Web pages: a Welcome page and an image-mapped page displaying SOHO's four basic models. Along the way, you'll learn how to place images, assign transparency to an inline GIF image, and create your own image map. You'll access all the ready-made graphic files from this book's CD-ROM.

Setting A Background Image

Start by opening a new page in PageMill; to do so, select File|New Page. If the Inspector is not showing, summon it from the View menu. Open the CHAP-3 directory from the CD-ROM, drag (copy) it onto your hard drive, and then drag the copied directory over to the side of your desktop. The CHAP-3 directory will be the root directory for this Web site project. Drag the SOHOSIDE.GIF file from that directory onto the background image well in the Inspector's Page tab. Your page should look like Figure 3.21. Note that the background image well can show only a portion of this short and wide GIF image. If you choose the wrong file, click on the Clear button underneath the well and try again.

Importing And Linking An Inline GIF Image

Now, bring in the SOHO logo icon file. Drag the SOHOICON.GIF file from the desktop to the upper-left corner of the PageMill window. Did you notice the three handles on the image? You can use them to stretch or scale the placed GIF, if absolutely necessary. Because this logo file was designed to drop right into the "barn siding," you shouldn't have to fiddle with it. Next, look at the Inspector. It automatically displays the height and width of the placed image. You can resize the image (to the pixel) here as well. Also, take the time to assign an alternate text label.

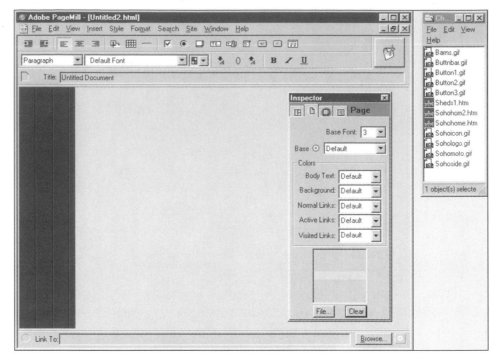

Figure 3.21 On this page, you can see the background image in place.

With the image still selected, type "aboutus.htm" in the Link To field at the bottom of the PageMill window, and press Return (Macintosh) or Enter (Windows). The page should appear as in Figure 3.22.

Assigning Transparency

Click to the right of the SOHO SHED logo to deselect it. The text insertion point should begin flashing directly to the right of the logo. Press Return (Macintosh) or Enter (Windows) to move to the next line. Now, you can bring in the company motto. Click and drag SOHOMOTO.GIF from the desktop into the PageMill window, just below the logo. When the image comes in, it will look like it's taking a chunk out of the barn siding (as shown in Figure 3.23). Take the time to label the image as "SOHO SHED. When your Small Office or Home Office just isn't big enough."

You really don't want to hack up the barn, so go ahead and assign transparency to the background color of the SOHOMOTO.GIF image. To assign transparency, you must first open PageMill's Image window by selecting Edit|Image|Open Image Window (or by pressing Cmd+D [Macintosh] or Ctrl+D [Windows]). The Image window provides a transparency tool (the magic wand) and an interlacing tool (the toggling disk/venetian blind), in addition to the image-mapping tools

RESIST TEMPTATION

Avoid resizing images in PageMill. Instead, rerender the image to the exact size in Photoshop.

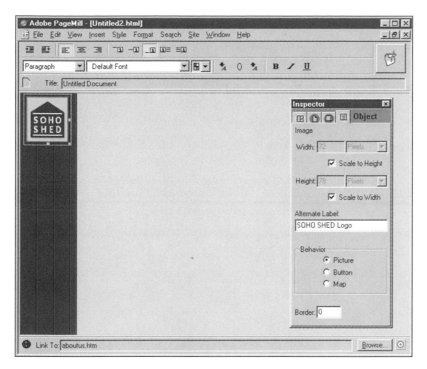

Figure 3.22 Always use the Inspector to label your images.

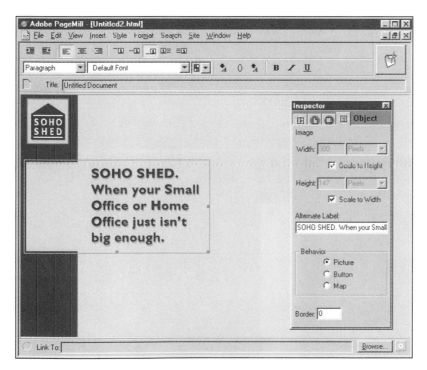

Figure 3.23 Ouch! What happened to the barn siding?

that are available within the Page Edit window. You assign transparency by selecting the background color (which you want to make transparent) with the magic wand. After you've assigned transparency (as shown in Figure 3.24), save the file by double-clicking on the Mona Lisa button at the top-left side of the Image window. When you save the file, it will overwrite the original file (which can get you into a loop if you've dragged the file directly from the CD-ROM because you cannot overwrite a CD). After you've saved the file, the page should appear as in Figure 3.25.

Of course, you have the option of assigning transparency in your favorite image editor, but PageMill conveniently gives you one last opportunity to set it as you build your page. For a GIF file to be properly transparent, it must have a consistent, nondithered background. Otherwise, you may end up with a spotty or splotchy "not-quite-so" transparent area. We'll cover more details on the subject of transparency online at www.geekbooks.com.

Creating Image Maps

Once deeply shrouded in mystery, the craft of creating image maps is now available to common folk. In just a few clicks and drags, you'll create an image map for a simple button bar. Start by deselecting the SOHO motto and press Return (Macintosh) or Enter (Windows). Click and drag BUTTNBAR.GIF from the desktop to just below the SOHO motto. The little button bar will drop onto the barn siding. Make it right align by clicking on the Right Align button at the top of the PageMill window.

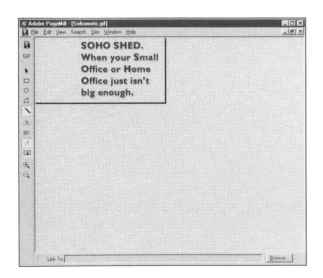

Figure 3.24 Although the background looks a little funky in the Out-of-Place image editor, it really is transparent!

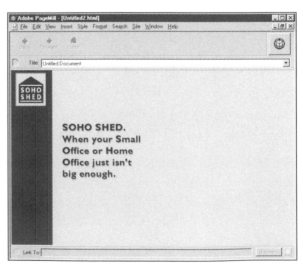

Figure 3.25 Now that's more like it. After the transparent image is saved to disk, it looks perfect on the Web page.

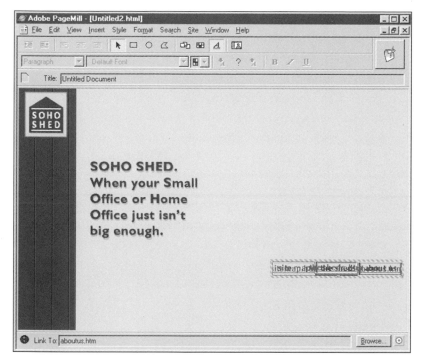

Figure 3.26 To resize a hotspot, just tug on its handles. Note that the hotspot information will obscure the image underneath when viewed in PageMill.

To access the in-place image map tools, double-click on the image. Select the Rectangle Hot Spot tool, and drag a rectangle around the Site Map button. Click in the Link To bar, type "sitemap.htm", and press Return (Macintosh) or Enter (Windows). Creating an image map is that easy! Now, repeat the procedure to create the last two buttons. Link them to thesheds.htm and aboutus.htm, respectively. Your page should appear as shown in Figure 3.26.

To finish the page, type "Welcome to SOHO SHED!" in the title bar, press Return (Macintosh) or Enter (Windows), and save the file as sohohome.htm. You're going to use the basic template of the page, with the background, button bar, and logo to complete the second page, aboutus.htm.

Delete the SOHO motto graphic from the page, and save the file immediately as aboutus.htm. Replace the old graphic with BARNS.GIF, and center the image. (You may need to fiddle around with different image alignment settings to alter the spacing between the logo and the barns.) Next, select Edit|Image|Open Image Window (or press Cmd+D [Macintosh] or Ctrl+D [Windows]) to access the Image window, make the background transparent, and save the image. Double-click on the image to access the image map tools. Then use the Polygon Hot Spot tool on each of the four barns. Just click, click, click around each barn

SLIDE ON OVER

With a small image map, resizing the individual hotspots can be tricky. Try sliding the hotspots around to access their resizing handles.

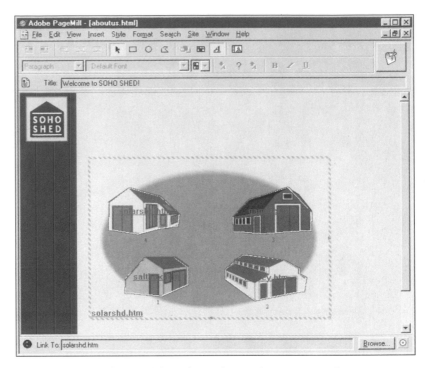

Figure 3.27 With four models to choose from in this image map, how are you going to keep visitors down on the farm, er, home office?

to create the hotspot. For the next step, double-click on the starting point of the hotspot outline to close it. Finally, from the top left and moving in a clockwise manner, assign the barns the URLs "solarshd.htm", "gambrel.htm", "horsey.htm", and "saltbox.htm". If you mess up a hotspot beyond repair, don't fret; just delete it and start over again. The results should look roughly like Figure 3.27.

Although the underbelly of the image map has a disconcerting appearance in Edit mode, all the noise disappears when you toggle into Preview mode. Check it out now.

Moving On

In this chapter, you learned how to work with graphics in Adobe PageMill. A successfully designed Web page includes a healthy mix of both text and graphics. You worked from the back (the background and navigational graphics) of a Web page through to the front (icons, illustrations, and photographs). A good practice is to attack the design of a page by taking into consideration how the different layers visually interact. A haphazard collection of graphics does not make an effective Web page.

In the next chapter, we'll explore the HTML layout controls provided by PageMill 3's Table tool. We'll delve further into the subject of graphics online at www.geekbooks.com.

CREATE A DEFAULT IMAGE MAP LINK

You can assign a default link for the image map to direct any clicks that do not fall on one of the hotspots. With the image (but none of its hotspots) selected, type the default link into the Link To bar.

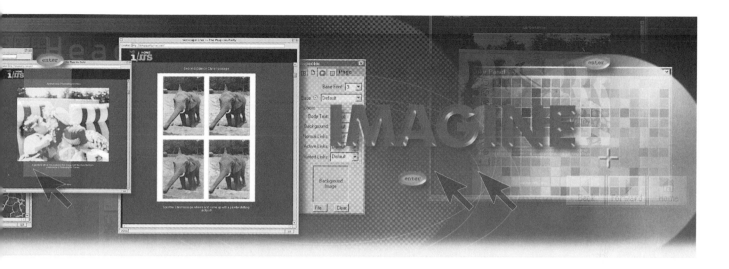

USING
TABLES
4

In this chapter, you'll take charge of PageMill's table editing features.

Typically, when people start building their very first Web pages, they often "hit the wall" and become frustrated by the complexity involved in creating anything but the simplest page layout. Fortunately, PageMill 3 makes it easy to implement some of the most intricate features of HTML's table controls. This chapter builds on what you've learned in the preceding chapters and allows you to quickly master these advanced features.

Learning how to control tables is key to the craft of advanced Web page design. With PageMill's visual controls, you can see exactly what you're doing as you're doing it.

Why Should I Use Tables?

HTML tables impart a high level of structure in your Web page designs. When tables were first implemented (back in Netscape Navigator 1.1), Web designers quickly became enthralled with their control over text alignment, individual column width, overall table width, borders, and various spacing attributes. In the early days, writing out all the HTML code necessary to build a nice-looking table was a tough hack. Thankfully, PageMill 3's Inspector and interactive design now make it easy to control each of these characteristics.

There are three basic reasons to use HTML tables. The first reason is implied by the name of the command, whereas the second and third, although they are every bit as important, may not be as obvious. You'll use tables to perform the following tasks:

- To create tables, such as spreadsheets, parts listings, statistical data, and financial reports (as shown in Figure 4.1)

- To constrain pages to a specific width

- To create multicolumn page layouts

Using Tables As Tables

When someone first mentions tables, you immediately think of the many types of information that are commonly presented in columnar form. The first thing that might come to mind is a spreadsheet, such as those from Microsoft Excel or Lotus 1-2-3. Perhaps you might think of the asset sheet from your company's annual report (as shown in Figure 4.1). If you're a sports fan, yesterday's box scores could be the ticket.

With PageMill 3, you can easily create HTML tables that can be highly customized to suit your needs. The Inspector's table controls allow you to take charge over the entire table as well as over individual cells.

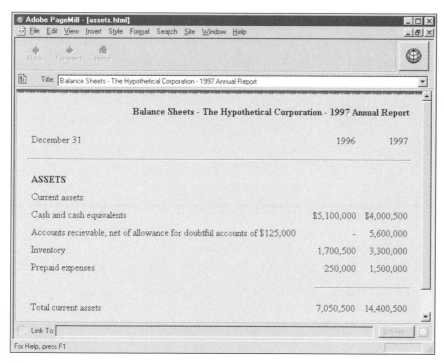

Figure 4.1 The Hypothetical Corporation uses its Web site to deliver its annual report to shareholders and the financial community.

Table height, however, has to be set interactively. With the entire table selected, you can change the following characteristics (as shown in Figure 4.2):

- *Width*—Can be set absolutely (as pixels) or relatively (as a percentage of browser width). You can click and drag on the table border to resize the relative width interactively, or you can change the width settings in the Inspector.

- *Height*—Optional. Can be set absolutely (as pixels) or relatively (as a percentage of browser height). You can click and drag on the table border to resize the relative height interactively, or you can change the height settings in the Inspector.

- *Caption*—Optional. Can be set to run either above the table (as a title) or below (as a footnote). Captioning is toggled on and off via the Inspector.

- *Border*—Runs around the outside of the table. Can be set anywhere from 0 (no border) to 500 (a huge, silly border). You'll rarely need to go wider than 5 (if that), although the wider the border, the more three dimensional the table will appear. The border is set via the Inspector.

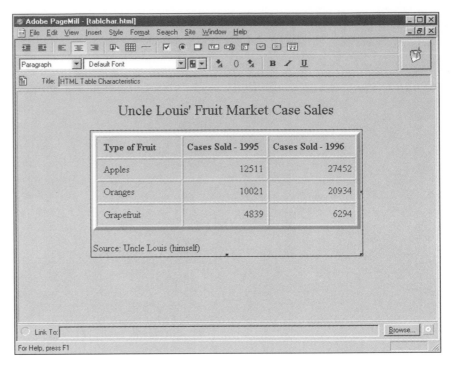

Figure 4.2 This simple table includes a border, cell spacing, cell padding, and a caption.

- *Cell spacing*—Determines the amount of space *between* cells. Appears as visible grid lines when the table border is set to anything larger than 0 and as white space when the border is set to 0. You might think of cell spacing as individual cell borders (keeping in mind that the attributes can be set for an entire table only, not specific cells). Cell spacing is set via the Inspector.

- *Cell padding*—No, it's not what we need in our offices after we've been working on our Web site for too long; it's the amount of white space added *inside* each cell. Cell padding is set via the Inspector.

You can apply cell controls to individual cells or groups of cells. Here's a rundown on cell controls (as shown in Figure 4.3):

- *Width Constraint*—Can be set absolutely (as pixels) or relatively (as a percentage of table width). Only one width per column is allowed. Cell width can be set interactively by clicking and dragging on cell borders or by entering the width via the Inspector.

- *Height Constraint*—Can be set absolutely (as pixels) or relatively (as a percentage of table height). Only one height per row is allowed. Cell height can be set interactively by clicking and dragging on cell borders or by entering the width via the Inspector.

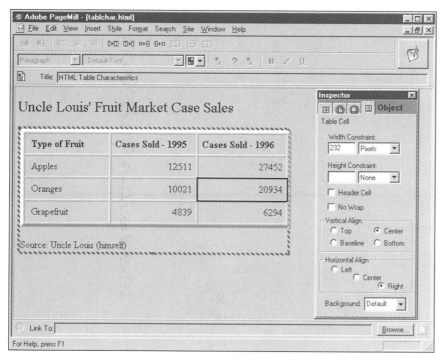

Figure 4.3 Individual cell controls are set via the Inspector.

- *Header Cell*—Automatically sets text in boldface, with a centered alignment. You set this option via the Inspector.

- *No Wrap*—Bases column width on longest line. You set this option via the Inspector.

- *Vertical Alignment*—Determines the top, middle, bottom, or baseline of a cell. You set this option via the Inspector.

- *Horizontal Alignment*—Determines the left, right, or center. You set this option via the Inspector.

- *Background Color*—Can be set to any valid color. Background tiles are not supported. You set this option via the Inspector.

You can also plug the settings directly into the table commands while you're working in HTML Source mode (as shown in Figure 4.4). HTML Source mode is a great asset when you're trying to fine-tune or troubleshoot a table. You can access HTML Source mode via the View menu or by pressing the Cmd+H (Macintosh) or Ctrl+H (Windows) keyboard shortcuts.

Working With Tables

PageMill 3 lets you work with tables from a variety of sources. You can open existing HTML tables (which have been created in other programs),

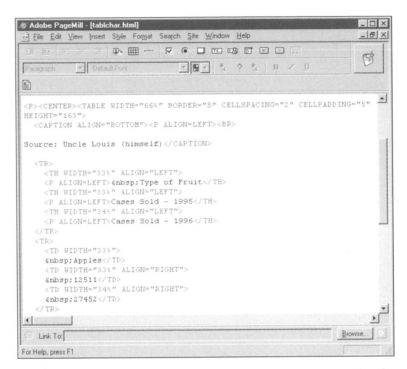

Figure 4.4 Don't get scared! You can make edits in HTML Source mode only if you want to.

you can use PageMill's conversion utilities to convert files, or you can create your own tables from scratch. If your word processing program supports HTML table export, you can save time by exporting a table and then opening the HTML file in PageMill to make the last few tweaks. Chapter 9 reviews a number of ways to get outside data into PageMill.

One of the coolest (and fastest) ways to get table data into PageMill is to cut and paste it from Microsoft's popular spreadsheet program, Excel. To move a table from Excel into PageMill, all you have to do is select the range of cells in Excel, copy it, switch to PageMill, and paste it in. After you place the table on the Web page, you can go in and tweak it to your heart's content.

Now, let's see what is required to create a table from scratch. To create a table in PageMill, you'll need to use the Insert Table button on the button bar (it's the one that looks like a little grid). If you click and drag on the button, a snappy grid will drop down (as shown in Figure 4.5), signifying table width and height in columns and rows, respectively. You can specify a maximum of 10 rows and 10 columns in this manner. When you release the mouse button, PageMill will draw the table with its default border, cell spacing, and cell padding (as shown in Figure 4.6).

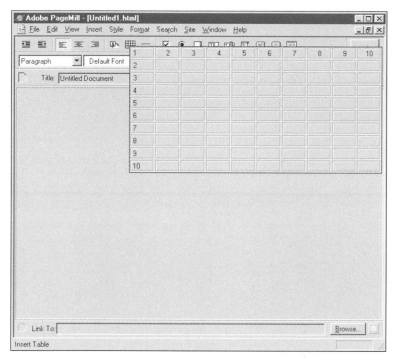

Figure 4.5 The drop-down grid looks like a flyswatter of sorts.

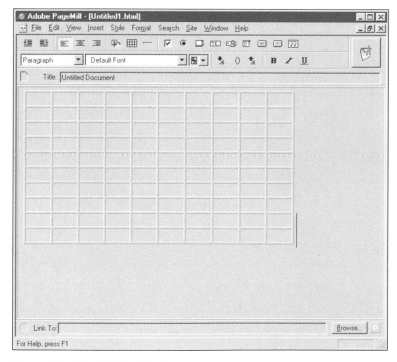

Figure 4.6 The 10×10 grid is drawn.

If you click on the Insert Table button (instead of clicking and dragging), you'll summon the Insert Table dialog box. This convenient dialog box allows you to specify more than 10 rows or columns (up to 99 of each) in addition to setting the cell spacing, cell padding, table border, and width (as shown in Figure 4.7). If you know how you want your table to look before you set it, you can save a bit of time by using the Insert Table dialog box (instead of going to the Inspector to set these characteristics after the table is already on the page).

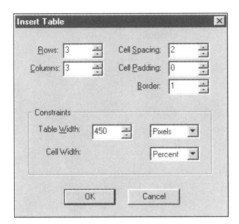

Figure 4.7   The Insert Table dialog box lets you set table characteristics before you drop the table on the page.

After you place the table on the page, you can enter the data or edit what's already there (if you opened an existing HTML file). The following handful of tricks will help you edit a table's contents:

- Edit the data in a cell by clicking an insertion point, by double-clicking to select a word, or by triple-clicking to select a line. To select all the data in a word-wrapped (multiline) cell, click an insertion point, and choose Select All, or press the Cmd+A (Macintosh) or Ctrl+A (Windows) keyboard shortcuts.

- Use the Tab key to navigate between table cells. Pressing the Tab key will move forward through the table cells. Pressing Shift+Tab will move backward through the table cells.

- To change the characteristics—such as the width, alignment, or background color—of a cell (or cells), you must first select the cell (or range of cells) by clicking and dragging from one corner of the selection to the opposite corner. An outline will appear around the cell (or cells), letting you know exactly what is selected. You then can make changes in the Inspector.

- After you select a cell , you can Shift+click to select additional cells.

- Edit|Table|Select More (Cmd+Shift+9 [Macintosh] or Ctrl+Shift+9 [Windows]) and Edit|Table|Select Less (Cmd+9 [Macintosh] or Ctrl+9 [Windows]) are two indispensable new shortcuts. You can use them to toggle between selecting the contents of a cell, selecting the cell itself, and selecting the entire table.

- You can access PageMill 3's table editing tools by selecting Edit|Table or by using the button bar.

- If working in a text editor suits your style better, you can always switch to the HTML Source mode (as shown in Figure 4.4).

Adding And Deleting Columns And Rows

The first four buttons in PageMill's table editing button bar (see Figure 4.8) allow you to add or delete columns or rows easily. To add a column or row, begin by selecting a cell, and then click on the appropriate button (or select Edit|Table). The column or row will be added to the table immediately after the selected column or row. In other words, columns are added to the right of the selection, and rows are added below the selection. The process of deleting columns or rows is straightforward as well. Just select a cell in the column or row you want to delete, and click on the appropriate button.

OKAY, THAT'S COOL, BUT HOW DO I...?

Unfortunately, HTML doesn't provide all the niceties that you may have come to expect from your spreadsheet program. For instance, you cannot perform decimal alignment on columns of figures. You'll have to cook up a design compromise to handle situations such as this one.

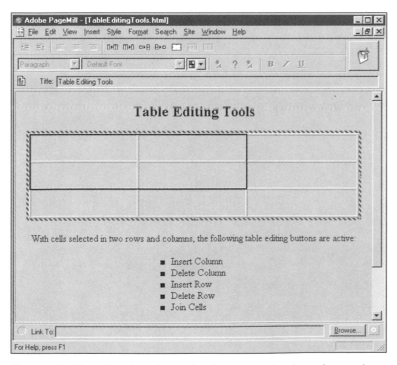

Figure 4.8 The table editing button bar becomes active dependent on the selected cells.

Joining And Splitting Cells

You're probably thinking, "Okay, now what do those last three buttons in the table editing button bar actually do?" Get ready to go back to high school biology class because you're about to learn how to join and split cells. Although this process is not truly comparable to the mystery of life, it is the HTML magic behind the most complex table and page layouts. Coding this kind of stuff by hand is a laborious chore that often leads to premature hair loss and intense stomach distress. Thankfully, PageMill 3 makes this task about as easy as it could possibly be (as shown in Figure 4.9).

To join two (or more) cells, all you need to do is select the cells and click the Join Cell button. If you take a look at the source code, you'll see that HTML uses **ROWSPAN="X"** and **COLSPAN="X"** modifiers to allow a joined cell to straddle rows or columns, where the *X* defines the number of cells to be straddled. These features are invaluable when you start building anything more than the most simple table and page layouts. Figure 4.10 demonstrates a common example of how you might use these features. The "Fruit Sold (by case)" heading straddles two rows, and the "Years" heading straddles three columns.

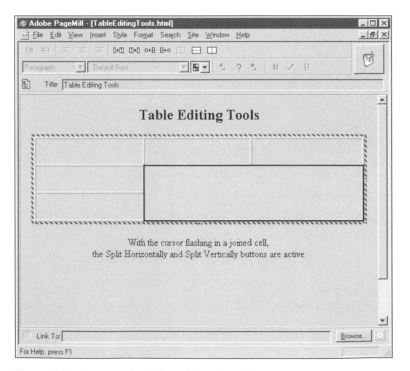

Figure 4.9 Joining and splitting table cells is a breeze.

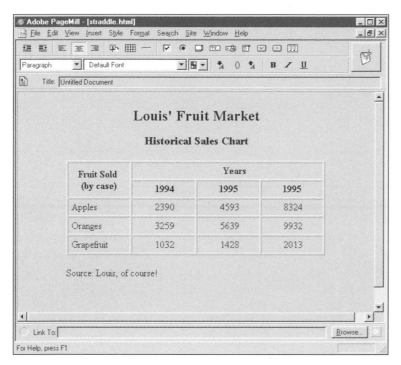

Figure 4.10 Creating a table like this without joining cells would be impossible.

To split a joined cell (either vertically or horizontally), click within the cell you wish to split and click the appropriate button. It's that easy! Now, let's take a look at why just about every Web page should use at least one simple table.

Building A Table

Let's take what we've just learned and replicate the table shown in Figure 4.10. Start with a new page and then follow these steps:

1. Click and drag on the Insert Table button to create a four-column by five-row grid. When you release the mouse button, PageMill creates a 4 by 5 table.

2. Click and drag to select the top two cells in the first column. Click on the Join Cells button to vertically (row) span the cells.

3. Click and drag to select the top cell in the last three columns. Click on the Join Cells button to horizontally (column) span the cells.

4. Following Figure 4.10, type the information into each cell. Click in the spanned cells to enter the data there. Use the Tab key to move forward through the other cells (press Shift+Tab to move backward).

HOW WIDE SHOULD I MAKE MY PAGES?

This is a subject of great debate among Web designers. While you may be using a high-resolution display, your audience may not be so lucky. Shoot for the lowest common denominator. Because many folks still use computers with a 640 by 480 display area, you should not make your Web pages too wide. Otherwise, your audience will have to scroll horizontally, and that's just not cool. You should stay safely within a 640 pixel wide area—600 pixels should do you well.

Some Web sites use extremely wide pages for special design effects. For example: Hitachi markets a line of large computer monitors. Their Web site at http://www.nsa-hitachi.com uses horizontal scrolling as a method to prove their point; that is, large monitors are more productive because they display a larger image area, hence less scrolling.

5. After you've entered all the data, click and drag to select the nine cells containing the sales data. Use the Inspector to set Vertical Align and Horizontal Align to center.

6. Click and drag to select the two spanned cells and the three cells containing the years. Use the Inspector to designate these cells as Header Cells and set the Vertical Align and Horizontal Align to center.

7. Click on the page to deselect the table; then reselect it. Use the Inspector to set a bottom-aligned caption. Try fiddling around with different Borders, Cell Spacing, and Cell Padding options to see how they affect the table.

8. On the table, select the default word "caption" and type a new caption. To push the caption away from the table, place the cursor at the beginning of the caption and press Shift+Return (Macintosh) or Shift+Enter (Windows) to add a line. Press Shift+Return (Macintosh) or Shift+Enter (Windows) to break "Fruit Sold (by case)" into two lines as well.

9. To interactively change the overall height of the table, click and drag downward on the bottom center of the table. You can interactively change the overall width of the table by clicking and dragging on the right side of the table. To scale both the height and width at the same time, click and drag on the left or right bottom corners of the table. To set the height or width of the table precisely (in pixels or as a percentage), use the Inspector.

10. Try changing column heights and widths interactively by clicking and dragging on the intercolumn grid lines. Then, try changing column heights and widths by selecting all the cells in a row or column and entering the height or width in the Inspector.

After you've finished creating this little table, try experimenting on your own. Drag in some graphics, try changing cell background colors, and give nested tables a whirl as well.

Using Tables To Constrain Page Width

Have you ever seen a Web page that looked totally unbalanced—one where the header graphic ended three quarters of the way across the browser window, but the text flowed out to fill the window, (as demonstrated in Figure 4.11)? That's an example of an unconstrained Web page and a prime reason why tables are essential when you're building anything but the most elementary layouts. Tables allow you to design pages that "stick" to a defined width. Although an unconstrained Web page allows its text to flow freely to fit the width of the browser window, you can set a specific pixel width for the text to flow (as in Figure 4.12) by adding a simple table to the page.

When creating a width-constraining table, you'll probably want to base the table width on the width of the widest graphic on the page. A good strategy is to have one overall page width that carries through every page on your Web site to provide a continuity of design. Otherwise, your pages will seem like they're jumping all over

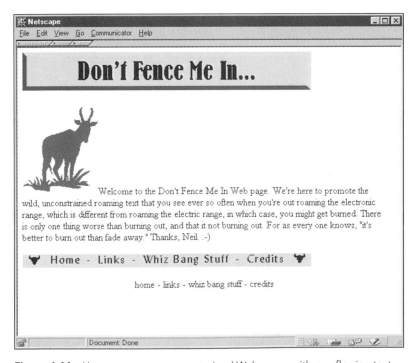

Figure 4.11   Here, you see an unconstrained Web page, with overflowing text.

Figure 4.12 And here's the same page, given a bit of manners with a simple width-constraining table.

the place. Try building some page-width-constraining tables now, using the table-building skills that you've just learned.

Working With Nested Tables

For intricate layouts, you'll often place tables within tables. These types of tables are commonly referred to as *nested tables.* Although that term might conjure up visions of those funny end tables at Aunt Edna's place, good old Edna never had the furniture flexibility that PageMill 3 provides when building complex Web pages. You won't end up with your proverbial drink and hors d'oeuvre in your lap.

Nested tables come into play when you place, say, a little spreadsheet into a page with a table-constrained layout. Tables can be dragged and dropped into other tables, or they can be cut and pasted. You have the option of dragging them from the Pasteboard as well as from other pages. Figure 4.13 shows a simple pair of nested tables, as you might see used on a baseball Web page. To nest a table within another table, click in the cell into which you want to place the table; then paste (or drag) the table into position. It's that easy!

After you nest the "inside" table in the "outside" table, you can assign the inside table's horizontal and vertical alignment within its cell. You

EVER WISH YOU HAD A RULER IN PAGEMILL?

Why guess? Check out Screen Ruler for Windows: http://www.kagi.com/microfox/

can also try some nifty design tricks by using different colored backgrounds for the inside and outside tables. Nested tables open up a whole new range of Web page layout possibilities. Try giving one a shot now. You'll be amazed at how easy they are to build.

Now that you've got the nitty-gritty on how to build tables, let's take a look at how you can use tables to build complex multicolumn pages.

Using Tables For Multicolumn Pages

The slickest Web page designs use the HTML table commands to create multiple-column layouts. Although we're all accustomed to multiple-column print publications, such as newspapers and magazines, multiple-column Web page layouts are a different beast altogether. Multicolumn Web pages most often consist of two- or three-column layouts. The dynamics of good Web page design frequently demand that the first column of a multicolumn page be used for a vertical navigational bar (as shown by *The Photoshop Plug-ins Book* table of contents page from the geekbooks.com Web site, in Figure 4.14).

Figure 4.15 shows how the skeleton of the page looks in the PageMill 3 Edit window. Notice the variation in spacing as it relates to the button bar. A dramatic difference may be noticeable between how a Web page appears in PageMill 3 and how the page appears in each Web browser. Comment markers (the exclamation mark icons), like those shown around the navigation buttons, help to make things less WYSIWYG in PageMill's Edit mode as well; they do not appear in PageMill's Preview mode, however.

Carving Images Into Tables

Want to tackle a tough graphic layout? Chop it up into little pieces in Photoshop, and then precisely

HOW TALL SHOULD I MAKE MY PAGES?

Ah, to scroll or not to scroll, that is the question. Although some folks will rant and rave that pages should be as short and concise as possible, there are many times when you need to present *lots* of information on one page. If you're building a long page, use anchored navigational links at the top of the page. Anchored links were covered back in Chapter 2.

Try to get the page's key information *above the fold*. Think how a newspaper looks on the newsstand. When you're walking past the newsstand, all you can see are the stories (and advertisements) that appear on the top half of a newspaper's front page. This same conventional wisdom applies to Web pages as well. Don't expect your visitors to happily go scrolling along—lest they end up strolling on by.

Use the 640×480 display as your lowest common denominator. Leave plenty of room for all of those browser buttons and extraneous real estate.

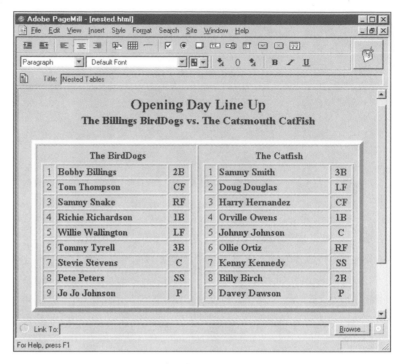

Figure 4.13 Batter up! Nested tables allow you to easily compile complex Web pages from several sources.

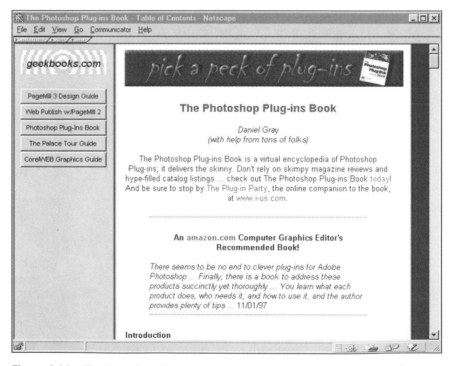

Figure 4.14 *The Photoshop Plug-ins Book* table of contents page uses a vertical button bar in the first column.

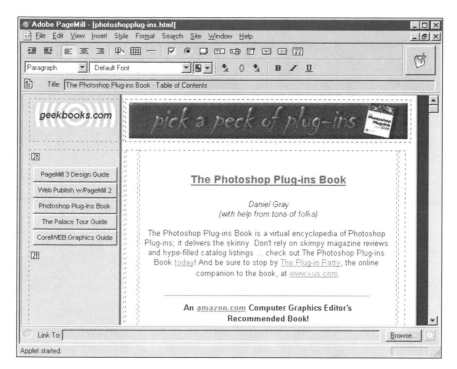

Figure 4.15 What's up with the spacing?

reassemble it in an HTML table in PageMill. Figures 4.16 through 4.19 demonstrate a series of steps you might take to slice and dice your way through a typical navigation graphic. Let's start with the original image in Photoshop (see Figure 4.16). Turn on Photoshop's Grid and Guideline features, and then drag out some guidelines to divide the image.

Use the rectangular selection tool to select the first area, and then copy the image area to the clipboard. Open a new file, paste the image into the new file, flatten the layers, and then save it. Repeat this procedure for each of the remaining chunks of the image. Figure 4.17 shows the image cut into five separate files.

A simple 480×313 two-column table was created for this image, with the Border, Cell Spacing, and Cell Padding all set to 0. These settings fit the overall width and height of the image precisely. The Vertical and Horizontal Alignment were set to top and left for both columns, respectively. The golfer was dragged into the first column, and the four remaining chunks were dragged into the second column. Each cell's Width Constraint was set for the exact width of its contents. Figure 4.18 shows the competed table in PageMill; it's definitely not

<!--USE COMMENTS-->

Carefully annotating in your HTML file by adding comment fields can help you to keep your sanity. To insert a comment, click Insert | Comment; then select the comment marker, and type your comment text in the Inspector. Comments are ignored by the Web browsers. **<!--this is what a comment looks like-->**

WATCH THOSE SPACES!

As you build your tabled graphic, be sure to eliminate any extra spaces because they will cause unsightly gaps in the layout. (The background will show through like grout around your bathroom tile.) If you use PageMill's HTML Source mode to remove the extra spaces, save the file from within HTML Source mode; as soon as you switch to Edit or Preview mode, PageMill will throw spaces back into the table.

PageMill 3 is unkind to table code created in other programs. If you've built a complex table in another program, be sure to encase it in <!--NOEDIT--> ... <!--/NOEDIT--> commands *before* opening the file in PageMill to prevent PageMill from causing havoc. Unfortunately, the table will not display in PageMill's Edit or Preview modes when encased in <!--NOEDIT--> ... <!--/NOEDIT--> commands.

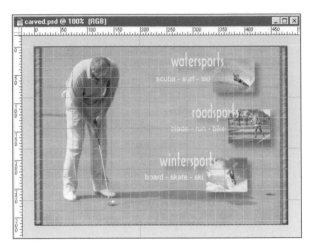

Figure 4.16   Here, you can see the original image in Photoshop, with the grid and guidelines turned on.

WYSIWYG. When the image is previewed in Netscape Navigator (see Figure 4.19), however, it's picture perfect.

This method is useful when you want to bring the individual sections of the graphic to life with either an animated GIF or JavaScript rollover. We'll dive into that subject in Chapter 7.

Changing Cell Color

Looking for some punch? Changing table cell colors, as shown in Figure 4.20, can make a dramatic difference in the way your information appears. The interaction between cell color and type color is critical. Keep in mind that your visitors may have their browsers configured to not display underlined hyperlinks.

Moving On

In this chapter, you learned how to implement complex Web page layouts through the use of tables. Tables are among the most powerful page layout commands in the basic HTML command set. With a little practice, you can create intricate HTML tables with the best of them simply by using PageMill. In the next chapter, you'll take your page layouts to the next level, as you learn how to create framed Web pages.

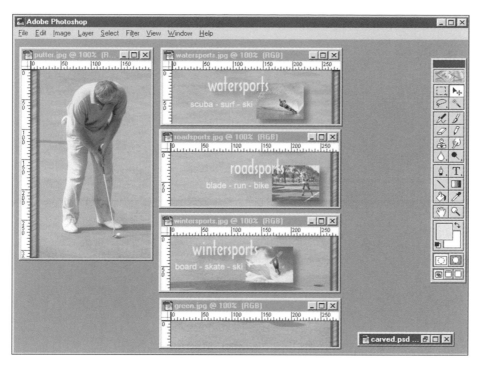

Figure 4.17 The image has been carved into five separate chunks.

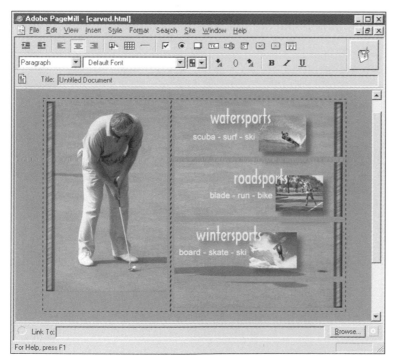

Figure 4.18 A simple two-column table is used in PageMill. Check out those crazy gaps.

NEED AN ELECTRIC KNIFE?

ShoeString's PictureDicer for Windows will do the tough stuff for you. The freeware version will carve up images *and* build the corresponding HTML tables. The shareware version (which was still in development as this was written) promises to generate JavaScript rollovers, as well. You can download PictureDicer from: http://www.ziplink.net/~shoestring/dicer01.htm

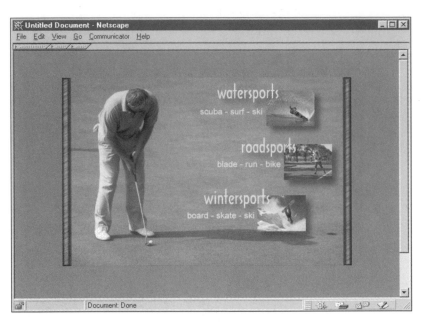

Figure 4.19 All looks well in Netscape Navigator!

Figure 4.20 The list of plug-ins is a nested table within the overall page template table.

FRAMING
YOUR SITE

What's the big deal about frames? Should you consider a framed layout?

Frames afford the Web page designer the ability to create modular Web sites with a persistent structure. This structure enables a flexible site, in which certain items such as headers, advertising banners, and navigational devices remain intact as your visitors scroll through the content and jump from page to page. This modular persistency can benefit your Web site in a number of ways:

- Logos and other ID graphics get more face time.
- Static advertising banners enhance the probability that the visitors will actually read the banner and, as the advertiser would hope, clickthrough.
- Consistent navigation can benefit the user interface.

How Do Frames Work?

In short, framed Web pages are nothing more than simple containers for other Web pages. It may help you to think of a framed layout as a little curio cabinet. You're allowed to build as many "shelves" as you want (although common sense says to never exceed four; use more and you'll be on thin Net ice) in your cabinet, although each shelf (frame) can hold just one item at a time. The curio cabinet is known as a *frameset,* with each shelf holding an individual Web page. When you click on a link on a framed page, the new page is displayed within the *target* window. You specify the target window when you create your links.

The frameset is a rather terse little file, basically consisting of a page title, along with references to the initial frame source files, as well as sizing, naming, and scrolling information. When you refer to the URL of a framed Web site, always refer to the URL of the frameset, not of the frames contained therein.

Slice And Dice

So you think you want to carve up your design into frames? Consider this move carefully; poorly implemented frames can ruin your visitors' experience. Always keep simplicity at the forefront of your designs. In practice, the best framed Web sites use either a two-, three-, or four-frame layout. Let's take a look at some basic examples of each.

Two Frames

Just want to keep your navigational structure separate from the content of your pages? With a simple two-frame layout, you can stuff the navigation and site identification into a top, side, or bottom frame. This solution can be clean and elegant. Figure 5.1 shows three basic two-frame layouts.

SEARCH ENGINES AND FRAMED WEB SITES

Some search engines fail to index framed pages properly. To accommodate these search engines, you should always make full use of **<META>** and **<NO FRAMES>** tags in the frameset. For more information on search engine strategies, check Chapter 8.

Figure 5.1 A two-frame layout is often the least obtrusive design.

Three Frames

Need to accommodate two persistent elements? A three-frame layout
can handle navigation and advertising in separate frames. Figure 5.2
shows some possibilities afforded by a three-frame layout.

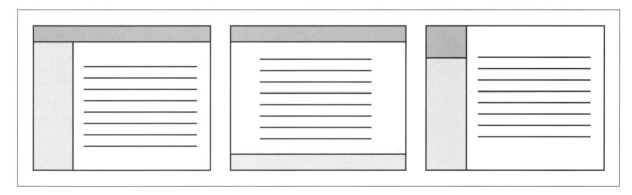

Figure 5.2 Three frames provide a wide degree of flexibility.

Four Frames

Into complexity? If you execute your four-framed layout carefully, you
can deliver your message effectively. Miss your mark, and you'll send your
visitors into a rage. Figure 5.3 shows some common four-frame layouts.

Thinking About Color

If you're considering a four- (or more) frame layout because of the
volume of information you need to present, you should pay heed to
the background color of each of the frames. You can reduce the visual
complexity of the interface by using the same background color for
two adjoining frames. This solution can be especially effective when
used with nonbordered, nonscrolling frames.

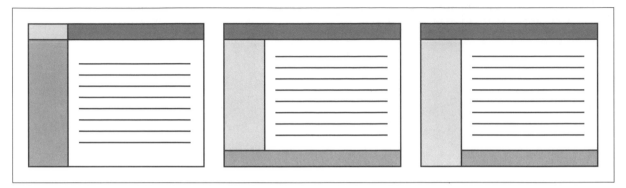

Figure 5.3 With four frames, the layout often gets cluttered.

Creating A Framed Layout

PageMill greatly simplifies the creation of framed Web sites. Building the frames themselves is actually rather easy; like most things PageMillian, all you have to do is drag 'em and drop 'em. Getting the targeting right, however, might make your eyes cross, unless you have a solid understanding of the basic principles. You would be wise to sketch out a diagram of how you would like your framed Web site to work *before* you go too far with page creation. Although sketching beforehand is always a good idea, it's especially so when you're creating framed sites.

Drawing Frames

You have a number of options when drawing a new frame. To split a window (or existing frame) in two quickly, choose Edit|Frame|Split Frame Horizontally, or press the Cmd+Shift+H (Macintosh) or Ctrl+Shift+H (Windows) keyboard shortcuts; this command will stack the new frame, as shown in Figure 5.4. The new horizontal frame will be placed below the existing frame.

If you want to create side-by-side frames, as illustrated in Figure 5.5, choose Edit|Frame|Split Frame Vertically, or press the Cmd+Shift+V (Macintosh) or Ctrl+Shift+V (Windows) keyboard shortcuts. The new vertical frame will be placed to the right of the existing frame.

You can also Option+drag (Macintosh) or Ctrl+drag (Windows) new frames out from the borders of the PageMill window. To do so, position the cursor over the horizontal border (to create a horizontal frame) or vertical border (to create a vertical frame), and hold down the Option (Macintosh) or Ctrl (Windows) key. The cursor will change into a little black arrow. While you're holding down the Option (Macintosh) or

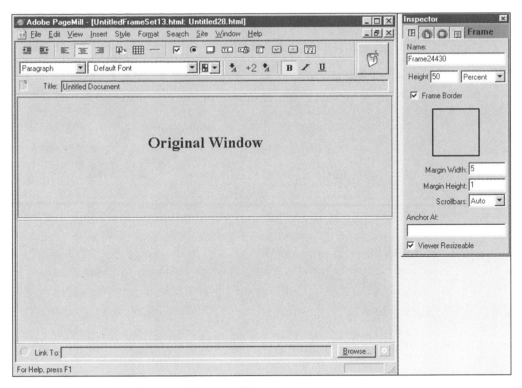

Figure 5.4 Here, a new frame is split horizontally.

Ctrl (Windows) key, drag the border to the position where you want the frame to appear. After the frames are drawn (no matter which method you used to create them), you can reposition the frame border by clicking and dragging it. Try creating some frames now, experimenting with each method.

Take a close look at the Inspector as shown in Figures 5.4 and 5.5. With the Frame tab chosen, you can fine-tune each frame. The first thing you should do is give each frame its own distinctive name. Performing this step is especially important *before* you start building your hyperlinks. If you change the name of the frame after it's linked, things could go awry. The name you specify in the Inspector will be the file name that PageMill uses when it saves the frame. Here's a run-down of the other options afforded by the Frame tab:

- *Frame Border*—Uncheck this box to get borderless frames.

- *Height*—You can set this option for horizontal frames, in percentage, pixel, or relative terms.

- *Width*—You can set this option for vertical frames, in percentage, pixel, or relative terms.

DROPPING FRAMES

Want to specify where the new frame appears? Use the Option+drag (Macintosh) or Ctrl+drag (Windows) method; the new frame will be placed on the side of window from which the frame was dragged.

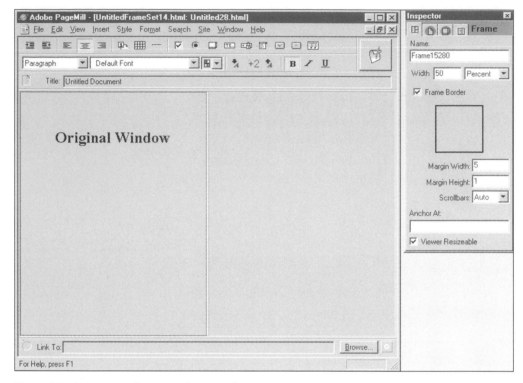

Figure 5.5 Here, a new frame is split vertically.

- *Margin Width*—This option determines the amount of space between the left and right sides of a frame and its contents.

- *Margin Height*—This option determines the amount of space between the top and bottom sides of a frame and its contents.

- *Scrollbars*—You can set this option to "yes", "no", or "auto". If the frame's content doesn't require scrollbars, be sure to set this option to "no".

- *Anchor At*—This option allows you to set up a framed page so that it opens at a specific point within a frame.

- *Viewer Resizeable*—Uncheck this box to prevent visitors from resizing specific windows (such as advertising banners).

After you've drawn a frame, you can draw additional frames within the first frame. Just click inside the framed area, and create the new frame using the methods described previously. Before you go wild and start drawing too many frames (as I did in Figure 5.6), you should sit down and consider the alternatives. You may be able to accomplish a similar layout through the use of tables instead.

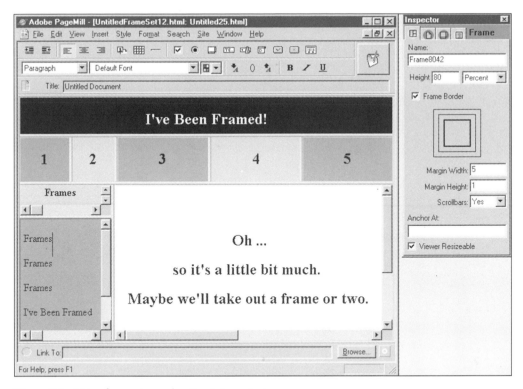

Figure 5.6 Using frames in moderation is important.

With the frames laid out and properly named, you should immediately choose File|Frameset|Save Frameset or press the Cmd+Shift+S (Macintosh) or Ctrl+Shift+S (Windows) keyboard shortcuts to save your frameset. After you start building inside the frames, you can also choose File|Frameset|Save Everything or press the Cmd+E (Macintosh) or Ctrl+E (Windows) keyboard shortcuts to save the frameset along with the individual frames in one fell swoop. PageMill will not store the individual frames, however, unless they contain some content.

Targeting A Frame

Creating a nifty-looking framed interface is one thing, but making it work (right) is quite another. PageMill affords you a number of options when you're targeting your framed links. Do you recall seeing a funny-looking bull's-eye, both on the Page tab of the Inspector (in red and white) and at the bottom of the PageMill window (a simple white circle button)? Surprise! They summon PageMill's targeting mechanism. The Inspector allows you to set the default target for each page, whereas the button at the bottom of the window allows you to set the target for each individual link, should you need to override the default.

WHAT'S THE DEAL WITH THE SQUARES?

Take a gander at the Inspector in Figure 5.6. Then, look back at Figures 5.4 and 5.5. Did you notice the squares in Figure 5.6? These nested squares make up the Frames Widget. They indicate how deeply an individual frame is nested and allow you to set the width and height for each frame. Click on the inner and outer squares to toggle between the width and height settings.

You can target a framed link in five basic ways:

- *New window*—Using this option, you can open the linked page in a brand new browser window, which leaves the original framed browser window intact.

- *Parent window*—Using this option, you can open the linked page in the current browser window, while wiping out the original frames.

- *Same frame*—Using this option, you can open the linked page in the same frame in which the link resides.

- *Same window*—Using this option, you can open the linked page in the same window. This option is similar to the parent window option.

- *Specific window*—Using this option, you can open the link in a specified window.

Now, you're ready to put that frame theory to work as you build a simple three-frame layout for the mythical Simple Links Web site.

Project: Building A Framed Web Page

Simple Links is a groovy little golf shop. The shop is just getting its online act together and has decided that a framed layout is the best solution for its Web site. True to the company's name, the three-frame layout Simple Links has chosen delivers its message with a minimum of fuss. Start this exercise by creating a new file; to do so, choose File|New or press the Cmd+N (Macintosh) or Ctrl+N (Windows) keyboard shortcut. Next, follow these steps:

1. Position the cursor over the left-side window border. Hold down the Option (Macintosh) or Ctrl (Windows) key—the cursor will turn into a right-facing arrow (as shown in Figure 5.7)—and drag toward the middle of the page to create a vertical frame. When you release the mouse button, the frames will be drawn (as shown in Figure 5.8).

2. You need to set the width of the left frame before you go any further. Click within the left frame to ensure that it is selected. On the Inspector's Frame tab, choose Pixels, type "108", and press Return (Macintosh) or Enter (Windows). The width of the left frame is now set at 108 pixels.

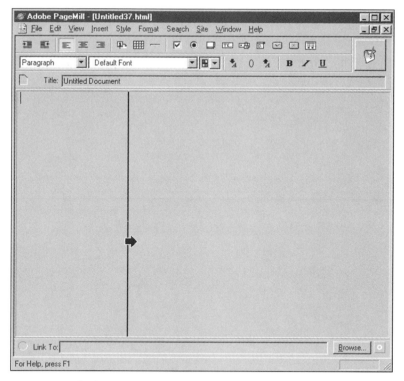

Figure 5.7 The frame-creation arrow points toward the center of the window (and away from the border you're dragging from).

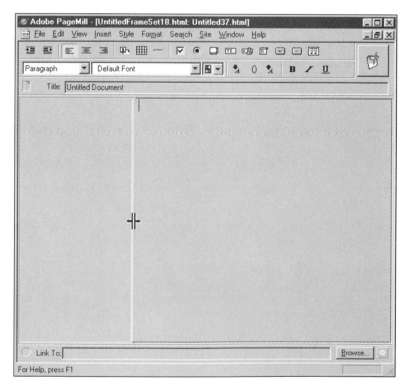

Figure 5.8 Instant frames! You can resize the frame by clicking and dragging on the border.

3. You're ready to create a smaller horizontal frame inside the left vertical frame. With the left vertical frame selected, choose Edit|Frame|Split Frame Horizontally. Two horizontal frames will replace the one skinny, vertical frame (as shown in Figure 5.9). Adjust the frame borders to make the top frame fairly small.

4. Now that all three frames have been drawn, you can name them. Click in each frame to select it, and then type a frame name in the Name field on the Inspector's Frame tab. Name the little frame "logo", the big frame "big", and the last frame "menu".

5. Before you do anything else, save the frameset by choosing File|Save All. You should put everything in a brand new folder named "simple". At this point, PageMill will save the frameset only, unless you've entered something on one of the frames. Save the frameset file as simplink.htm.

6. Drop in the logo and add a title. You'll need to get the simplink.gif file from this book's CD-ROM. Copy it from the CHAP-5 folder on the CD into the simple folder on your computer's hard drive. Then, drag simplink.gif into the little frame at the top left. The logo looks pretty good, but the back-

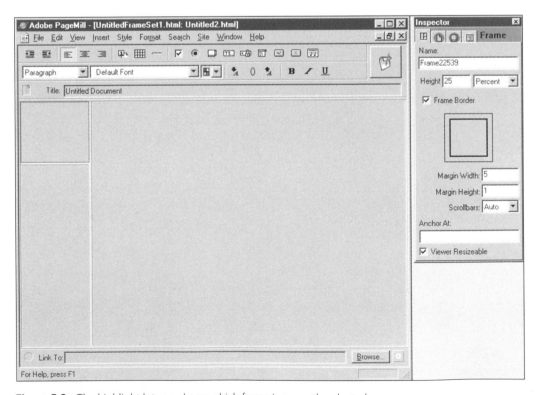

Figure 5.9 The highlight lets you know which frame is currently selected.

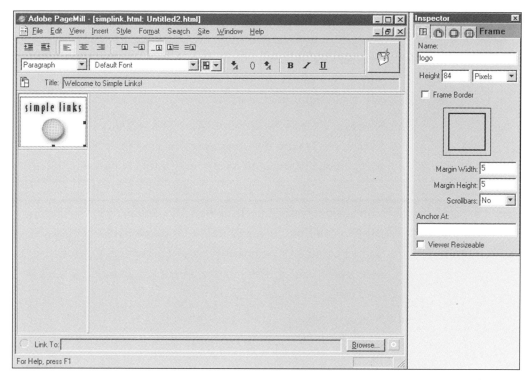

Figure 5.10 Once you've centered the Simple Links logo, you'll want to adjust the frames to fit.

ground of that frame should really be set to white. Click on the Page tab on the Inspector, and select the white color chip on the background button. In the Title field, type "Welcome to Simple Links!" and press Return (Macintosh) or Enter (Windows).

7. You've got to get rid of those hideous scrollbars and set the frame height. To do so, first click on the Frame tab on the Inspector. Select No from the Scrollbars drop-down list. For the Height option, first select Pixels and then type "84". Set both Margin Width and Margin Height to "5". Make sure that Frame Border and Viewer Resizeable are unchecked. Select the logo and click the Center button on the button bar. The page should appear as shown in Figure 5.10. Choose File|Save Frame As to save the frame as logo.htm.

8. You're ready to begin creating the navigational text. In the skinny window on the bottom left, type the following words and separate each by pressing Return (Macintosh) or Enter (Windows): "welcome", "products", "news", "people", "links", "help". Set them to bold and align them all flush right. Use the Color Panel and Inspector's Page tab to set the body text to yellow, the background

---

ARGH! I CAN'T SEE EVERYTHING!

Editing a small framed area (especially when you want to look at the HTML) can be nerve-wracking, but it doesn't have to be. PageMill conveniently allows you to edit a frame in its own window by choosing File | Frameset | Open Into Window.

color to dark blue, the normal link color to white, the active link to bright green, and the visited link color to light blue. Next, set the base font size to 4, and click on the Frame tab. For the Scrollbars option, select No. Finally, make sure that Frame Border and Viewer Resizeable are unchecked.

9. Select each one of the menu links and use the Link To field to link them to pages named welcome.htm, products.htm, news.htm, people.htm, links.htm, and help.htm, respectively. You can find these prebuilt pages in the CHAP-5 folder on this book's CD-ROM. Drag them into the simple folder before you start linking.

10. Ready, steady, go. You can now target those links. With the menu frame selected, you can do them all with one move on the Inspector's Page tab. For the Base Target list, click and drag down to the "big" window, as shown in Figure 5.11, and release the mouse button. You've now targeted the big frame. (After you've targeted a frame, its name will appear in the Base Target field.) Take a moment and select File|Save Frame As to save the frame as menu.htm.

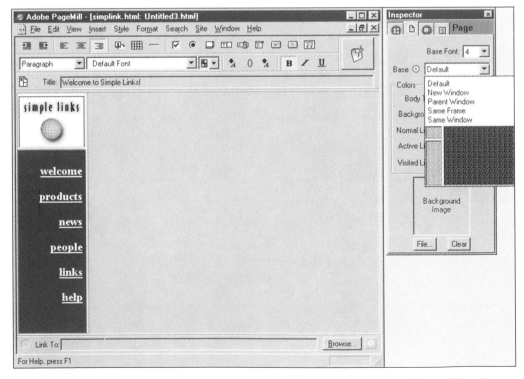

Figure 5.11 The Inspector allows you to set the overall target for an entire page of framed links. You can override it by using the target at the lower right of the PageMill window.

Figure 5.12 Sure, this site is simple, but that's why it's Simple Links!

11. Now for the fun stuff. Switch to Preview mode and try those links. When you're done clicking around, click on the Welcome link, switch back to Edit mode, click in the big window, and uncheck Frame Border on the Inspector's Frame tab. Select File|Save All. By following these steps, you can set up the Welcome page so that it is the first page your visitors will see when they hit the site, as shown in Figure 5.12.

Although you'll probably want to use this technique to point most of your internal links to your framed layout's "big frame," you might use the other types of targeting for plenty of reasons. If you have a page that was not designed to be viewed within a frame, you'll most likely want to target the full-window parent frame. If you're linking to another Web site, you might want to target the new site to open in an entirely new window; this way, your site's window will remain open, increasing the chances that your visitors will stay a while longer.

Here are some additional frame pointers:

• Name each frame with an identifiable label. Otherwise, PageMill will assign a nondescriptive name, such as frame1137468.

HOW CAN I EDIT A FRAMESET IN HTML SOURCE MODE?

Unfortunately, PageMill does not allow you to edit a frameset in HTML Source mode. You'll have to open the file with an ASCII text editor such as BBEdit, Simple Text, Notepad, or WordPad instead.

REMOVING A FRAME

To remove a frame, drag the frame border to touch the opposite side of the frame (you'll see it change color slightly), and release the mouse button. A message will appear, asking whether you really want to "Remove the adjoining frame from this document?" Click on OK to kiss it good-bye.

- Pay careful attention to each targeted link. Don't run the risk of sending your visitors off to Web Sheboygan without a return ticket.

- If a frame does not require the use of scrollbars, turn off the option via the Inspector.

- Disable the Viewer Resizeable option on frames that you deem to be of utmost importance, such as those containing advertising banners or site IDs.

- Use the Inspector to assign sufficient margin width and height so that your text and images don't bump into the frames.

Where Have All The Framed Sites Gone?

Frames made quite a splash when they were first introduced in Netscape Navigator 2.0, but the initial popularity among cutting-edge Web designers wore off for a number of reasons. Here's a handful of hypotheses:

- The inability of older browsers to display frames necessitated that Web site developers produce nonframed versions of their framed pages. Doing so often meant more work but questionable return on the developers' investment in time.

- The navigational shortcomings of certain framed Web sites were exacerbated by neophyte Web surfers who were unaware that holding down the mouse button (Macintosh) or right-clicking (Windows) would allow them to go back in a frame.

- Early on, a number of sites went overboard with frames. After a torrent of visitor frustration and outrage, many sites backed off. Framed sites are back on the upswing.

- Serious techno-tweaks have a barnyard full of tricks to play with Java and JavaScript. The initial "whoa, cool" phase has run its course.

- In general, the search engines don't like frames. Careful META tagging and no frames messaging is essential with framed sites.

Moving On

In this chapter you learned that frames allow you to design Web sites with a great deal of depth. A compact, modular layout provides information at a glance, without the incessant need to scroll. Frames present design challenges, however, that make your work as a Web site architect even more crucial. You must allot ample time to plan, execute, and test these designs carefully. In the next chapter you'll learn how to build HTML forms, which represent the first step in building a interactive Web site.

BREAKOUT!

Does another Web site have a link to your site, yet the site displays your pages within its frames? Fear not; you *can* fix it! The International I Hate Frames Club has a handful of nifty JavaScripts to break your site out of someone else's frames. Check them out here: http://www.wwwvoice.com/f-java.htm

You'll also find a frame-breaking JavaScript on the PageMill 3 CD-ROM in the Goodies|JavaScript folder: js_page_breakframes.html

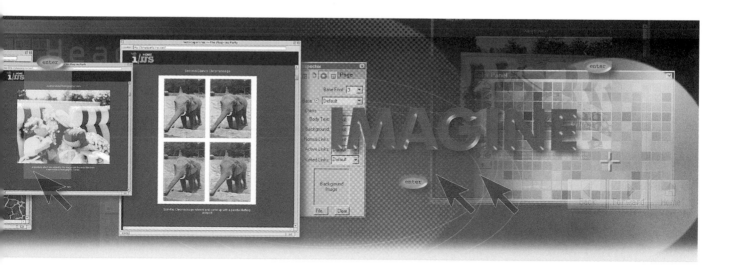

FORMING
CONCLUSIONS
6

In this chapter, you'll learn how to build forms, and you'll read about some schemes that create interactive Web sites without any programming.

At no time in history has demographic information ever been so rapidly extracted. HTML forms make it fast and easy to gather data. And PageMill's form creation tools allow you to whip out forms in record time. The program helps to enable data mining for the masses.

When Should I Create A Form?

There are many reasons to add HTML forms to your Web site. If your site contains a huge amount of information, you might use a search feature to query the database. You might be building a mailing list of potential customers, or perhaps you're interested in taking a survey of visitors to gauge their opinions. Whatever the situation, you'll probably need to use a form on any page where you would like your visitors to enter variable information for the purpose of interaction with the site.

Let's look at two real-world examples of HTML forms. They'll give you some perspective on what forms can do for your Web site.

Car Talk is an extraordinary Saturday afternoon radio show hosted by the Tom and Ray Magliozzi (a.k.a. the Tappit brothers, Click and Clack). In the real world, *Car Talk* can be found on National Public Radio, and on the Web, it can be found at http://www.cartalk.com. This site is every bit as fun and informative as the radio show. Take a look at the Car Talk Classifieds ad search form, shown in Figure 6.1. This nifty form allows visitors to the Car Talk site to search for the car of their dreams by defining a number of criteria, including minimum and maximum price, make, body style, mileage, age, and location. When you submit your query, the database returns descriptions of any vehicles that meet your specifications. Car Talk Classifieds is the place to go to search for that classic set of wheels.

Mo Hotta Mo Betta (http://www.mohotta.com/) is a mail order purveyor of hot and spicy foods, including hot sauces, salsas, chilies, peppers, snacks, and "mo hot stuff." The San Luis Obispo, California-based firm does the majority of its sales through a whimsical printed catalog. Although the Web site contains a nice selection of goods, the catalog features an amazing array of products to entice the widest range of customers. Thus, compiling a mailing list for the catalog is an important part of the Web site. Figure 6.2 demonstrates how Mo Hotta Mo Betta includes a prominently featured mailing list form.

If all you want to do is provide a means of visitor feedback (rather than feed your database), HTML's Mailto feature is the easiest type of

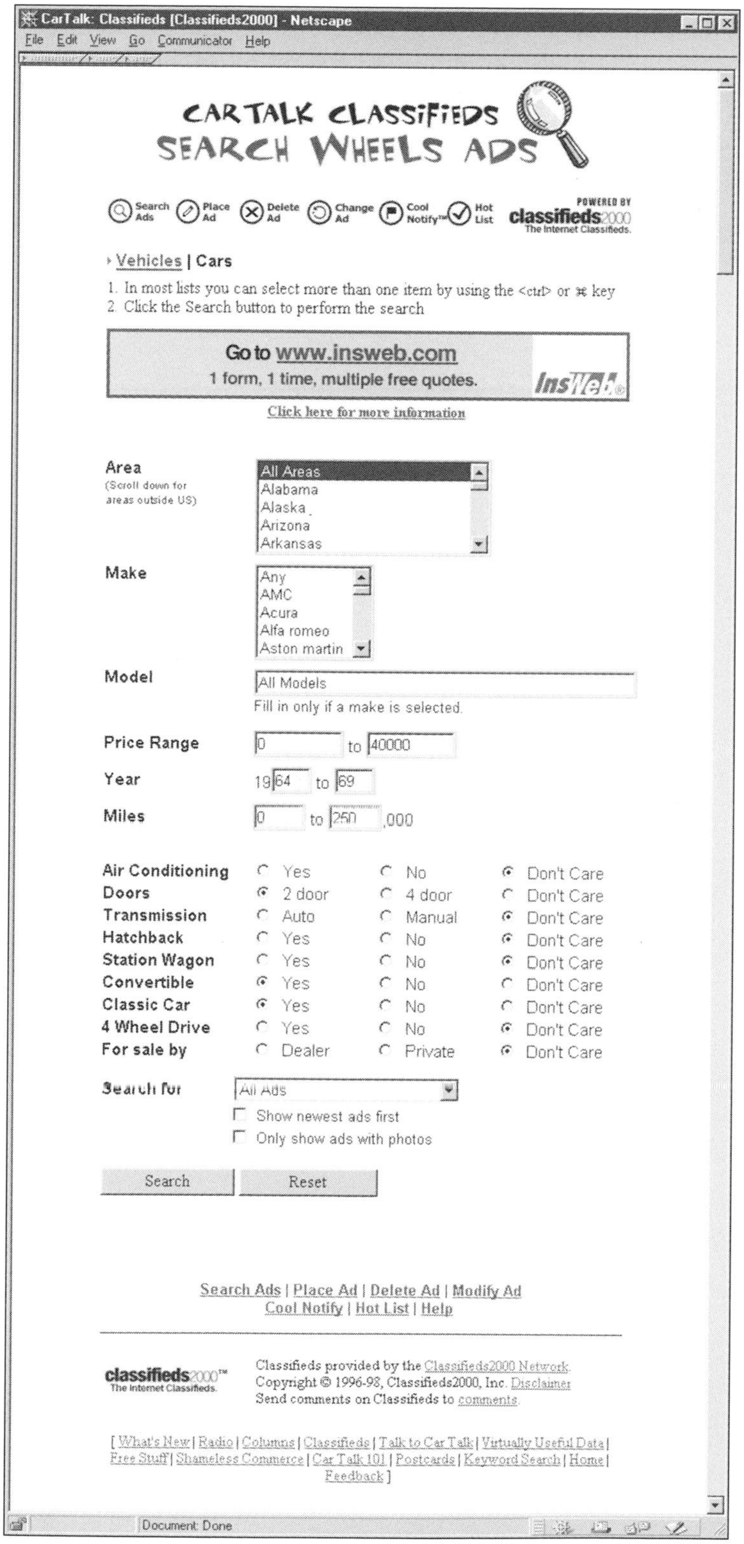

Figure 6.1   Using the Car Talk Classifieds Search Wheels Ads, you can look for that perfect old Pontiac convertible, just like the one you used to know and love.

Figure 6.2 Hey, pepperheads...looking for some hot stuff? Go to http://www.mohotta.com/ and sign up now!

feedback loop to implement. Although HTML forms are far more powerful, using Mailto links is the fastest way to solicit email from your visitors. When visitors click on a Mailto link, they are presented with a window that lets them send email directly to a prespecified address. If you need more than just unformatted email, however, you can look into the options afforded by HTML forms and CGI scripts. You might also want to look into Java or JavaScript solutions.

Form Creation Tools

HTML provides all the mechanisms you'll need to knock out a great-looking form. And PageMill makes those forms incredibly easy to create. The program's form creation tools allow you to build complex forms without touching any serious HTML code. All you need to do is click a form object button on the button bar (or make the appropriate selection by choosing Insert|Form) to bring a form element onto the page. Of course, you'll still have to assign names and values to the various fields, but that task is a far cry from hacking this stuff out by hand.

After you place a form object on the page, you can easily alter or move it around with just a flick of the mouse. Figure 6.3 illustrates the following features:

- *Checkboxes*—These critters are often set as groups, which allow any, all, or none of the group to be selected. To set a number of checkboxes as a group, use the Inspector's Object tab to assign the exact same name to each of the items. You can also create and name the first checkbox and then Option+drag (Macintosh) or Ctrl+drag (Windows) to create additional members of the group.

- *Radio Buttons*—You can use radio buttons when asking a "yes/no/maybe" type of question.

THE FORM IS ONLY HALF OF THE EQUATION

To use standard forms on your Web site, you'll need to have a program running on your Web server that knows what to do with the submitted information. These programs are often referred to as Common Gateway Interface (CGI) scripts.

You can also build forms by using Java applets or JavaScripts. Java and JavaScript can eliminate the need for a CGI script. This capability can give you more control over the entire process. Although this chapter mainly deals with HTML form capabilities built into PageMill 3, we'll take a quick peak at Java and JavaScript form solutions toward the end of the chapter.

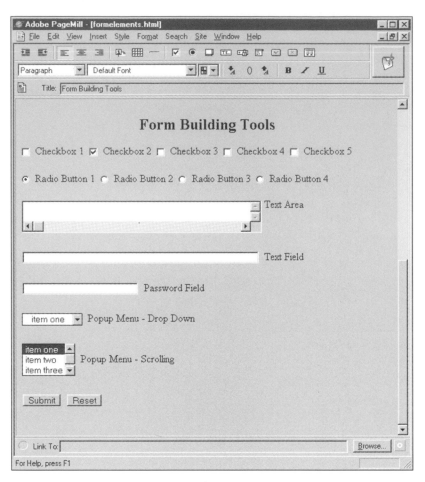

Figure 6.3 PageMill makes laying out forms easy. The real trick is making them work at the server.

Although similar to checkboxes in that they can be set as groups, radio buttons allow only one button in a group (at a time) to be selected. To set a number of radio buttons as a group, use the Inspector's Object tab to assign the exact same name to each of the items. You can also create and name the first radio button and then Option+drag (Macintosh) or Ctrl+drag (Windows) to create additional members of the group.

• *Text Area*—Use text areas for entering more than one line of text. Although you can quickly resize text areas by pulling on their handles (or by entering specific values on the Inspector), by default, they do not provide text wrapping. You can allow the user's text to wrap within the field by switching to HTML Source mode and entering the following within the text area command:

```
WRAP="PHYSICAL"
```

- *Text Field*—Use text fields when you need your visitors to enter only a single line of text. You can quickly resize text fields by pulling on their handles (or by entering specific values in the Inspector).

- *Password Field*—These special text fields are used for entering passwords. When visitors type in password fields in their browsers, only bullets or asterisks are displayed.

- *Pop-up Menus*—Although pop-up menus are drop-down menus by default, you can set them as scrolling list selections by dragging the bottom handle downward. You can also change a drop-down menu into a scrolling list by selecting Allow Multiple Selections on the Inspector's Object tab. A drop-down menu will allow visitors to select only one item, whereas the scrolling list selection field can allow visitors to select more than one item (as long as Allow Multiple Selections is selected).

- *Submit Button*—This button sends the visitors' variable information to the Web server and is required on every form. The text on the button can be altered by double-clicking the button and then double-clicking the text to select it. You can also switch to HTML Source mode and enter the desired text in the VALUE="submit" field (replace the word *submit* with the text of your choice).

- *Reset Button*—This button is a convenience feature that allows visitors to clear the form automatically. The text on the button can be altered by double-clicking the button and then double-clicking the text to select it. You can also switch to HTML Source mode and enter the desired text in the VALUE="reset" field (replace the word *reset* with the text of your choice).

- *Hidden Field*—Visitors never see some fields (unless they take a peek at the HTML source code). If you select Insert|Hidden Field, a cryptic little *H* appears in a box on the page. This icon is visible only in PageMill's Edit mode. You'll need to add a name and value via the Inspector.

Each form object has a name and a value, and you have complete control over how these variables are labeled. It is essential that you assign consistent names and values to each. Don't confuse the title that you see on the Web page with the name of the object. Although your visitors to your site will see the title, the CGI script will see the object's name. Although they may be named identically, they may not. In any case, don't forget to give each object the proper name and value.

CHECK THEM OFF!

PageMill allows you to preset checkboxes and radio buttons so that they are checked (through either the Inspector or by double-clicking on each while in Edit mode).

Can I Have More Than One Form On A Page?

Yes! Whereas PageMill 2 supported only one form per page, PageMill 3 allows you to have multiple forms per page. To add additional forms to a page, position your cursor where you want the new form to begin, and click the Insert Form Break button. Although the Form Break marker is quite ungainly, it appears only in PageMill's Edit mode, as shown in Figure 6.4.

Where Does The Info Go?

Aye, here's the rub. A form merely provides the means of gathering information. You'll need to have a CGI script running on your Web server before you can do anything with the submitted data. The CGI must know what to do with this information, and it must be in sync with the form so that it understands what to do with the various names and values. In most cases, you must huddle up with your Webmaster to find out what kind of support he or she can provide with regard to scripting. Note that CGI scripts are server specific. A script written for one platform may not run on another (for example, Unix Perl may be useless on a Windows NT server).

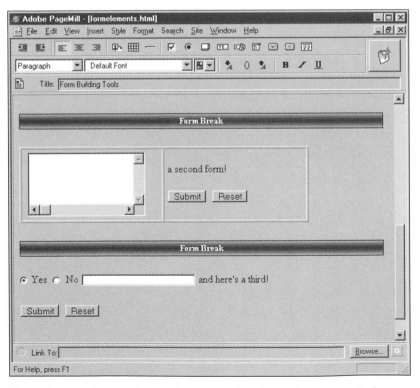

Figure 6.4 Don't worry. These ugly Form Break markers will not appear in the browser.

In the bad old days, the only way to create a CGI script was to write it with a programming language such as AppleScript or Perl. Thankfully, times have changed. Nonprogrammers will be thrilled to learn that several applications are now available to build scripts without writing any code. Maxum NetForms for Macintosh and O'Reilly's PolyForm for Windows 95/NT are two programs that you can use to create interactive forms instantly without any programming whatsoever.

How does the Web server know which CGI script to use? Take a quick look at the Inspector's Form tab. The Action field should be filled out with the name and location of the appropriate CGI, such as /cgi-bin/blahblahblah. cgi, where /cgi-bin/ is the directory, and blahblahblah.cgi is the name of the script itself. You'll have to select either Get or Post, but you must contact your Webmaster to determine which to use because different servers have different requirements.

Creating CGIs Without Hacking Any Code

Although PageMill does a bang-up job of creating Web page forms, it doesn't provide anything to handle the data on the other (server) end. In the early days, we were all hostage to the (largely Unix) scripting gurus whom we relied upon to create custom CGI scripts. Now applications have quickly come to market to automate the script creation process, allowing us mere mortals to complete our own interactive form designs. CGI scripts are server-specific beasts. A script created for a Unix server will not necessarily run on a Windows NT server, a Macintosh script won't run on a Unix server, and so on. We'll take a look at a number of packages, such as Maxum's NetForms, that can have your site performing as if it were tended by the high priests of Unix themselves.

Revving Up Mac Servers With Maxum

Maxum Development is the premier developer of Macintosh-based Web server add-ons. Its popular NetCloak and NetForms products are among the most widely deployed server products in the industry and have helped the Macintosh to establish a respectable foothold as a viable Web server platform. The company's focus is on extending Web sites' functionality by making them "dynamic, interactive, secure, accessible, and fast." NetCloak and NetForms cover the first two bases, by providing a means to create dynamic documents on the fly and by delivering an easy-to-implement solution for interactive forms, respectively. The Maxum Web site (http://www.maxum.com) contains downloadable demo versions of its applications along with online manuals, FAQs, and a host of other goodies.

NetCloak

Remember the dreaded Romulan Cloaking Device from the original *Star Trek* TV series? It allowed the Romulans (or whoever had captured the device) to sneak about space invisibly with nary a hint of their presence. NetCloak runs in a similar manner—"below the radar"—allowing Macintosh Web servers to deliver customized content based on a set array of parameters. When visitors hit a NetCloaked server, they get custom pages, which are built on the fly just for them. How does this happen? Each time a client (browser) sends a request to a server, the request carries a certain amount of information with it. This information (which normally just gets dumped into the server log file) includes the following:

- *Client domain*—Indicates the IP address from which the browser is accessing the site.

- *Referring document*—Indicates the exact page from which the browser was referred.

- *Client type*—Specifies the browser version and platform.

NetCloak works by implementing its own little set of HTML commands. These commands access the NetCloak CGI running on the Web server. By using this client data, the server can run a script to deliver a customized page based on locale of the users, the source of the incoming links, or the types of browsers. This capability allows you to pull some pretty cool tricks. If you're running an international site and want to serve up pages in multiple languages, you can set up NetCloak to deliver pages based on the domain. A domain ending with .es (Spain) would get a Spanish page, and so on. If you want to issue a special greeting to folks who have jumped from a specific site, you can make use of the referral information. (This trick is great for handling clicks from ad banners at multiple locations.) If you want to serve up different versions of your site for different browsers, you can use the client information to deliver terse text pages for Linux browsers and full-blown, Java-stuffed, framed nightmares to Navigator and Explorer users.

The program definitely has an air of Big Brother about it. If you want folks coming only from a specific domain to see the contents of a page, you can cloak it from the rest of the world. All other visitors will see a page at the same URL, but they will see a page with different content. You can also provide the same function based on a username and password. NetCloak uses three basic commands—show, hide, and insert—to work its magic. By combining these commands with variable information, you can deliver a high level of customization without hacking a Perl script. In addition to domain, referrer, client, username, and password data, the variable information includes the following:

- Time of day
- Day of week
- Date
- Access count
- Countdown
- Random number
- Redirect
- User-entered variables

The time, day, and date variables allow you to serve up different pages at different times, as well as on different days and dates. Your site

WHAT'S PERL?

Perl is a powerful Unix script programming language (although versions are available for other operating systems) that's often used to create CGI scripts for Web servers.

might have a special page that runs only during business hours or perhaps when your business is closed. This functionality allows you to set up special holiday or weekend greeting pages without worrying about being around at midnight to "turn on the page." You might even want to add a bit of eye-opening fun to your pages by delivering a one-liner (or two) based on these variables.

NetForms

Face it. The Web is a huge information appliance, constantly spewing out product data and sucking up prospect information. The faster your organization can inhale those leads, the faster you can go about the business of selling. NetForms will put a big, powerful engine behind the sleek and elegant forms you'll design in PageMill. The real beauty of a form comes to light only when it's fully functional. NetForms lets you design how a form *works*, not just how it *looks*. The program is based around four functions:

- *Createdoc*—Creates new HTML files on the fly by allowing users to simply fill out a form.

- *Insertfile*—Pops submitted data into an existing HTML file. This function is great for building guestbooks.

- *Textstore*—Stores submitted data in an ASCII text file for inclusion in a database.

- *Sendmail*—Provides email autoreply.

Each of these four functions fulfills crucial Web site needs. The Createdoc function lets nontechnical users create their own Web pages without requiring any knowledge of HTML whatsoever. All users have to do is fill out a form and click on the Submit button. This function is ideal for creating applications such as online classified ads or even for fun projects such as online recipe books.

Textstore is the marketeer's dream, putting 500 horsepower under the lead-generating hood. After visitors submit information, the data is quickly whooshed off to an ASCII file without requiring any manual data entry.

And have you ever looked twice down the snail-mail chute, just to make sure that your letters haven't gotten snagged on the way down to the mailbox? Although HTML's built-in mailto command provides a fast way to encourage visitors to drop you a line, it's lacking in one respect. When people send email via a Mailto link, they don't get any type of warm and fuzzy response telling them that the mail has been sent. Using NetForms' Sendmail function with a Response directive allows you to set up an autoreply function to thank visitors immediately for their valuable input.

TagBuilder

Maxum's utility TagBuilder allows you to drag and drop all the features available in both NetCloak and NetForms conveniently into PageMill. TagBuilder saves time by automating the HTML code-generation process, allowing you to focus on the specific parameters of each code rather than worry about keying in the beginning and ending tags.

Using O'Reilly & Associates' PolyForm

O'Reilly's Windows-based PolyForm (http://polyform.ora.com/index.html) is a "Web Form Construction Kit," designed for use with Windows 95 and NT servers that are Windows CGI 1.1 compliant, such as O'Reilly's WebSite, Microsoft ISS, Netscape's Communications and Commerce servers, and Quarterdeck's WebSTAR. The package consists of both server software (the CGI) and the PolyForm application (which allows you to create the forms themselves).

PolyForm's ScriptWizard allows novices to quickly build custom forms by starting with prebuilt forms for information requests, feedback, order forms, and time sheets. The output from the forms can be saved on the server as text or data files, or they can be sent as email. A thank-you confirmation can be sent to visitors, through either a simple prebuilt page or by sending them to a specific URL. You can choose to have a copy of the information sent as email. The Wizard-built forms may be used as is, or they can be highly customized, depending on the application at hand.

After you build a form, you can open it in the PolyForm Control Panel to double-check the settings. The Control Panel centers around four function tabs: Form, Save to File, Send to Browser, and Email Options. You can customize the forms by entering specific information in the fields before generating the forms (after which, you can hack the HTML to your heart's content). Although PolyForm is a departure from the PageMill environment, it offers powerful capabilities that go far beyond what you can do with PageMill alone.

 ## Building A Form

In this exercise, you'll build a guestbook form for your Web site. This form will include text field, text area, radio button, and drop-down and scrolling list functions, as shown in Figure 6.5.

As you begin building the form, you'll quickly see how easily you can create, adjust, and rearrange the different form elements. You'll want to start with a brand new page.

1. Let's begin by adding a simple heading. Type "Please Sign Our Guestbook". Change the format to Larger Heading, and then press Return (Macintosh) or Enter (Windows). Next, insert a Horizontal Rule. Press Return (Macintosh) or Enter (Windows).

2. Add five (one-line) text fields. To do so, select the Paragraph style, click the Insert Text

Field button, type "Name", and then press Shift+Return (Macintosh) or Shift+Enter (Windows). Next, click on the Insert Text Field button, type "City", press the spacebar, click on the Insert Text Field button again, type "State", and then press Shift+Return (Macintosh) or Shift+Enter (Windows). Click on the Insert Text Field button one more time, type "Country", and press Shift+Return (Macintosh) or Shift+Enter (Windows). Finally, click on the Insert Text Field button, type "Email address", and press Return (Macintosh) or Enter (Windows).

3. Adjust each text field so that it appears as in Figure 6.5 by dragging on its right side handle. Select each field and type its name in the Inspector's Object tab. You can also use the Inspector to set the size (length) of each field precisely.

4. Back on the Web page, type "Tell us what you like (or don't like) about our Web site". Press Shift+Return (Macintosh) or Shift+Enter (Windows). Click on the Insert Text Area button, and adjust the text area so that it is approximately 7 rows by 54 columns. Check the size with the Inspector's Object tab, and type "tellusaboutit" in the name field.

5. It's radio button time! Click an insertion point after the text area, and press Return (Macintosh) or Enter (Windows). Type "When do you think you might visit us again?" and press Shift+Return (Macintosh) or Shift+Enter (Windows). Click on the Radio Button button. Then, click to select the new radio button, and use the Inspector's Object tab to assign it the name "nextvisit" and the value "tomorrow". Option+drag (Macintosh) or Ctrl+drag (Windows) the button four times to create a group of five buttons. Insert the text ("tomorrow", "in a few days", "later this

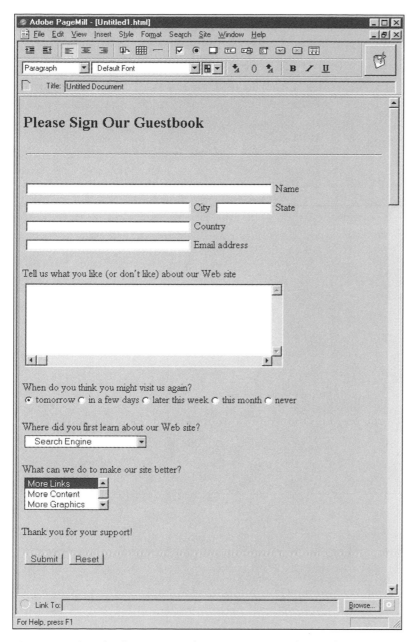

Figure 6.5 Guestbooks are among the most common Web page forms.

week", "this month", and "never") on the page and in the value field for each button, as shown in Figure 6.5.

6. Add a drop-down menu. To do so, press Return (Macintosh) or Enter (Windows). Type "Where did you first learn about our Web site?" and press Shift+Return. Click on the Insert Popup button, and then double-click to select the new pop-up menu. Highlight the default text and type the following, pressing Return or Enter after each line:

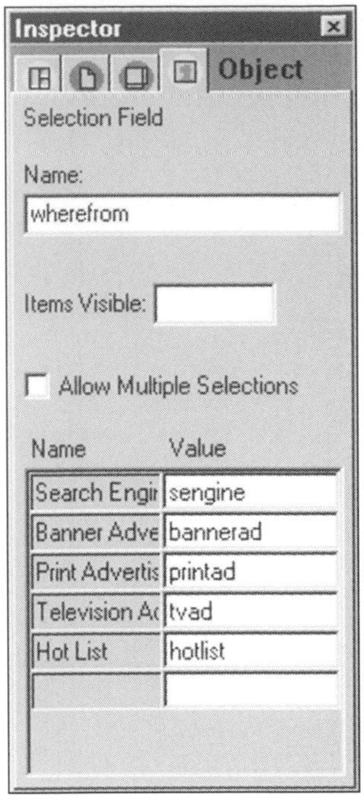

Figure 6.6 Every form object must be assigned a name and a value.

"Search Engine"

"Banner Advertisement"

"Print Advertisement"

"Television Advertisement"

"Hot List"

Click on the page to deselect the menu, and then click once to select it again. On the Inspector's Object tab, give it the name "wherefrom" and assign values to each of the five sources, as shown in Figure 6.6.

7. Add a scrolling list selection to the form. To do so, press Return (Macintosh) or Enter (Windows). Type "What can we do to make our site better?" and press Shift+Return (Macintosh) or Shift+Enter (Windows). Next, click on the Insert Popup button, and double-click to select the new pop-up menu. Highlight the default text and type the following, pressing Return or Enter after each line:

   "More Links"

   "More Content"

   "More Graphics"

   "Less Graphics"

   "More Shockwave"

   "More Software"

   Click on the page to deselect the menu, and then click once to select it again. Drag the menu's bottom handle down so that the top three entries are showing. On the Inspector's Object tab, give it the name "whatelse" and assign corresponding values to each of the six choices. Make sure that Allow Multiple Selections is checked and that the Items Visible field is set to 3. Take the time to experiment with different sizes.

8. To finish the form, add a thank-you line and those crucial Submit and Reset buttons. To do so, press Return (Macintosh) or Enter (Windows). Type "Thank you for your support!" and press Return (Macintosh) or Enter (Windows). Next, click on the Insert Submit Button button, press the spacebar, and click on the Insert Reset Button button. On the Inspector's Object tab, name the Submit button "submitInspector". (The Reset button doesn't need a name because it works only at the browser level.)

Can I Use A GIF Or JPEG Image As A Submit Button?

No problem! Just place the image on the page, select it, and specify it as a button on the Inspector's Object tab.

9. You're done, so save your file! If this were a real working form, you would have to set an Action on the Inspector's Form tab. This Action lets the server know what CGI script to use with the incoming data.

Try your new form in PageMill's Preview mode. Then, try opening the form with Netscape Navigator or Microsoft Internet Explorer to see how it performs. Although some of the earlier browsers (AOL's in particular) had problems dealing with forms, just about all the browsers today support the HTML 2.0 form specification to which PageMill writes its forms.

A Word About Java And JavaScript Forms

These days, server-based CGI forms are not the only game in town. In fact, Java and JavaScript forms have become some of the most popular ways of gathering information and providing interaction. While Adobe PageMill's form creation tools do not automatically create Java or JavaScript forms, you can easily incorporate these highly interactive elements into your Web pages.

The Goodies folder on the Adobe PageMill 3 release CD-ROM contains a host of ready-to-go JavaScripts. Check out the Appendix or open up the goodies/javascript/index.html file in your Web browser to get a gander at all the cool JavaScripts. When you find one you like, just follow the instructions to cut and paste the JavaScript into PageMill. You'll need to make sure that you encase the JavaScript in NOEDIT tags to keep PageMill from messing with the code. Once you've pasted the JavaScript into PageMill, you'll notice that it does not appear in the Edit or Preview mode. Save the file, preview it in your browser (or switch to Internet Explorer preview), and the form should appear.

You can create extremely specialized Java applet forms. The Java applets on the PageMill 3 release CD-ROM, however, seem limited to special effects. You can use applications such as Interleaf Jamba (a demo version is included on the PageMill 3 Design Guide CD-ROM) or Lotus Bean Machine to quickly build custom Java applets. We'll cover the subject of Java and JavaScript in more depth in Chapter 8.

Moving On

In this chapter, you learned the ins and outs of Web page forms. PageMill makes quick work out of standard HTML form creation and allows you to integrate Java and JavaScript-based form solutions, as well. In the next chapter, you'll learn more about Java and JavaScripts as we bring those dead sites to life!

PLATFORM ISSUES

Java and JavaScripts will act differently on different platforms (and in different browsers). If you're considering using these elements in your Web pages, you should test your pages thoroughly before deploying them.

PAGEMILL SITES
DONE RIGHT!

This section provides a full-color showcase of great PageMilled Web sites from around the world. You'll find sites from America, Canada, Australia, and Europe, along with my very own Plug-in Party site. But it doesn't end there... I'll be providing hot new PageMilled links online at www.geekbooks.com!

Web Site
AGS Sports and Travel

URL
www.ags-sports.com.au

Owner
AGS Sports and Travel

Designer
Julian Matthews

Tools Used
PageMill, Photoshop 4,
Illustrator 6, SimpleText

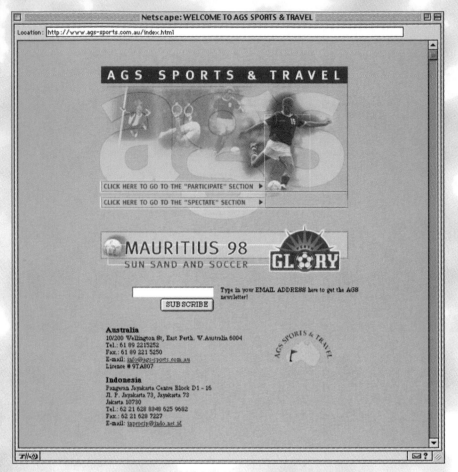

AGS Sports and Travel is an Australian travel agency specializing in sports-related bookings. The bright green home page provides straightforward navigation to the site's main Participate and Spectate sections. "PageMill lets us design the AGS site very efficiently," says designer Julian Matthews. "The AGS site uses frames extensively. Doing it with PageMill was a breeze."

AGS site navigation is carried in both the top and left side frames. The calendar page uses a large table to present event date and location information.

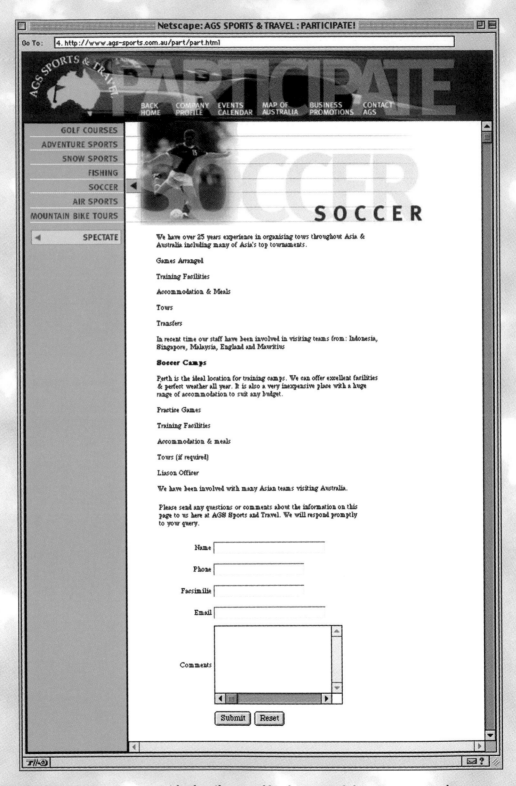

The Participate pages provide details on golf, adventure, fishing, soccer, and mountain biking activities, among other sports. Page designs are tested in both Netscape Navigator and Microsoft Internet Explorer before going live.

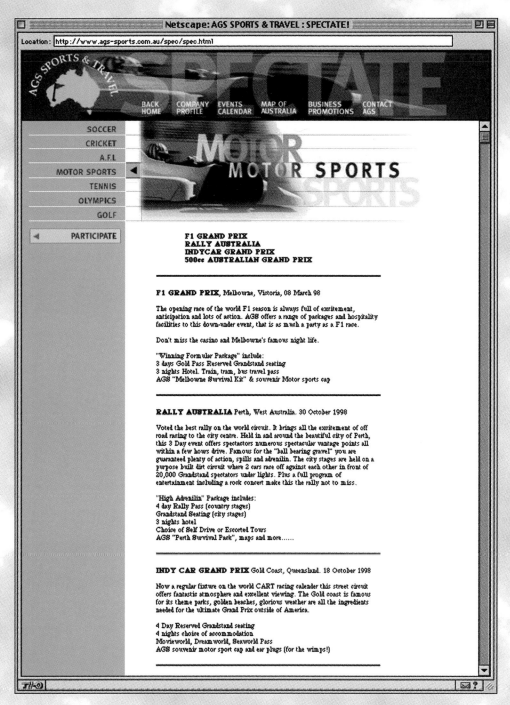

The Spectate pages deliver the details on sporting event packages. The site uses stock photography from PhotoDisc to great effect.

Web Site
Bob Staake Humorous
Illustration & Cartoon

URL
www.bobstaake.com

Owner
Bob Staake

Designer
Bob Staake

Tools Used
Photoshop 3.0,
PageMill 2.0

Bob Staake is a professional illustrator and cartoonist. His Web site is a bright, whimsical reflection of his work. Though the site is eclectic by nature, the navigation is consistent. "The intuitive navigation bar on the left is a static element on each of the pages and enables surfers to effortlessly zig and zag through the site," says Bob. "I have found that 'advertising' other interior pages on the home page forces the surfer to almost automatically delve deeper into the site. More importantly, I establish the rather ridiculous 'Bob' theme on my home page—a convenient hook that will run from page to page."

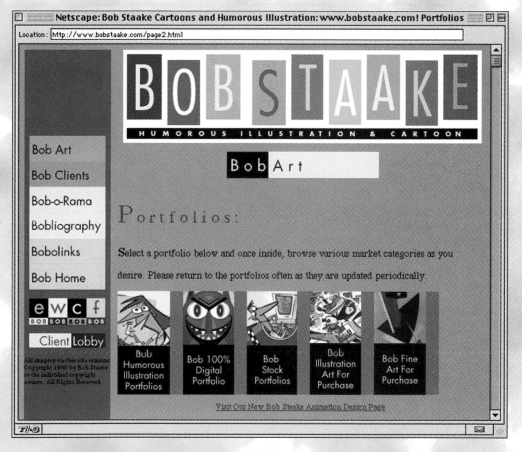

The Bob Art portfolio page allows visitors to jump between the five portfolios. "Since this was originally intended as a portfolio site to exhibit my work to publishing, corporate, and advertising clients, I knew this page would be the primary embarking point," says Bob. "In additional to the portfolios of my work, I also thought it was essential to promote my 'other' art on this page as well."

This rock and roller is an example of Bob's Photoshop illustration work, and is one of 27 greeting cards he recently created for Gibson. Notice that the background colors change from page to page, though all come from a consistent palette.

The Bob Art Time Machine lets visitors experience Bob's style over the years. "I really have wanted to exploit a Web site's ability to tell a *big* story via a few megabytes," explains Bob. "By adding features like my 'Time Machine,' clients come away feeling as if they really learned something about me—and I feel features like this do a lot to 'humanize' me in their eyes. Beyond that, clients respond that they simply love the interactive features that I have peppered through my site."

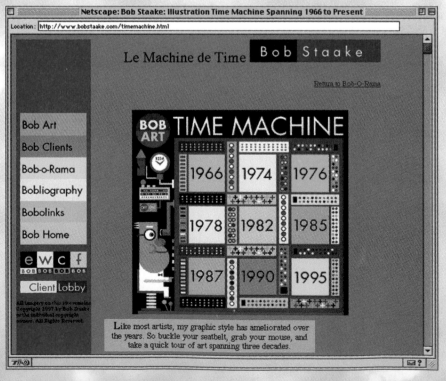

It's important to leave the door open for expansion. Bob Staake's approach fits the needs of the site. "Not knowing how my site would expand, I saw a need from the beginning to create an area that could be added to modularly," says Bob. "My Bob-O-Rama page now functions as a 'catch all' for the site's weird games, activities, smarmy self-promotional prose, and mindless diversions." Bob-O-Rama is certainly a success, having become the most heavily trafficked area on the site.

Web Site
Calgary Board of Education

URL
www.cbe.ab.ca

Owner
Calgary Board of Education

Designer
Laura Diemert

Tools Used
Power Macintosh 9600,
PageMill 2.0,
BBEdit Lite 4.0.1,
Photoshop 4.0, Acrobat 3.0,
Flash 2, DeBabelizer 1.6.5

The Calgary Board of Education Web site portrays a forward-looking learning organization. The home page establishes persistent site navigation using a rollover menu created in Macromedia Flash. A JavaScript determines whether visitors have the Flash plug-in; if it doesn't find the plug-in, an imagemap menu is substituted for the Flash menu. The headings are repeated at the bottom of the page as text links.

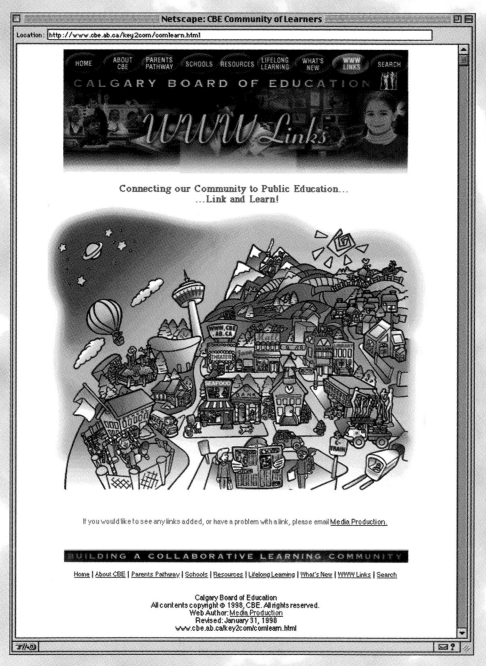

"The Calgary Board of Education believes that learning does not stop once a child leaves the walls of a school, and therefore highly values the community around us," says site designer Laura Diemert. "In order to introduce others to our community, and to provide an enjoyable exploratory environment, we created the 'Key to the Community' area." The page features a large imagemapped illustration, created by Tracy Hass. "Tracy supplied us with a black-and-white line drawing which we took into Photoshop and then dropped color into on a seperated layer," explains Laura. "It was then saved as a JPEG, and easily made into an imagemap in PageMill."

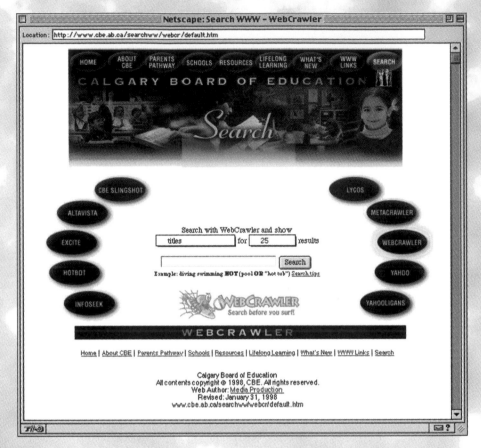

The Search page provides convenient links to the most popular search engines.
The Calgary Board of Education even has its own search engine (Slingshot).
The Search page graphics were created in Photoshop and sliced into individual
pieces, then reassembled as a table and imagemapped in PageMill.

The Calgary Board of Education site makes use of Adobe Acrobat PDF documents. "After a document has been formatted for print, it only takes a few minutes to repurpose it into a PDF, and drag and drop it into a PageMill layout," explains Laura. "You save the viewer the time they would have to wait for a printed copy, or for an HTML layout to be formatted. Although a plug-in is required to view PDFs, many browser have this plug-in resident, or viewers have taken the time to install the free plug-in as it is a widely used technology."

Web Site
Empire N.A. Farm Equipment

URL
www.empirecaseih.com/

Owner
Bob Bottens

Designer
Jason Bramer

Tools Used
Power Computing
PowerCenter Pro 210,
PageMill 2.0, Photoshop,
Illustrator, GifBuilder, Fetch

Special Features
CGI forms

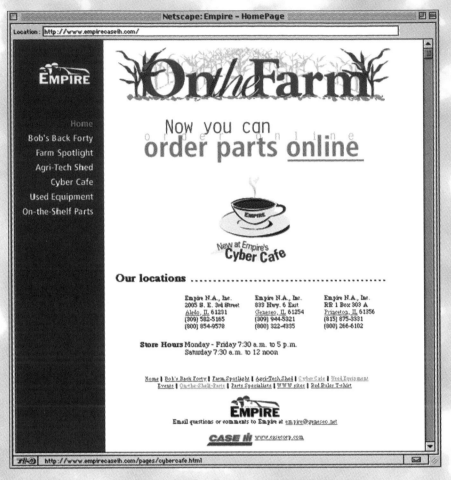

Illinois-based Empire N.A. Farm Equipment is blessed with an attractive, to-the-point, business Web site. Its utility starts right where it should: at the home page. "Empire's home page gives the viewer control of navigation from the very beginning," says site designer Jason Bramer. "You can get to every page of the site from here." The site employs a basic layout and uses a banner image originally created for a printed mailer. The graphic was created in Adobe Illustrator, then transformed into a tasteful animated GIF with Adobe Photoshop and GifBuilder. Site icons were also created in Illustrator and converted into GIFs using Photoshop.

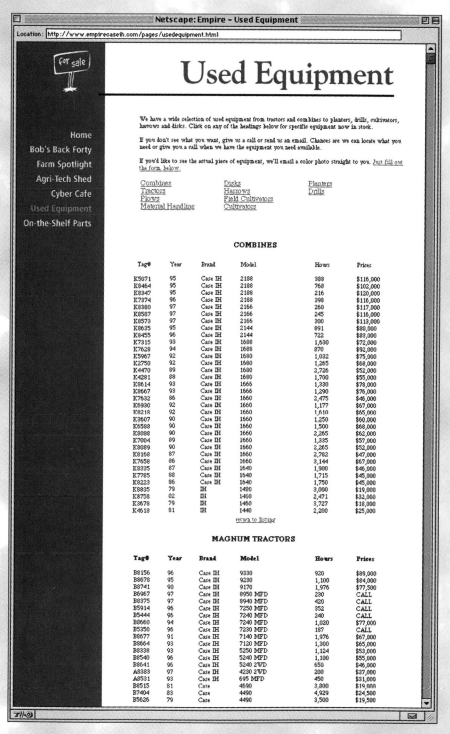

The Used Equipment page displays Empire's stock on hand. The page features an extensive table of combines, tractors, and other goodies. A form at the bottom of the page provides a link to the person in charge of Empire's used equipment, via a CGI script.

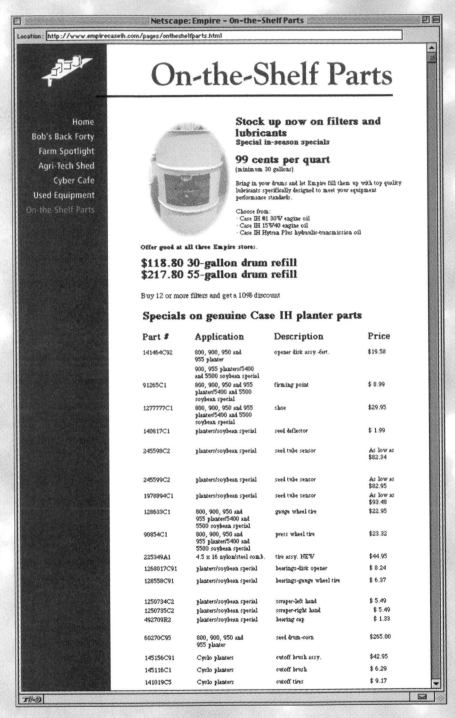

The On-the-Shelf Parts page highlights parts specials and provides the means to order parts online. A CGI script allows customers to send order information directly to Empire's parts manager.

Web Site
GackleAndersonHenningsen,
Inc.

URL
www.gah.com/

Owner
Greg Gackle

Designer
Jason Bramer

Tools Used
Power Computing
PowerCenter Pro 210,
PageMill 2.0, Photoshop,
GifBuilder, Fetch

Special Features
JavaScript mouseovers

The GackleAndersonHenningsen, Inc. Web site's big-city looks belie the
design firm's Bettendorf, Iowa roots. "Our home page was designed to be
very subtle, yet grab one's interest," explains site designer Jason Bramer.
"The main image is an animated GIF created in Photoshop and compiled in
GifBuilder. The copy on this page loads faster than the animation, and lets
the viewer begin reading as the animation loads."

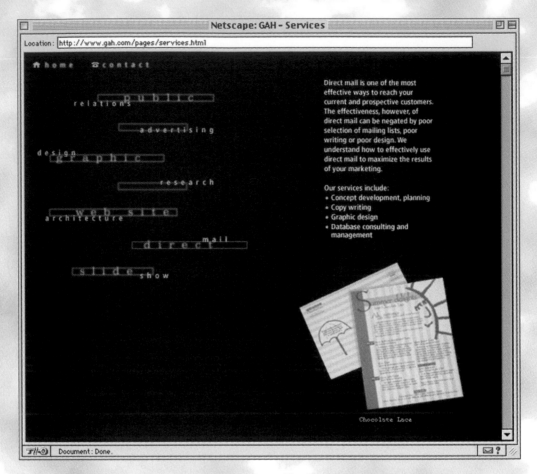

The Services page uses JavaScript mouseovers effectively. The page's borderless frames and solid black background provide a clean canvas. "This makes for less confusion in trying to locate information," says Jason. "The mouseovers are used to give a little visual stimu-lation. We kept these subtle as well so the page doesn't seem crammed with extras."

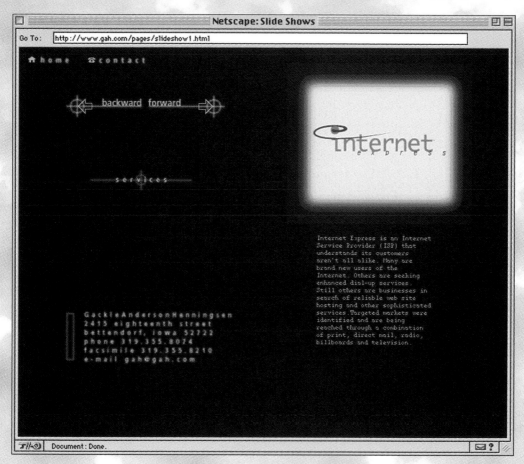

The three Slideshow pages present a number of client projects through a series of animated GIFs created with Photoshop and GifBuilder.

Web Site
OzNoise

URL
www.oznoise.com.au

Owner
Vivid Interactive and Design
Australia

Designer
Julian Matthews

Tools Used
PageMill, Photoshop 4, Illus-
trator 6, Director 6,
SoundEdit 16, SimpleText

Special Features
Shockwave Streaming audio

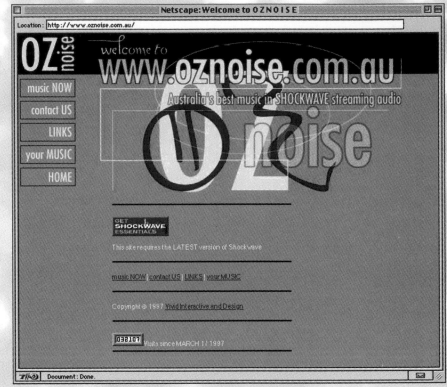

The Australian OzNoise Web site delivers the skinny on new tunes from down under. The home page sets the stage with a distinctive typographic treatment and bold gold and black backgrounds. "We wanted to create an audio site that featured unsigned or independent Australian bands and artists," says site designer Julian Matthews. "A surfer can hear entire songs from each band and then email them with a request for more information, ask how to purchase their CDs, or request a lock of hair."

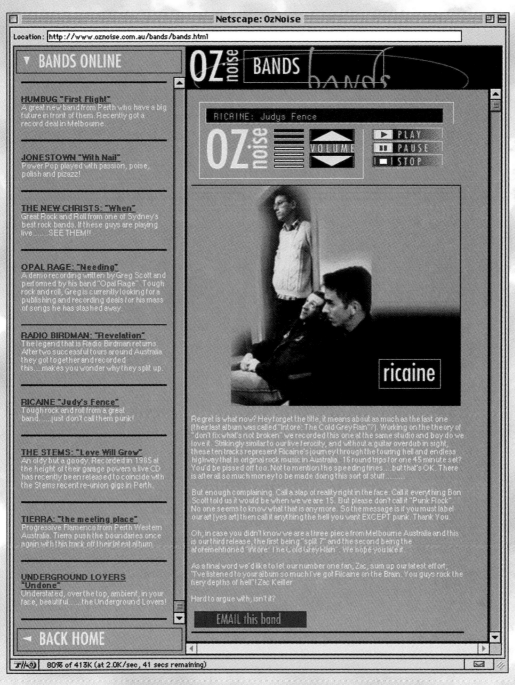

The Bands page lets visitors listen to songs via the Shockwave plug-in. "The reason we chose 'Shockwave Streaming Audio' at the time the site was done was for its ability to 'embed' the movie and graphical interface into the page so it existed as a whole with the other elements on the page," explains Julian. "The Shockwave files are only 18k and stream near FM radio quality sound over even a 28.8k modem."

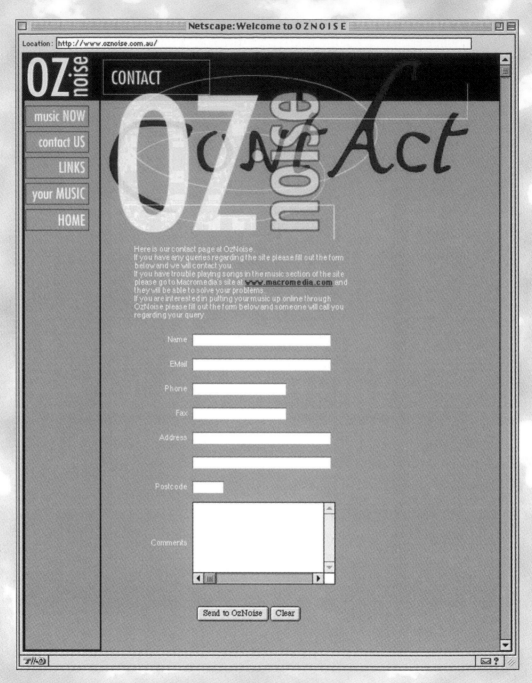

Whereas some form pages can appear utilitarian (at best), the OzNoise Contact page solicits visitor feedback in an attractive layout.

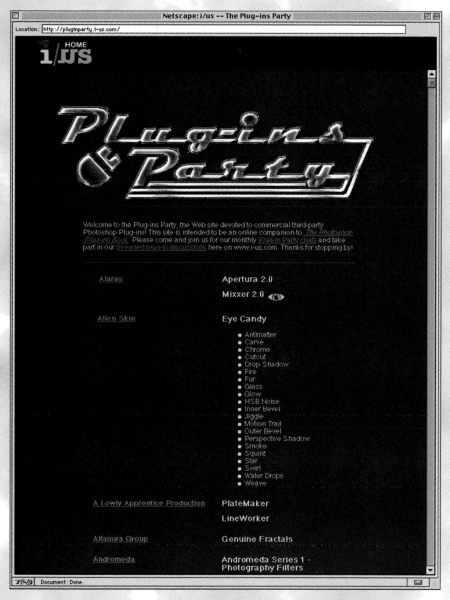

Web Site
The Plug-in Party

URL
pluginparty.i-us.com/

Owner
Daniel Gray

Designer
Daniel Gray

Tools Used
Power Macintosh and
Pentium computers,
PageMill, Photoshop, and
every plug-in known to man
(well, almost)

I was originally going to support one of my previous books, *The Photoshop Plug-ins Book,* on my own Web site, but instead decided to build the Plug-in Party on the www.i-us.com Web site due to its high level of print and Web designer traffic. Symbiotic community relationships provide a positive buzz for everyone. The Plug-in Party home page is a big scrolling jump list of developers and plug-ins. Example pages are linked with eye-cons. I kept the example pages as simple as possible, and chose an uncommon, yet unobtrusive background to best show the plugged-in imagery.

I created a pair of four-up comparative illustrations to demonstrate the intense palette manipulations created by Second Glance Chromassage.

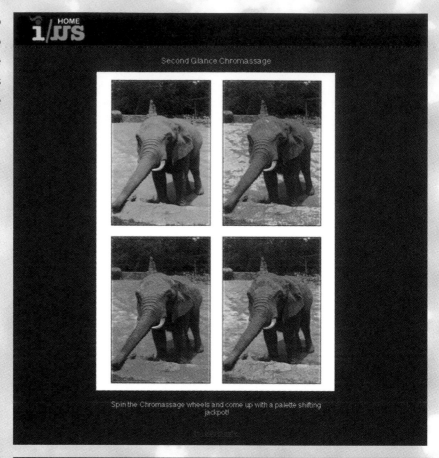

This is a favorite picture of my kids. Andromeda's Halo filter gives the image a painterly effect.

Here's another indulgent look at the rugrats. Alaras Mixxer is a powerful
tool for creating duotones and other high-end print effects.

Xaos Tools Terrazzo is the king of the pattern makers. Turning a giraffe's hide into a seamless background was a snap.

WildRiverSSK is one of the most versatile special effect plug-ins. This huge page demonstrates dozens of sample effects with the WildRiver SSK MagicMask filter.

Web Site
The Prometheus Chamber
Orchestra

URL
www.dslproductions.com/
prometheus

Owner
Wilson Hermanto/
Douglas Ladendorf

Designer
Douglas Ladendorf

Tools Used
Power Macintosh 8500/120,
Umax Vista-S6E scanner,
PageMill, Photoshop,
Illustrator, BoxTop PhotoGif
and ProJPEG, SiteJaz,
SmartGIF, GifBuilder,
BBEdit Light, Sound Edit16,
Director 6

Special Features
Shockwave streaming audio
of orchestra selections

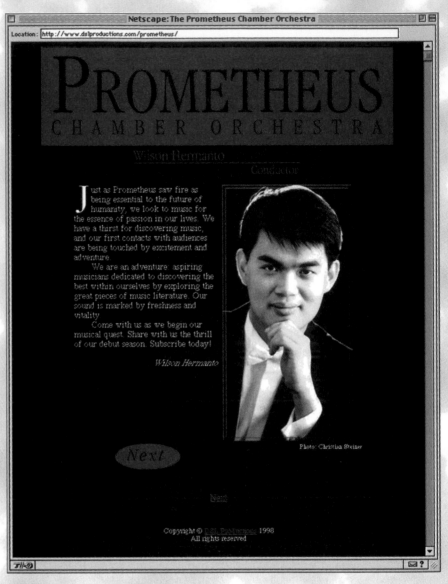

The Prometheus Chamber Orchestra site uses an unpretentious, yet elegant design. "The introduction page was inspired by a flier for the orchestra, which was printed in black and red on white," explains site designer Douglas Landendorf. "I decided this color scheme would work very well for the Web site, and took that as my jumping-off point. The black and red conveys both a sense of mystery and a connection to the fire that Prometheus gave to humanity." Douglas used only black-and-white photos to enhance the classical nature of the design.

Throughout the Prometheus Chamber Orchestra site, tables are used to provide 10 percent margins, allowing the pages to air out. The site is devoid of standard Web design fare, such as beveled buttons or JavaScript rollovers. "As far as I know, no one has had trouble figuring out what to do without a bevel or roll-over," says Douglas.

Douglas uses a GIF animation sleight of hand on the site's index page to provide a sense of movement and energy. "I divided three black and white photos into quadrants and alternated them at different rates to create a kind of slide show effect (using SmartGif and GifBuilder)," explains Douglas. "Each quadrant was put in a table cell with borders, padding, and spacing set to 0. This brings them back to a seamless image that flows together." A lowsrc version of the image loads immediately, while the GIF animation streams to the browser. "I found that some browsers would load one quadrant completely before going on to the next, defeating the effect of the lowsrc," says Douglas. "To work around this I secretly cached the lowsrc images on the first page."

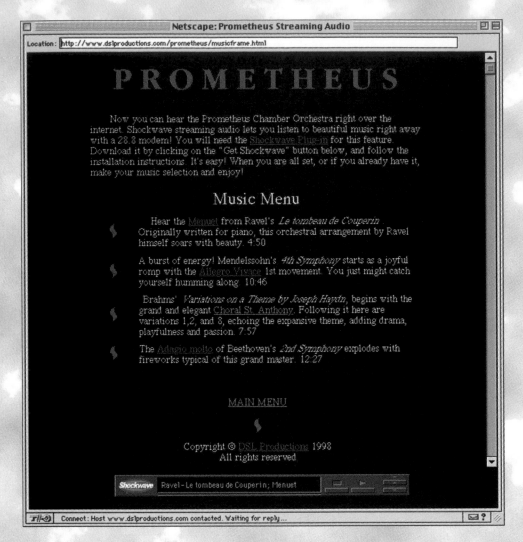

Like the OzNoise site, the Prometheus Chamber Orchestra site uses Shockwave streaming audio. "After auditioning the available streaming technologies, I found Shockwave to be the most reliable and best sounding," says Douglas. "My target audience uses a 28.8 modem or better. The sound is quite good, and gives the visitor an idea of what the orchestra can do. The music was taken off Hi8 tapes I shot with the help of an audio engineer, as well as DAT recordings. Selections were digitized and 'Shocked' with SoundEdit16. Once uploaded to the server, they are called within the **<embed>** tag to be opened with the player (a Director movie)." The music page features a menu in the main frame, with the nifty Shockwave player in the bottom frame. This arrangement allows selections to load quickly.

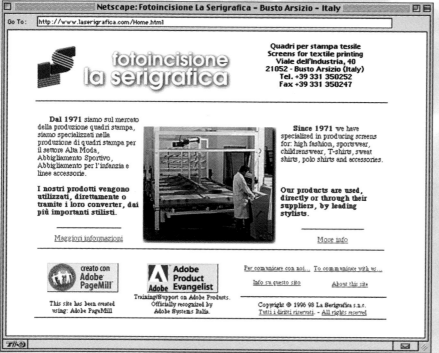

Web Site
Fotoincisione La Serigrafica
s.n.c.

URL
www.laserigrafica.com

Owner
Fotoincisione La Serigrafica
s.n.c.

Designer
Enzo Borri

Tools Used
PageMill 2.0, SiteMill 2.0,
Illustrator 6.0, Photoshop 4.0

Special Features
To ensure the best compatibility with any browser, there
are no special features except
for an animated GIF of the
company logo

Fotoincisione La Serigrafica s.n.c. is an Italian serigraphic (screen) printer.
Prior to building the www.laserigrafica.com site, designer Enzo Borri devel-
oped Adobe Systems' Italian Web site. "During the development (of the
Adobe site), I had to follow guidelines especially written to make all the
foreign sites follow the same look of the main Adobe site," explains Enzo.
"I had the opportunity to learn a lot about site design by studying the
Adobe guidelines and after studying other good sites." This site avoids
frames, heavy images, complex backgrounds, Java, and other design tricks.
"The result is a very clean site, which is easy to navigate and compatible
with any kind of browser, from WebTV to old versions of Netscape Navigator and Internet Explorer," says Enzo.

The Samples page (www.laserigrafica.com/us/samples.html) is the most graphics-intensive page of the site. "There are many images but there's no other way to show an image other than by using an image!" exclaims Enzo. Photoshop Actions are used to create the page headings.

BRINGING A DEAD
SITE TO LIFE

7

In this chapter, you'll learn how to implement animation, Java applets, JavaScripts, Shockwave, sound, and QuickTime movies in PageMill.

I think I can safely say that if you're reading this book, you're a child of the animated age. We've all grown up with the common experience of cartoons; we just had different reference points—whether they are Heckle and Jeckle, Tom and Jerry, or Itchy and Scratchy. This chapter will ease your entrance to the world of animated Web pages. Together with the book's CD-ROM, it will provide the basic tools needed to create your own animated effects, whether you're working on a Macintosh or a PC.

After you've seen your first animated Web page, you're bound to start dreaming about how you can bring that same excitement to your own designs. Although animation might seem to be a daunting craft to master, rest assured, you can quickly learn how to add animation to your Web site. The trick is to determine which way to proceed. You can choose from a number of methods to add animation to your Web site, from the easy to implement (and totally free) to the heavily technical (and consequently costly).

This chapter will demonstrate how GIF animations, JavaScript, Java applets, Shockwave, QuickTime, and sound files can spice up your site. PageMill 3 makes incorporating these elements easy.

Animation Basics

You don't have to be the next Chuck Jones to successfully pull off an animated Web page. Just don't think of animation solely in the terms of your childhood cartoon heroes. There are different levels of animation—some achievable, some not. Although you won't create animations of a Loony Tunes caliber, you'll be able to create awesome sequences without having to enroll in art school.

Web page animations are created when the browser displays a series of *cels* (or frames—think of a strip of film) in sequence. These cels can consist of images, text, or a combination of both elements. Although the types of animation you can create from scratch are limited only by your imagination, proper execution can take a good bit of time.

Let's take a look at some examples.

Figure 7.1 shows the five different images used in a simple animation. The cels are sequenced (1, 2, 3, 4, 5, 4, 3, 2) and looped so that they appear to pulse in and out. As the browser displays the subsequent cels, the viewer gets the impression that the warning sign is flashing in a subtle manner.

The pulsing sign technique is easy to accomplish and can be delivered by any one of a number of methods. Start with an unblurred original in Photoshop, and apply different levels of Gaussian blur. You'll often see variations of this technique used as JavaScript rollover buttons.

Let's start with the most rudimentary types of Web animation: server push and client pull.

Server Push And Client Pull

The first Web page animation technologies were very basic. Like so many Web techniques, what was cutting edge just a few years back now seems quaint, at best. While one technique has been eclipsed, however, the other is still used to provide a number of quick-and-dirty animations.

Server Push

In the bad old days before Netscape Navigator 2.0, *server push* was the primary means to animate Web pages. This technique uses CGI scripts to push (send) a series of image files from the server to the client's browser. The image "moves" as each succeeding file is downloaded. Server push animations work best with tiny, limited palette animations. The smaller the individual files (animation frames) are, the faster the animation will download and play.

Server push fell out of favor because of its propensity to "eat the pipe." With a server push, the connection between the server and the browser is open until either the server stops sending data (when an animation sequence ends) or the Web surfer says, "Stop, I've had enough!" by hitting the Stop button. If the animation loops, or constantly cycles, it can consume bandwidth at a torrid pace.

Client Pull

Client pulls are similar to server pushes in that they are both schemes to download multiple files. The difference is as their names imply—server pushes are fired from the server, and client pulls are prompted from the browser. Client pulls are initiated by HTML coding, which forces the client to tell the server, "Send me this particular file in x seconds." With server pushes, the pipe is open until broken. With client pulls, the pipe is reopened each time the client requests a new file. Server pushes can be faster, as you do not have to renegotiate a connection each time. The trade-off is made in the loss of pipe.

Figure 7.1 These five frames are sequenced to create a pulsating warning sign.

NETSCAPE ON PUSH AND PULL

You can find more background information on both server push and client pulls on Netscape's Web site at http://search. netscape.com/assist/net_sites/ pushpull.html. You'll even find a fun little server push animation of the Netscape mascot, Mozilla, at http://search.netscape.com/ assist/net_sites/mozilla/index.html

HOLD THE LINE WITH PLACEHOLDERS!

To prevent PageMill from messing with HTML coding that you've created with another program, you can protect the coding by encasing it within a *Placeholder*. (Note: You should always add your Placeholder before you bring the file into PageMill.) In an ASCII editor, type <!--NOEDIT--> before the coding you wish to protect, and type <!--/NOEDIT--> immediately after the text. Once the file has been opened in PageMill, a little Placeholder pylon (road hazard cone) will appear in both Edit and Preview mode. A quick check in HTML Source mode will show that the code is, in fact, untouched. The Placeholder tags are really just HTML comment tags and are ignored by all the browsers.

Of the two techniques, only client pulls remain in vogue. Server pushes were outdated by a series of animation techniques (primarily GIF89a, Java, and Shockwave). Client pulls, however, are fun little devices that allow the Web site designer to deliver a sequence of complete Web pages in a manner reminiscent of the old Burma Shave highway billboards (although you should use this procedure with artistic discretion). You can also use client pulls to create automatic "forwarding" pages when you move a page from one URL to another. When a browser hits the old URL, the forwarding page tells it to reset its bookmark, and (after a set amount of time) automatically sends the new page down to the browser.

Implementing Client Pull In PageMill

Adding client pull animation is easy. To implement a client pull animation, you'll need to hop into PageMill's HTML Source mode and insert a META Refresh code into each Web page to summon a subsequent page. The META Refresh tag is inserted within the page head, just before the page title. The tag looks something like this:

```
<META HTTP-EQUIV=REFRESH CONTENT="X;
  URL=http://www.servername/filename.html">
```

Pretty simple, eh? Note the two variables: time and **URL**. **X** equals the number of seconds before the next page is loaded. Try building some basic client pull page animations of your own. Be sure to insert the complete URL.

Next up, let's take a look at the next step in our animation timeline, GIF89a.

GIF Animation

If you're looking for an inexpensive, fast, and simple way to get your Web site hopping, look no further. Unlike techniques such as server push, GIF89a animations can bring movement to your site without costing you much time, cash, or bandwidth. They're easy to implement in PageMill; just drag them and drop them into your pages as you would any other GIF image. You can use GIF89a animations for everything from bullets and buttons to image maps. PageMill 3's Preview mode allows you to see exactly how the animation will appear on the finished page.

Although the multipart GIF89a format has been in existence since the dark ages of 1989 (hence the name), GIF89a animations were only introduced to the World Wide Web community by Netscape Navigator 2.0 in late 1995. When Netscape took the wraps off GIF89a Web page animation, one of the first places it came into vogue was on advertising banners. Ad agency Web designers quickly discovered that they could use GIF animations to accomplish many of the design tricks that were previously possible only with server pushes.

The best way to learn about animated GIFs is to cruise the Web in search of some good examples. We've taken the time to scope out some of the best sites for you to take a gander at GIF89a, the poor Web designer's animation format of choice. Check the appendix for a list of cool animation Web sites.

Creating GIF89a Animation

Many of the things you've learned about creating great GIF files apply to animated GIFs as well. You want to ensure speed and stability while providing a pleasant experience for your visitors. Animation adds a new list of things to watch for:

- *Keep them small.* By now, this tip should be obvious. The bigger the size of the image and the more frames, the longer it will take to download. Be realistic about what you can accomplish.

- *Don't interlace the images.* Interlacing is cool for static GIFs but not for animated GIFs. The "underwater look" just doesn't cut it.

- *Watch your interframe delay times.* You can specify this time in increments of a hundredth of a second, or you can designate it to be "as fast as possible." Quite often, you'll need to slow things down a bit to make your animation run smoothly. Keep in mind that "as fast as possible" will result in different timing on different machines.

- *Use looped animations judiciously.* An incessant animation can be irritating. Avoid using infinite loops.

- *Throw out the garbage.* Use the proper disposal method lest your animation be plagued with not-so-happy trails of digital litter.

Animated GIF Builders

Here's a list of popular Animated GIF creation applications:

- Universal Animator (Macintosh and Windows)
  http://www.autofx.com/

- Fireworks (Macintosh and Windows)
  http://macromedia.com/

- GIFmation (Macintosh and Windows)
  http://www.boxtopsoft.com/

- GifDANCER (Macintosh)
  http://www.paceworks.com/

- GIF Movie Gear (Windows)
  http://www.coffeecup.com/

- GIF Animator (Windows)
  http://www.ulead.com/

- Photo Cell (Macintosh)
  http://www.secondglance.com/

- WebPainter (Macintosh and Windows)
  http://www.totallyhip.com/

- *Limit the number of animations on a page.* More than a few animations on a page can be overkill. Use your best judgment.

- *But above all: Go wild!* If you have a killer idea for an animation, by all means, try it. If it doesn't work out on the first, second, or even third shot, keep plugging away until you make it work.

Implementing GIF Animations In PageMill 3

Placing a GIF animation in PageMill is no different than placing a standard GIF file. Just drag and drop, or use the Insert Object command. Your visitors will not need any special plug-ins to view animated GIFs as long as they are using Microsoft's Internet Explorer or Netscape Navigator, versions 2.0 or higher. These days, that's just about everyone.

Let's take a step forward and look at two of today's animation heavy hitters: Java and JavaScript.

Is It Difficult To Use Java And JavaScript?

The answer to this question depends on how you go about it. The following section provides an overview of the technologies and how they can be incorporated into your PageMilled Web pages. As you read through the section, you will understand the principles and learn to apply them in real-world situations. Average folks *can* use these technologies. They're not rocket science! Sure, you'll go through the requisite period of head scratching. But you'll quickly blast through your befuddlement.

I'm not suggesting that you learn how to program or script, if that's not what you want to do. These days, you don't have to be a software engineer to take advantage of these technologies. You don't need to write programs by hand to use Java applets and JavaScript on your Web pages. Instead, you can realize the power of Java and JavaScript by incorporating *finished* applets and scripts. You can also find a number of ways to create customized Java applets and JavaScripts without having to touch any code.

Java

There has never been a programming language quite like Java. I'm not saying that there have never been similar languages; Java definitely bears a resemblance to its relatives in the C family. Java is different because of the incredible hype that swirls around it. Java's promise of cross-platform compatibility has been at question from the start, however, as various entities (most notably Microsoft) have attempted to usurp control of the language and gain the favor of the software development community.

As a Web site developer, you probably won't deal with the actual programming involved in creating a Java applet. In many cases, you'll either use a prebuilt applet or have an engineer create an applet specifically for the application at hand. It's important, however, that those applets run in a cross-platform environment.

As I write this piece in the spring of 1998, the desktop computer world is exceedingly dominated by Microsoft Windows. Apple Computer's market share has sunk well into the single digits. The market is ripe for change, however, and public discontent with Microsoft is on the rise. A number of operating systems stand at the ready: Red Hat Linux, BeOS, and Apple's Rhapsody. Will any of these operating systems grab the crown from Microsoft? It's hardly thinkable, but stranger things have happened.

What is unquestionably clear, though, is that the revolution brought upon by the Internet was made possible through open standards. In the future, as

JAVA AND JAVASCRIPT— WHAT'S THE DIFFERENCE?

Java was originally developed by Sun Microsystems, with the intent of creating a totally cross-platform programming language. The dream was "write once, run anywhere." Java applets are little programs that are downloaded along with a Web page. The Web page coding usually contains parameters that control how the applet behaves.

JavaScript isn't Java at all. JavaScript was originally developed by Netscape and released to the world as LiveScript. Netscape changed LiveScript's name to JavaScript shortly after it was released in order to ride the coattails of the Java buzz. JavaScript is scripting language contained entirely in the Web page code and is executed in the browser. JavaScript doesn't have any external applets (although a JavaScript can call a Java applet into play).

WHITHER ACTIVEX? (OR IS IT JUST PLAIN WITHERED?)

ActiveX was Microsoft's answer to Sun's Java. More hype than substance, ActiveX suffered a dearth of development—so much so, that c|net's popular news.com Web site ran a feature on February 19, 1998, titled "inActiveX."

Although PageMill includes the ability to insert ActiveX controls and files into Web pages, the scarcity of ActiveX in real-world Web development makes the topic hardly worth covering in these pages. The technology looks to follow Microsoft Bob into the best-forgotten annals of Redmond history.

in the past, a range of disparate machines will be connected via the Net. It is absolutely essential that the applets you embed in your Web pages run on the widest range of computers. Pure Java is the clearest way to that goal.

Creating Custom Java Applets

In the beginning, the creation of Java applets was the sole province of the software engineer. Much has changed, however, in the few years since Sun's upstart programming language rode to hype-filled fame and glory. Nontechnical folks can now choose from a staggeringly large number of prebuilt Java applets. And the tools are here for nonprogrammers to create their own custom applets. Cool beans...*JavaBeans,* that is.

Although the PageMill 3 CD-ROM includes a wide range of JavaScripts, Adobe went light on the Java. We've stepped in to fill that void. This book's CD-ROM includes demo versions of Interleaf Jamba as well as Java applets from Modern Minds.

Interleaf Jamba

Looking to brew your own specially blended Java applet? Interleaf Jamba lets you create powerful Java applets without programming. This Windows application provides an innovative visual applet development environment; you can actually see and understand what you're doing. Whoa! You can create interactive animations, navigation bars, and powerful information-gathering forms—all without writing code.

Jamba's wizards help expedite the applet development process as you learn the application. Once you're familiar with Jamba, however, you'll probably want to build your applets from scratch. Jamba's wizards include the following:

- *Attention Getters*—Banners and Ticker Tapes

- *Cool Navigation*—Animated Buttons and Image Maps

- *Hot Information*—Guest Books and Email

- *Power Presentation*—Web Books and Presentations

The Jamba interface is shown in Figure 7.2.

Modern Minds Ultimate Button Bar And WildView

We combed through hundreds of Java applets to find the Modern Minds Ultimate Button Bar and WildView collections. They are two of the most versatile applet collections known to man. Well, okay... they won't slice bread, but they're definitely cool. Both applets come with extensive electronic documentation and are fully operable in demo mode.

The Ultimate Button Bar's forte is as its name implies. This collection allows you to build a wide variety of text- and image-based navigational button bars. It contains three basic applets:

- *ImageURLButtonBar*—Lets you create image-based (GIF or JPEG) buttons.

- *TextURLButtonBar*—Lets you create text-based buttons; allows images to be used as backgrounds.

Figure 7.2 Jamba, Jamba, Jamba.

More Java Applet Builders and Customizable Applets

Here's a handful of commercial Java applet builders and customizable applets:

- 1st JAVATab&Tree
  1st JAVANavigator
  http://www.auscomp.com/

- BeanMachine (Windows)
  http://www.lotus.com/

- IMC ActionLine (Macintosh)
  http://www.imcinfo.com/

- PaceWorks ObjectDANCER (Macintosh)
  http://www.paceworks.com/

- PageCharmer (all platforms)
  PageMover (all platforms)
  http://www.pagecharmer.com/

- WebBurst (Macintosh and Windows)
  WebBurst FX (Macintosh)
  http://www.powerproduction.com/

- *LiteTextURLButtonBar*—Lets you create text-based buttons; similar to the TextURLButtonBar, but with fewer features and, subsequently, a faster download.

WildView offers a host of possibilities. You can use it to create animated image maps, scrolling text, rotating ad banners, complex navigational systems, menus, catalogs, and slide shows. The WildNews demo, shown in Figure 7.3, uses scrolling text as well as rotating photographs.

Implementing Java In PageMill

Java applet files have a .class extension. Begin by moving the applet (and any supporting files) into your Web site's root folder. To embed the Java applet into the Web page in PageMill fashion, select Insert|Object|JavaApplet. In the Insert Object dialog box, select the applet and click on Place. Java applets come in as 100×100 pixel objects. Use the Inspector's Object tab to change the default Height and Width to the applet's true size.

Each applet has its own set of parameters. Although you can use the Inspector's Object tab, as shown in Figure 7.4, to specify the parameters from scratch, you can usually just copy and paste the parameters more easily (and with far less frustration) from the applet's electronic documentation into PageMill's HTML Source mode. After all that good stuff has been placed in the page, you can always use the Inspector to fine-tune the settings. Using Source mode to edit the parameters may *still* be easier, however, because the Inspector offers teeny-tiny little Name and Value fields. In fact, you might just want to forgo PageMill's Insert|Object|JavaApplet method and just cut and paste the whole kit and caboodle into Source mode.

You can view Java applets in PageMill's Edit and Preview modes. The Active Content tab of PageMill's Preferences dialog box includes four Java options:

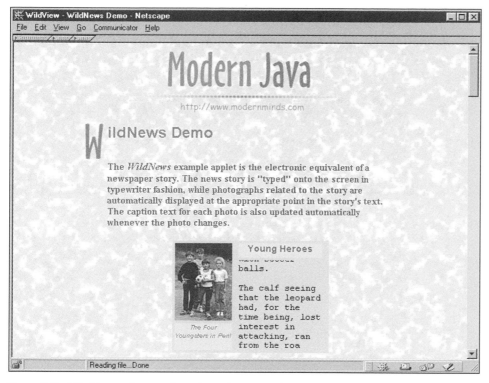

Figure 7.3 WildView pulls a number of popular Java tricks into one cool package.

- *Enable Java Applets*—Check this box to preview applets in PageMill.

- *Run Applets in Edit Mode*—Check this box to preview applets in PageMill's Edit mode.

- *Reload Applets When Switching to Preview Mode*—Check this box to reload applets each time you switch from Edit to Preview mode.

- *Use CLASSPATH Environment Variable*—Leave this box unchecked, unless specified.

Java applets (and their supporting files) absolutely must be stored properly within your Web site's file structure. Make sure that you put them in the correct place locally (on your computer's hard drive) and that you use PageMill's Site Upload function to move all those files to your Web server.

Coffee getting cold? Let's get a fill-up and some piping hot JavaScript.

JavaScript

JavaScript provides the means to create dynamic Web pages. You can add this interactivity by simply cutting and pasting the JavaScripts into your HTML pages. Thankfully, you don't have to look near and

MORE COOL JAVA BUTTONS

Looking for more Java button options? Take a gander at 1 Cool Button Tool (Windows): http://www.formulagraphics. com/

WHAT'S UP WITH THAT APPLET?

Click on View | Show Java Console to display PageMill's Java Console and get a readout of what your errant applets are up to.

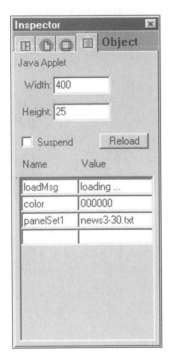

Figure 7.4 The Inspector works fine for minor parameter tweaks. Source mode is a better bet for heavy edits.

far for those scripts; the Adobe PageMill 3 CD-ROM contains a large selection of canned JavaScripts from The JavaScript Source in the Goodies/JavaScript folder. We've included a handy list of those scripts in the appendix, so you can find the script you need at a glance. (You can also view a complete list of scripts on the CD-ROM by opening Goodies/JavaScript/completescriptdirectory.html in your Web browser.)

Pasting a canned JavaScript into a Web page is one of the fastest ways to add interactive functionality to your site. Let's take a look at some of the things that this technology can do. JavaScript allows for the following functions:

- Browser detection
- Information displayed in the browser's status bar
- Enhanced navigational menus
- Feedback based on mouse position, such as interactive "rollover" buttons
- Forms (without the need for CGIs)
- Local time and date information, and actions based thereon

Reviewing Some JavaScript Basics

Although this section is not intended to teach the intricacies of JavaScript (you can find shelves of books for that use), a quick peek at the various script elements will help you to find your way around a script. To understand a bit about how JavaScript works, let's take a look at a (slightly modified) script from the PageMill 3 CD-ROM. The following Daily Redirection script displays a different page for each day of the week. When a browser calls the page in which the JavaScript is located, the script checks for the current day and redirects the request to the appropriate page.

```
<SCRIPT LANGUAGE="JavaScript">

<!-- This script and many more available at
The JavaScript Source!!  -->
<!-- via the Internet U R L:
http://www.compfund.com/javascript/  -->
<!-- Begin
function initArray() {
this.length = initArray.arguments.length;
for (var i = 0; i < this.length; i++)
this[i+1] = initArray.arguments[i];
}
```

```
var DOWArray = new
initArray("Monday","Tuesday","Wednesday","Thursday",
"Friday","Saturday","Sunday");
var today = new Date();
var day = DOWArray[today.getDay()];
if (day == "Monday") window.location = "Mon.html"
if (day == "Tuesday") window.location = "Tues.html"
if (day == "Wednesday") window.location = "Weds.html"
if (day == "Thursday") window.location = "Thurs.html"
if (day == "Friday") window.location = "Fri.html"
if (day == "Saturday") window.location = "Sat.html"
if (day == "Sunday") window.location = "Sun.html"
// End -->
</SCRIPT>
```

JavaScripts must be encased in **<SCRIPT>** ... **</SCRIPT>** codes to be able to execute. Some scripts, such as the Daily Redirection script, are placed entirely within the **<HEAD>** ... **</HEAD>** section of your Web page. Other scripts insert some code within the **<HEAD>** ... **</HEAD>** section, with the remainder of the code placed in the main **<BODY>** ... **</BODY>** section. A well-commented script will explain where each section of the script should be placed. The JavaScripts on the PageMill 3 CD-ROM are fairly self-explanatory.

Here is a handful of basic JavaScript pointers:

- Scripts start with <!-- and end with -->.

- Comment lines start with //.

- Comment blocks (longer passages) can be contained within /* and */.

- JavaScript is case sensitive.

- Every command that is opened should be closed.

Creating Custom JavaScripts

If you want to create your own custom JavaScripts but don't have the wherewithal to code them by hand, you're in luck. You can create scripts in a number of cool ways without touching any code. It took a while for the software developers to catch on, but they've now developed some slick programs for creating rollover buttons and the like. If you're so inclined, be sure to check out the following:

- *Astound Dynamite* (Windows)—http://www.astound.com

- *Macromedia Fireworks* (Macintosh and Windows)—http://www.getfireworks.com

- *PageSplitter*—(Macintosh. Windows under development)—http://www.pagesplitter.com/

BROWSER INCOMPATIBILITIES

JavaScripts can appear and function differently from browser to browser and from platform to platform. If your Web site is meant for the world at large, be sure to test your pages with multiple browsers. If your Web site is on an intranet, where everyone is using the same exact browser, you can forgo this exhaustive testing.

CHECK THE PAGEMILL 3 CD-ROM

Want to read more on the topic of JavaScript? You'll find an HTML version of Chapter 1, "An Overview of JavaScript," from David Flanagan's *JavaScript: The Definitive Guide, 2nd Edition* (O'Reilly & Associates).

PAGESPLITTER!

You'll find a demo version of PageSplitter on this book's CD-ROM.

PROTECT THAT CODE!

Let's say that you create some really great JavaScripts. How do you prevent them from being stolen? Because JavaScript is placed into the page code, folks can view the source and steal your mojo. Fortunately, you can take countermeasures. Here are four resources that you can use to obfuscate your code:

- The !Impressions! Web Design PageParser
  http://www.ozemail.com.au/~jbp/impressions/pageparser.html

- Jammer
  http://www.geocities.com/SiliconValley/4274/jammer.htm

- JavaScript Scrambler
  http://members.tripod.com/~tier/jss.html

- JMyth Code Encryption Utility
  http://www.geocities.com/SiliconValley/Vista/5233/jmyth.htm

You shouldn't feel that you absolutely *have* to buy a program, however. The power of the Net brings these great features to your computer, with nary a download or a trip out to the local computer superstore. In the following sections, I describe a pair of wonderful online resources for interactive JavaScripting.

Instant JavaScript

Want a slick drop-down JavaScript navigation menu or some cool mouseover buttons? c|net's Charity Kahn has developed some amazing utilities for creating custom JavaScripts online. Simply enter your data into the forms, and let the bot do the work. After the bot creates your code, all you have to do is cut it and paste it into your Web page. Nice! Be sure to check out the Browser Detective, Cookie Cutter, Menu Maker, Mouseover Machine, and Window Builder. The Mouseover Machine, as shown in Figure 7.5, enables you to create interactive navigation bars easily. Just fill in the blanks. After you've plugged in the file names and submitted the form, you'll be rewarded with the JavaScript code. Copy and paste the code into your page, and you're navigating, baby.

You can find Charity's Cool Tools at http://www.cnet.com/Content/Builder/Programming/Kahn/index.html.

More Rollovers...Woof!

Neil McCorrison's Easy OnMouseOver Image Changer Creator is another cool automatic JavaScript rollover generator. Tell it how many buttons you want, the size of each button, the base image, the rollover image, the status bar text, and the link for each.

You can find Neil's Easy OnMouseOver Image Changer Creator at http://neil.simplenet.com/javascript/.

Implementing JavaScript In PageMill

You can bring JavaScripts into a PageMilled page in several ways. Although PageMill allows you to

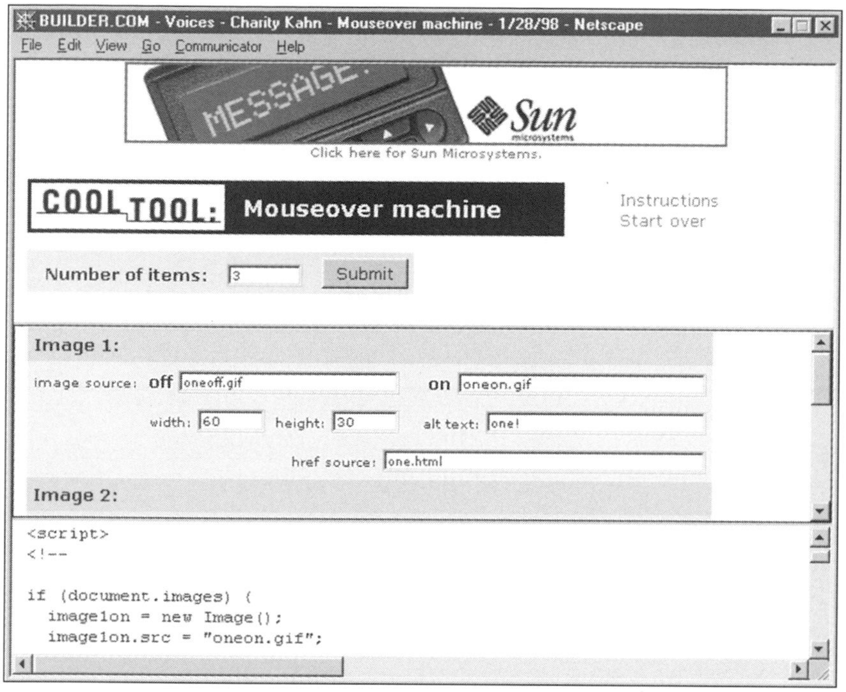

Figure 7.5 Creating rollover buttons with Charity's Mouseover Machine is a breeze.

insert JavaScripts into placeholders, I would recommend doing battle in either PageMill's HTML Source mode or, preferably, in an ASCII text editor. Although you can use the text editors that come with the Macintosh system (SimpleText) or Windows (Notepad), you'll be happier with a full-featured text editor, such as BBEdit (Macintosh) or NoteTab (Windows). We'll look at both BBEdit and NoteTab in Chapter 9.

Unfortunately, some JavaScripts do not display in PageMill's Edit or Preview modes. And by and large, the interactive features won't work in Preview mode, either. JavaScripted page previewing should be done in either PageMill's Internet Explorer preview or in the browser of your choice. Figures 7.6 through 7.8 show how a calendar script appears in PageMill's Source and Edit modes as well as in the browser.

Next, we'll take a look at Macromedia's Shock-wave, a technology that combines slick animation techniques with sizzling soundtracks and scintillating scripting.

Macromedia Shockwave

Macromedia's Shockwave first rumbled through the Web in late 1996. The technology raised quite a stir in the Web community by bringing the power of Macromedia Director and the creativity of its massive user base (well over 250,000 users) to the Internet. Director is the most

DOC JAVASCRIPT EXPLAINS ROLLOVERS...

Read all about Universal JavaScript Rollovers at http://webreference.internet.com/js/column1/

PLACEHOLDERS OR NOT?

If you insert your JavaScript code into a placeholder, it *definitely* won't show in PageMill's Edit mode. Properly encasing the script between **<SCRIPT><!--** and **--></SCRIPT>** is the way to go.

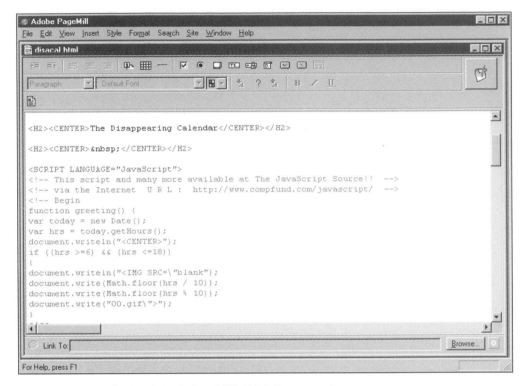

Figure 7.6 Here's the JavaScript in PageMill's HTML Source mode.

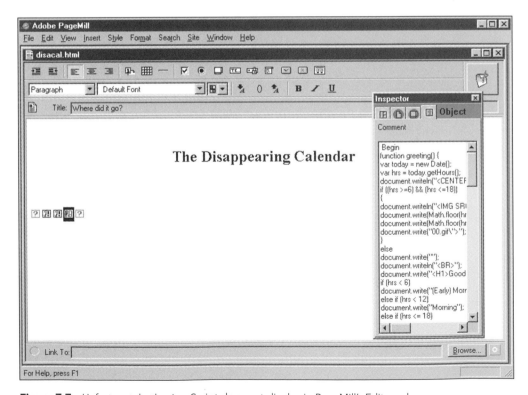

Figure 7.7 Unfortunately, the JavaScript does not display in PageMill's Edit mode.

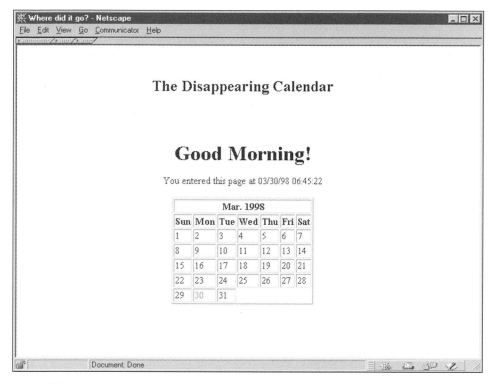

Figure 7.8 Fear not...the JavaScript looks fine when viewed in Netscape Navigator.

prevalent tool in the multimedia industry, and Macromedia boasts
some of the most talented third-party developers in the world.

Shockwave adds an enhanced level of interactivity to Web pages. Although you can set up a standard GIF animation as a hot link or even
an image map, after the visitor clicks on the image, the image (itself)
doesn't do anything. It merely sends the visitor off to the linked Web
page or anchor. The most basic Shockwave animations, however, can
be programmed to do something when clicked on (other than simply
jumping to another page). A button might beep, appear as if it were
clicked on, or an additional animation sequence may be triggered.
And best of all, you can add Shockwave animations to Web pages
created with PageMill 3 by simply dragging and dropping the file from
the desktop into your page.

For visitors to experience Shockwave animation, they must have the
Shockwave plug-in installed in their browsers. The plug-in has proven
to be one of the most popular on the Internet; Macromedia claims that
its site has served up millions upon millions of copies of the installation files. When you incorporate native Shockwave into your Web site,
you are taking a leap of faith; you're betting that your visitors will

USING OTHER FOLKS' CODE

When you're just starting out
with JavaScript, you're probably
going to borrow someone else's
code rather than hack it out by
hand. This should not present a
moral dilemma *if* you *only* borrow code that's been designated
as freeware. You should *never*
borrow code unless you know
that it's okay with the author.
Fortunately, you can find some
Web sites that feature volumes
of freeware JavaScript code. The
appendix contains a host of
online JavaScript resources.

THE MANY FLAVORS OF SHOCKWAVE

Macromedia started out by creating Shockwave files from Director, their flagship multimedia application. They soon added versions for FreeHand (vector graphics), Authorware (computer-based training), and xRes (high-end bitmaps). The most dramatic addition, however, was Macromedia Flash, which brought interactive vector animations into the loop.

You'll find demo versions of Macromedia Director and Flash (for both Macintosh and Windows computers) on this book's CD-ROM.

have Shockwave installed or that they will be sufficiently intrigued to download and install the plug-in. Thankfully, Shockwave is now bundled with Netscape Navigator and Microsoft Internet Explorer.

Macromedia Director

Shockwave animations that have been created with Macromedia Director are delivering everything from arcade game action to interactive edutainment via the Internet. Because Director is the tool of choice for so many professional multimedia developers, these firms have naturally flocked to the World Wide Web to hawk their skills. The high caliber of Shockwave animations available on the Web today is staggering. Acclaimed CD-ROM developers are literally giving their Shockwave games away as an enticement to pull visitors into their Web sites.

Creating Director Shockwave Files

To create your own Director Shockwave sequences from scratch, you'll have to get your hands on a copy of Director 4, 5, or 6. Director movie files need to be processed through Macromedia's Afterburner utility (which is provided free of charge to registered Director users via Macromedia's Web site) to create a Shockwave file. It doesn't matter what platform you create or play back on. Shockwave is a cross-platform technology, fully supported on both Macintosh and Windows. Figure 7.9 shows a Director project in the works.

You don't have to have Director to add Shockwave to your site, however. You can easily incorporate existing Shockwave files from third-party sources. A vast array of ready-made Shockwave animations is available on the Internet for the picking. Of course, you'll have to be respectful of the creators' copyrights, but that should go without saying. Copyright doesn't have to be a problem. In fact, many of the smaller Shockwave goodies are freeware.

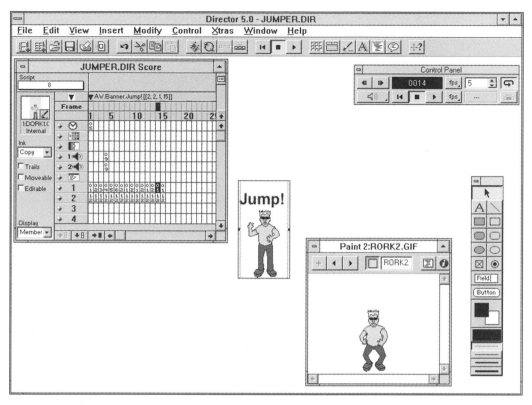

Figure 7.9 Director's environment provides complete control over multimedia elements.

One place on the Web is filled with Shockwave tidbits galore. Its name is Shock-Bauble. I first wrote about the Shock-Bauble Web site (http://www.adveract.com/shokbobl/abtboble.htm) in *Web Publishing with Adobe PageMill 2,* the predecessor to this book. The Shock-Bauble Web site was created by @dver@ctive, an interactive media developer located in Chapel Hill, North Carolina. The Shock-Bauble Web site is a cool thing indeed, but these days, you don't even have to hook up to the Internet to enjoy those cool trinkets—they're on the PageMill 3 CD-ROM.

Shock-Baubles are compact animations, with most files weighing in at under 12K. These tasty little tidbits are, for the most part, freeware. If you use one of the Shock-Baubles on the site, in most cases, you owe only a wink and a nod to the developer (although a small credit on your Web page is a nice touch, as is an email message thanking the bauble's creator).

The nifty little keyboard, shown in Figure 7.10, is an excellent example of what can be accomplished with Director's Lingo programming language. You don't need to study up on your code; just grab the file and drag it into PageMill.

DIRECTOR TO JAVA CONVERSION

These days, you can forgo the Shockwave plug-in by creating Shocked Java files. Check out Narrative Enliven (http://www.narrative.com/) or Macromedia's Director Export Xtra for Java (http://www.macromedia.com/software/director/java/).

Figure 7.10 Tinkle the keys?

The Shock-Bauble site includes work from developers in the U.S., Europe, and Australia (among other locales). Shockwave is truly an international phenomenon, with "shocked" sites shaking to the surface around the globe. The appendix features a selection of some of the best Shockwave Web sites we've found.

Implementing Director Shockwave Files In PageMill

Director Shockwave files have a .dcr extension. Begin by moving the Shockwave file into your Web site's root folder. To embed the Shockwave movie into the Web page, select Insert|Object|Other File. In the Insert Object dialog box, change Files of type: to All Files (*.*). Select the Shockwave file and click on Place. Shockwave files come in as 88×88 pixel objects. Use the Inspector's Object tab to change the default Height and Width to the Shockwave object's true size. (Each of the Shock-Bauble Web pages in the Goodies/ShockWave/FREESTUF folder should include Height and Width information.)

To preview Director Shockwave movies in PageMill, you must have the Shockwave plug-in loaded in PageMill's Browser Plug-ins folder. Your Web server may have to go through a simple one-time configuration to serve Shockwave files, if it has never served any before. Check Goodies/ShockWave/Using_sb.htm on the PageMill 3 CD-ROM for the full details.

Macromedia Flash

Macromedia Flash changed the game in Web page animation, as its big brother Director did before it. Flash actually began life as FutureSplash Animator. Macromedia acquired FutureSplash in early 1997 and quickly relaunched Animator as Flash. Unlike most techniques that are based on bitmap animation, Flash uses vector animation. This capability allows for smaller files that download more quickly. Synchronized sound is supported in the form of WAV and AIFF files. This capability allows for everything from simple buttons noises through more complex arrangements.

You might think of the difference between Macromedia Director and Flash as the difference between Adobe Photoshop and Illustrator. Director and Photoshop both deal with bitmaps. Flash and Illustrator both deal with vector art (although they can incorporate bitmaps). Whereas one provides its images in bit-by-bit detail, the other delivers its images with bold, object-oriented graphics.

Creating Flash Shockwave

To create Flash Shockwave files, you'll need to have access to a copy of Macromedia Flash. Being the hard-working, ever-caring folks we are, we've seen fit to include demos of Flash on this book's CD-ROM (in both Macintosh and Windows versions). Flash, like Director, uses a timeline to choreograph movement, as shown in Figure 7.11.

Implementing Flash Shockwave In PageMill

Flash Shockwave files have an .swf extension. Begin by moving the Shockwave file into your Web site's root folder. To embed the Shockwave movie into the Web page, select Insert|Object|Other File. In the Insert Object dialog box, change Files of type: to All Files (*.*). Select the Shockwave file and click on Place. Shockwave files come in as 88×88 pixel objects. Use the Inspector's Object tab to change the default Height and Width to the Shockwave object's true size.

To preview Flash Shockwave movies in PageMill, you must have the Shockwave plug-in loaded in PageMill's Browser Plug-ins folder.

Next, it's time to listen up for some tips on using sound in your Web site.

Sound

PageMill allows you to add sound files easily to your Web pages. Sound files generally have one of the following extensions: .aif, .aiff, .au, .wav, mid, or .midi. For your visitors to hear sounds on your Web pages, their computers must be set up with the appropriate hardware

CHECK THE PAGEMILL 3 CD-ROM

Adobe has included a large number of goodies from the Shock-Bauble Web site on the PageMill 3 release CD-ROM. Take a peek in the Goodies/ ShockWave/FREESTUF folder.

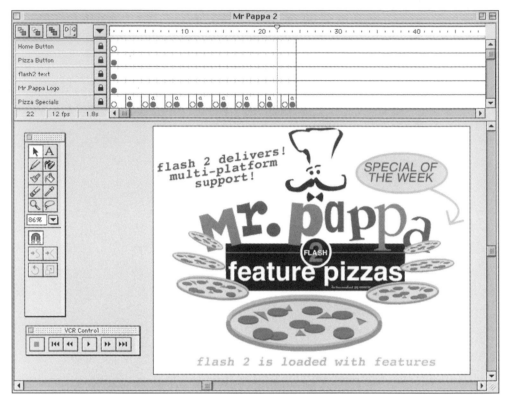

Figure 7.11 If you're familiar with vector illustration techniques, you'll feel at home with Macromedia Flash.

and software. Whereas Web browser-equipped Macintosh computers have the built-in hardware ability to play analog sounds (AIF, AIFF, AU, and WAV), Windows computers must be equipped with sound cards.

MIDI files are different from the other formats in two important ways. You can think of them as digital sheet music in a way. MIDI files are programs that provide instructions on how a song will play. Analog sound files are recordings, in the same vein as tape recordings. MIDI files may require an additional plug-in to play at the browser.

Creating Sound Files

You'll need the appropriate software to create your own sound files. Fortunately, you won't have to spend a dime to get started. If you're working on a Macintosh, you can use the Mac's Sound Control Panel to record. Then, you'll want to use SoundApp (a cool little freeware program) to convert it to WAV format. If you're working with a Windows computer, you can use the built-in Windows Sound Recorder to create and save the file in WAV format.

Of course, as your needs and expectations increase, you'll want to edit and enhance your recordings. Fortunately, a host of shareware sound applications is available. We've included a list of Internet sound resources in the appendix.

Implementing Sound In PageMill

Begin by moving the sound file into your Web site's root folder. Select Insert|Object|Sound; then select the sound you want to insert into the page and click on Place. The sound will appear in PageMill as a gawky 88×88 pixel white square (in both Edit and Preview mode), as shown in Figure 7.12. Fear not; that isn't how it will appear in the browser. Instead, the browser will display a player console graphic; Netscape Communicator's player console is shown in Figure 7.13. For the player console graphic to display properly, however, you must adjust its horizontal and vertical dimensions in the Inspector. (Otherwise, the browser will display an 88×88 pixel chunk of the graphic.) Select the sound object. On the Inspector's Object tab, set the Width to 145 and the Height to 60.

With the player console graphic, your visitors can play the sound at will. You can also configure sounds so that they play as background

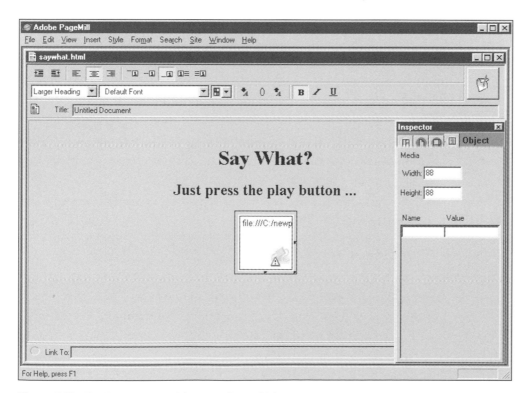

Figure 7.12 Don't worry; your visitors won't see this!

Figure 7.13   After you make the size adjustments, the entire player console graphic will be displayed.

music. (The player console graphic will not be visible.) To create background music, enter the following parameters into the Name and Value fields in the Inspector's Object tab:

autoplay	true
loop	true
hidden	true

You can also add imageless QuickTime as sounds. Let's take a look at how Apple's QuickTime format fits with PageMill.

QuickTime Movies

Want to put some real moving pictures on your Web site? Using QuickTime movies is the most popular way to deliver video clips via the Web. The medium allows you to show everything from your Frisbee-catching family dog to your latest whizzy invention in glorious full motion. And these movies work great in cross-platform situations. As with the other forms of animation, you can easily add QuickTime animation to Web pages in PageMill by simply dragging and dropping the files from the desktop. (You can also use the Place command or copy and paste.)

WANT THE PLAYER CONSOLE IN ITS OWN WINDOW?

If you want to have the player console pop up as a separate window (rather than within the Web page), choose Edit|Make Link to link to the sound instead of embedding the sound.

QuickTime movies are typically very large because they usually contain both sound and video. Adding a QuickTime clip to a Web page is a powerful way to convey information, but if the QuickTime movie is huge, you should always make it an optional choice for your visitors. Put the clip on a separate page, and make sure the link to that page includes a polite warning about the file size. In other words, don't put a 4MB file on the front page of your Web site.

Creating QuickTime Movies

Creating QuickTime clips is a relatively hardware-intensive task. You'll need a video capture board in your PC or Mac (or an AV-Mac) and a VCR or camcorder in addition to a video-editing application such as Adobe Premiere. Of course, if you have a buddy who already has all these goodies, you're probably in luck. Once again, we don't have the room to cover this huge topic in depth. If you're interested in QuickTime, Apple provides a host of resources at its QuickTime Web site at http://www.apple.com/quicktime/.

Implementing QuickTime Movies In PageMill

You can choose to have your QuickTime movies play within the Web page or in a separate window. You can easily implement either method. Using a separate window can be more polite, however, as your visitors won't have to sit through lengthy downloads if they don't *really* want to view the movie. You can preview QuickTime movies from PageMill's Preview mode. By default, the QuickTime plug-in is installed with PageMill. Here are a few pointers on working with QuickTime files in PageMill:

- Begin by moving the QuickTime file into your Web site's root folder.

- To place a QuickTime movie into a Web page, select Insert|Object|Other File. In the Insert Object dialog box, change Files of type: to All Files (*.*). Select the file and click on Place.

- To have a QuickTime movie play in a separate window, select Insert|Object|Other File. In the Insert Object dialog box, change Files of type: to All Files (*.*). Select the file and click on Link To.

Moving On

Adding just the right amount of sound and fury can change your site from a collection of static pages into an action-packed fun ride. As a Web designer, you are responsible for determining what type of animation to add to your pages, if any. Whether you decide on adding

GIF89a, Java, JavaScript, or Shockwave animation depends on your competencies, resources, and circumstances. Poorly executed and gratuitous animations are a distraction at best. Well-executed animations, on the other hand, are an invaluable addition.

As with so many design decisions, less is more and more is less. True elegance in Web page design is a direct result of simplicity. But what good is a well-designed Web site, if no one knows about it? In the next chapter, you'll learn how to bring in the crowds.

GET THE
WORD OUT!
8

In this chapter, you'll learn how to attract traffic to your Web site, while steering it to success.

Even if put the most incredible Web site ever imagined on the Internet, you can't be assured of true success unless its message reaches your intended audience. The secret is to get the word out and then promote, promote, promote. The form that your promotion takes depends on the type of Web site you're building. And like so many projects, your promotional efforts are almost always budget dependent.

You don't need to allocate a single cent of real money to promote your Web site, but should you decide to shell out the bucks, you'll want to send them in the right direction. In most cases—whether or not the project has a real budget—you'll begin your promotional efforts by focusing on the no-cost venues.

Registering With The Search Engines

The first way your audience will find your Web site is through a *search engine*. Search engines are Web sites that have been designed to catalog the contents of the entire World Wide Web. They fulfill the needs of the Web community, providing an organized way of using this wonderful resource, which draws millions of information-hungry visitors every day. In many cases, advertising revenue is what keeps the search engines up and running. Those little advertising banners displayed at the top and sometimes in the middle of search engine pages are easy to endure when you realize the great service they afford. Certain search engines are not financed solely through advertising revenue, however. Some charge for their searches and offer subscription plans for enhanced levels of service.

Search engines use *automated robots* to crawl around the Web on a nightly basis; they check for new pages in cyberspace and gather updated information on pages that have already been cataloged. These software robots are often referred to as spiders, crawlers, worms, or bots. The information they gather is distilled and displayed at no cost to the user. Digital's Scooter, which scurries from site to site gathering up information for Digital's high-powered AltaVista database, is one of the busiest spiders on the Web. Other big-name spiders include Inktomi Slurp (HotBot), ArchitextSpider (Excite), and Gulliver (Northern Light).

Some Of The Most Popular Search Engine Sites

Table 8.1 shows a short list of the most popular Internet search engines, along with their URLs. Each has a different approach to organizing and delivering information. If you can't find what you're looking for on one site, keep jumping until you do.

Table 8.1 The most popular search engines.

Search Engine	Address
AltaVista	http://altavista.digital.com
Excite	http://www.excite.com
HotBot	http://www.hotbot.com
Infoseek	http://www.infoseek.com
LookSmart	http://www.looksmart.com
Lycos	http://www.lycos.com
Magellan	http://www.mckinley.com
Northern Light	http://www.northernlight.com/
Open Text Index	http://www.opentext.com
search.com	http://www.search.com
WebCrawler	http://www.webcrawler.com
Yahoo!	http://www.yahoo.com
2ask	http://www.2ask.com/

The robots may find your site by chance, but you don't have to wait for them to come looking. You can (and should) ask the spiders to come crawling to your URL. This step is essential in launching a new Web site, as well as when substantially revamping or moving a site. Submitting your URL is akin to sending out invitations for a party. People will show up on your doorstep only if they know there's a gig. Accordingly, if you move your site and leave no forwarding address, as in the case of a hostile parting of ways with an erstwhile ISP, visitors will think your Web site has fallen off the face of the earth. And if you open a whole new section on your site that is thinly linked to the existing site, you can't count on a visit from the spiders unless you give them a nudge and tell them where to look.

Each engine has its own online URL submission form to fill out, and each treats this task a little differently. Going from search engine to search engine, registering your Web site's specific information, can take the better part of a day. Although this job may seem tedious, registering is an essential step toward your site's ultimate success. Best of all, it's completely free! The AltaVista registration form, shown in Figure 8.1, includes a "No SPAM Please" warning for would-be index spammers. Be true to your Web site, your visitors, and the search engines. Spamming the search engines with erroneous information is flat out wrong.

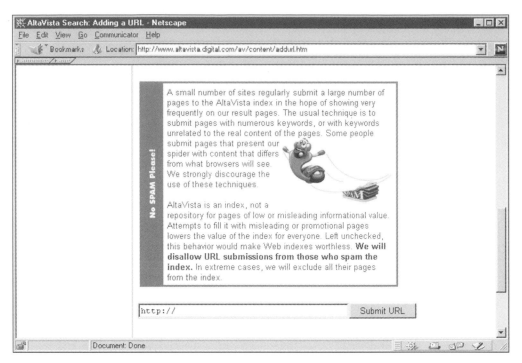

Figure 8.1 In the AltaVista registration form, simply fill in the URL address, click on Submit URL, and AltaVista does the rest.

You can find alternatives to registering with the search engines one by one. Services such as Submit It! (http://www.submit-it.com/), PostMaster (http://www.netcreations.com/postmaster/), and WebPromote (http://www.webpromote.com/) allow you to perform a wholesale submission. For a small fee, these services can submit your URL to hundreds of sites. Submit It! and PostMaster also offer limited free submissions. Figure 8.2 shows the basic Submit It! Free form. Submit It! Free Classic provides a more detailed form. Here's a quick rundown on how the free services work:

- Submit It! Free submits your URL to AltaVista, Excite/NetFind/ Magellan, Infoseek, HotBot, Lycos/Net Guide, Open Text, and WebCrawler.

- Submit It! Free Classic requires that you fill out a short form. It allows you to submit your URL quickly to What's New on the Internet, Infoseek, WebCrawler, InfoSpace, Northern Light, Starting Point, ComFind, Yellow Pages Online, The Internet Archive, What's New Too!, LinkStar, Pronett, Bizwiz, WebDirect!, Nerd World Media, AltaVista, Mallpark, AAA Matilda, and The Web Magazine.

- PostMaster 2's free submission feature submits your URL to i-Explorer, LinkStar, Magellan, Pronet Business Centre, Yahoo, ViaNet Links, Anzwers, Excite NetSearch, HotBot, Infoseek, Lycos, Open Text, WebCrawler, and Postmaster What's New.

Using a bulk submission service can save lots of time, which is great if you don't have time to lose. But there's something to be said for *knowing* that you entered exactly the information required for each specific search engine. You might, for example, want to write a specific description or announcement of your site for one search engine suited to its particular audience. Each site also has its own indexing categories (and personality); it's very important to fill out the form as completely as possible. The more categories you can squeeze your Web site into, the better.

Many folks will tell you that it's not worth the effort to register with anything other than the most popular search engines. The vast majority of search engine hits come from these sources (in no particular

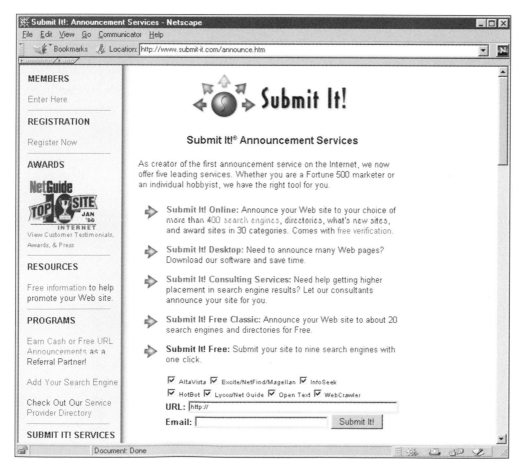

Figure 8.2 The Submit It! Free registration form lets you submit your URL to a number of search engines in one fell swoop.

AWESOME SEARCH ENGINE ADVICE

Looking for the search engine skinny? When it comes to fine-tuning your site for each search engine, it's a game of nuance. Check out Bruce Clay's Search Engine Ranking Tools page at http://www.bruceclay.com/web_rank.htm

order): HotBot, Infoseek, Yahoo, WebCrawler, Excite, Northern Light, AltaVista, and Lycos. Do you have a dime (or the time) to spare? If so, it *may* be worthwhile to have your Web site automatically registered with hundreds of lesser Web sites.

Some search engines, such as Excite and Magellan, offer more than just robot-gathered lists. These sites provide reviews of Web sites, complete with satirical comments and numerical ratings. Several of the hybrid print/zines do the same. You'll need to register your site's URL with these services, and keep your fingers crossed that they like your stuff if they choose to review your site.

Spider Watch: Keeping Track Of The Crawlers

After you've registered your site, you may want to keep an eye on the robots to make sure they've done their job. The best-run Web sites are capable of generating server statistics that should include information about the audience you've attracted. At the very least, your Webmaster should be able to provide you with a file listing of the server logs. Utilities can turn this raw dump into a structured listing. You can use this information in a variety of ways, but three of the most important items that you can learn are who's hitting your site, what pages they're hitting, and from where they're being referred. In this case, you should not be concerned with the raw level of hits. You should look only at the HTML page accesses, not at any graphic file accesses.

The robots should begin hitting your site within a few nights after you submit your URL. Depending on their backlog, some may not hit your site for weeks. After they've discovered your site for the first time, they will return time after time, each on its own mysterious (and often nocturnal) schedule. If you have access to your site statistics, you should watch to see whether the robots are hitting, and also watch to see whether they are referring people to your site.

Give the robots a couple of weeks to do their initial work. Then, go to each search engine, and check to see that your site is indexed by doing a search on a number of keywords. If your site doesn't show up in the search list, and if you're not seeing hits from that site, you have a good indication that the robot has not cataloged your site. Allow the robot a few more days to do its work; then check back again. If your site doesn't show up after a few weeks, you might want to try registering your URL again with the search engine.

Take note of how the various search engines list your pages. You should be cognizant of the title that you give each page in PageMill. This title will be picked up by the spiders and used to catalog your page. It's the single most important element with regard to search engine listings. Neophyte Web designers commonly overlook the proper titling of their Web pages. It's a small touch, albeit an essential one.

With most search engines, you'll have to register only your primary URL (or home page). After the spider finds your front door, it will continue to crawl around your site, cataloging the linked public pages. The spiders are not smart enough to gain access to pages in nonpublic areas, however. If you maintain a number of password-protected pages, you can rest assured that the common robots will not be able to log in. Anything's possible though, and a logging robot is likely to surface eventually.

If, for some reason, you don't want the robots coming to your Web site, you can set up a special file (robots.txt) to tell them to stay away. If you want to prevent specific pages from being indexed, you can add a <META NAME="ROBOTS" CONTENT="NOINDEX"> tag to those pages.

Stats For Fine-tuning Content

While we're on the subject of statistics, it's worth mentioning that all the data in the world is useless if you don't do something with it. This axiom holds true for your server statistics as well. You need to watch your audience. You need to see where they go and take note of where they don't go. If your audience is attracted by sugar, then you had better get ready to lay out plenty of the sweet stuff. If they want spice, you had better figure out what kind.

Web sites are opportunities in the making for social scientist wannabes, as people are infinitely more exciting to watch than lab rats. Having the ability to watch the hoards run through your site is essential in implementing an effective strategy. Thankfully, adding tracking and site management features does not have to be an expensive proposition.

Use META Tags

Before you register your Web site with the search engines, you should use HTML META tags to ensure that your pages get the best possible ranking. Creating META tags isn't rocket science. It just takes a little common sense.

HITS: RAW VS. REAL

Raw hits will report on every file access, including both HTML pages and graphic files. These numbers reflect a skewed approach to Web site statistics due to the wide variance in the number of graphic files per actual Web page. It's more important to look at real HTML page accesses, which provide a concise picture of true site traffic.

How Do The Major Search Engines Stack Up?

Check out Internet World's Search Engine Features Chart. It delivers the goods on the most important search engines (AltaVista, Excite, HotBot, Infoseek, Lycos, Northern Light, and WebCrawler). You can find it at http://searchenginewatch.internet.com/webmasters/features.html.

If you've taken a look at your pages in HTML Source mode, you've probably seen PageMill's infamous META tag: <**META NAME="GENERATOR" CONTENT="Adobe PageMill 3.0 Win"**>. PageMill adds that tag whether you like it or not. You can remove it with a text editor, if you like, but the next time you open and save the file with PageMill, the program will add the tag again.

Although you can use scores of META tags, there are just a handful of truly important ones. You should be most concerned with three:

- *Description,* for example <**META NAME="description" CONTENT="A concise summary of what the page is all about."**>. Get right to the point. Don't ramble. Don't mislead. With most search engines, this text will appear underneath the page title in the relevancy listing.

- *Keywords,* for example <**META NAME="keywords" CONTENT="pine, maple, oak, sassafras"**>. You should use only words that are truly relevant to the page. Avoid stuffing any bogus words here or any undue repetition of words.

- *Robots,* for example <**META NAME="ROBOTS" CONTENT="NOINDEX"**>. Use this tag if you don't want the spiders to index your page.

We all want our Web sites to rise to the top of the charts. Unfortunately, each engine has a different algorithm for determining search relevancy. Some META tag gurus have stated that it's worthwhile to craft and submit a specific page for each search engine. Many of the spiders read META tags; Excite, however, ignores them. Here are a few relevant URLs:

- *HotBot Likes META Tags*—http://help.hotbot.com/faq/pages.html

- *AltaVista Likes META Tags, Too*—http://www.altavista.digital.com/av/content/addurl_meta.htm

- *Excite Ignores META Tags*—http://www.excite.com/Info/listing.html

Creating META tags is a fairly trivial task. You can hack them out by hand in a text editor, or you can create them with a specialized tool. In either case, you'll have to paste them into your pages in PageMill's HTML Source mode. In the following sections, we'll take a look at some of the alternatives.

Create META Tags Online

WebPromote's groovy META Tag Builder (http://metatag.webpromote.com/) lets you create META tags online, as shown in Figure 8.3. Just plug in your site description and keywords. When you're done, WebPromote will embed the META tags into the page you submitted and then email the *complete* HTML page back to you. Simply cut and paste the entire page from that email message into a new document (in either PageMill's HTML Source mode or in a text editor), and save the file.

Create META Tags On Your PC

Want to create those META tags on your own computer? SiteUp Internet Promotions Meta-Tag Generator for Windows 95 (http://www.siteup.com/meta.html) is a handy freeware application that lets you build tags quickly and painlessly. Just type in the page title, author name, keywords, and description, as shown in Figure 8.4. When you click on Generate, the Meta-Tag Generator will place your META tags into a new window, as shown in Figure 8.5.

Figure 8.3 WebPromote makes quick work out of creating META tags.

WEB SERVER STATISTICAL SOFTWARE

In the bad old days, Webmasters relied on Perl scripts to parse the raw data in the server logs. These days, a host of programs can turn those logs into finely finished reports, complete with snazzy color-coded charts. Your ISP may provide statistics as part of its Web site hosting package. If not, you should look into a third-party application. Here's a list of programs you might want to check out:

- *WebTrends*—http://www.webtrends.com/
- *Hit List*—http://www.marketwave.com/
- *Bolero*—http://www.everyware.com/
- *Bazaar Analyzer Pro*—http://www.aquas.com/
- *net.Analysis Pro*—http://www.netgenesis.com/
- *NetIntellect*—http://www.NetIntellect.com/
- *SurfReport*—http://netrics.com/

We've included two demo versions of WebTrends (Windows) on this book's CD-ROM.

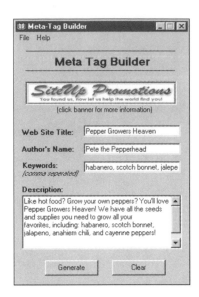

Figure 8.4 Fill out this simple form...

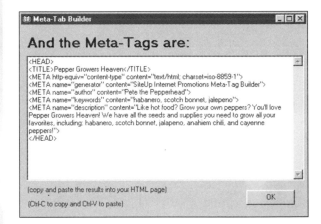

Figure 8.5 ...and you'll be rewarded with a spiffy set of META tags.

Promote Your Web Site

Don't overlook any of the free promotional opportunities that are available to you on the Net. Remember to post announcements about the opening of your Web site only to those newsgroups and mailing lists that are appropriate for the subject matter. Keep the posts brief and to the point. Don't sell...tell. Let folks know what your site is about and where they can find it. Avoid spamming the lists at all costs.

Once your site has been registered with the search engines, and you're satisfied the robots are doing their job, you'll need to look at promotional opportunities, from buying traditional print advertising to buying *webvertising*. Bringing attention to your site does not necessitate spending tons of additional money on advertising, however.

Take a look at every printed piece your organization publishes, from business cards to marketing collateral and traditional advertising. Consider adding your URL to each place your organization's phone number appears. If people in your audience are looking for more information on your organization, they will see that you have a Web site and will have the correct address at hand.

Cool Places To Put Your URL

The following are some of the best spots to sneak in your URL:

- T-shirts (discreetly—the hippest place is on the left sleeve, just above the hem)

- Hats (across the back is the coolest)

- Pens and other promotional trinkets

- Stationery

- Business cards

- Press releases

- Print advertisements (including the Yellow Pages)

- Television advertisements

- Email signatures

- Any place you list your organization's phone number or address

Uncool Places To Put Your URL

If you plaster your URL in the following places, get ready to get flamed:

- T-shirts (when all you have is a big URL).

- Delivery vehicles (see Figure 8.6). Don't run a giant URL; keep your Web address the same size as your phone number.

- Big bumper stickers. (Little stickers can be cool.)

- Inappropriate or unrelated newsgroups and mailing lists (not to mention cross-posting).

SO WHAT ARE *ALL* THE META TAGS?

To find the site that delivers the details on META tags, go to http://vancouver-webpages.com/META/

CHECK THE LIST OF MAIL LISTS!

To see what mailing lists your news release may apply to, you should check out the Publicly Accessible Mailing Lists Web site at http://www.neosoft.com/internet/paml/bysubj.html

- Radio advertisements. (Having to listen to a disc jockey read a long URL is unbearable.) The only really cool radio URL is http://www.cartalk.com.

- Everywhere.

Schemes To Draw A Crowd

After you've taken all this good advice to heart and tried to hold the line on your promotional costs, you may be tempted to spend some more money in the hopes of drawing a substantial crowd. Contests, giveaways, and other schemes are bound to crank up your hit rates and pull in the people, but they might not pull in the people you want to attract. Some folks will come to your site just for something free—just because it's there. You'll get a marked increase in hits, but they won't be as profitable.

If you decide to run a promotion of this type, online or off, make sure that you hype it for everything it's worth. Get your news releases out early, and work the editors. Editors often appreciate a phone call or email message to see whether they've actually received a press release. When you make such a call, offer to answer any questions they might have. You may need to send out another release because busy editors sometimes lose loose papers on their desks. Time your events so that you can get maximum coverage in both print and electronic realms.

Advertise With Banners

Thinking about an investment in Web advertising banners? Ready to blow some big bucks? Before you do, stop by the Ad Resource Web site

Figure 8.6 Putting a big URL on your delivery van is not cool...even if you run it flopped on the grill so that folks can read it in their rearview mirrors.

(http://www.adresource.com/) to do some research on the subject. Ad banner pricing varies wildly. If you have the "champagne wishes and caviar dreams" of Robin Leach yet the beer and pretzel budget of Homer Simpson, you'll be in for a shock. Ad banner rates are usually described by the cost of CPM (impressions by thousands). Your CPM costs can range anywhere from $10 on up (with the emphasis on *up*). And you can expect substantial minimum purchase requirements.

DoubleClick

At the high end of the scale, the DoubleClick Network (http://www.doubleclick.net/) shuttles banner ads to viewers with, perhaps, the Web's most sophisticated ad delivery system. DoubleClick's potential targets include browser type, company size, domain, frequency, geography, operating system, service provider, and SIC code. As such, DoubleClick provides the highest degree of control over who sees an ad banner, and when they see it. You can even target a specific company or college. These results all come at a cost. Minimal DoubleClick campaigns start in the thousands of dollars.

LinkExchange

Beer and pretzel budgets can be accommodated at LinkExchange (http://www.linkexchange.com/). Although the company rode to fame on its cooperative banner program, in which banners are exchanged for free between members, LinkExchange now offers LinkExchange Express, a paid advertising banner program. LinkExchange Express lets you specify who sees your banner, but the model is based on the site on which your banner is placed rather than the information provided by the visitor's banner. So what's the hook? Minimum LinkExchange Express ad campaigns can be initiated for less than a hundred bucks.

Moving On

A thorough understanding of the topics covered in this chapter will help you to steer your Web site to success. Web publishing is a dynamic medium that allows you to change your direction quickly while en route. The most successful Web sites are designed by folks who know their audience intimately and can build and promote a dynamic site that rapidly adapts to changing needs. In the next chapter, we'll cover the mechanics of Web site maintenance.

WANT TO FIND OUT WHO'S LINKED TO YOUR SITE?

If your Web server can produce a list of referring URLs, you can identify where your visitors are finding your Web site. If you don't have the ability to check your site stats, however, you can always use the search engines. Just type in your Web site's name and submit the inquiry. The search engine will cough up a list of other Web sites that mention your site. Just follow these links to see what they have to say about you!

PROMOTING YOUR PAGE

For more great information on how to bring in the crowds, check out "How to Publicize Your Web Page" on Oregon State University's Web server at http://www.orst.edu/aw/stygui/propag.htm

DEALING WITH SITE MAINTENANCE

9

In this chapter, you'll learn how PageMill's built-in site management features make your Webmastering life a breeze.

Web sites are dynamic creatures. They live, breathe, and grow. As your site matures from a seedling into a sapling, you need to plan for its expansion. As its branches grow, you have to decide which to encourage and which to prune. A well-organized site will make your life easier and just takes a little thoughtful planning. You don't even have to be insanely compulsive to do a good job! With the right tools, organizing your Web site can be as easy as trimming the hedges.

Adobe PageMill 3 provides an integrated site management environment. Earlier versions of PageMill relied on Adobe SiteMill for site management chores. SiteMill's functionality has been built into (and expanded on) in PageMill 3.

Site Management Issues

Although Web site management is not a trivial matter, it does not have to become an all-consuming task, either. A sensible layout will enable you to create a site that allows for easy expansion. As you plan your site, you'll have to make some important decisions. The key is to conceptualize and implement an effective file hierarchy.

The following are some of the primary issues in site management:

• How is the site organized?

• Where are the images stored?

• How are the links maintained?

• How are orphan files found and eliminated?

This chapter will help you to understand the issues that face a growing Web site. You will see how a typical site evolves while discovering how tedious it is to implement change in a manual scenario. After learning how bad these problems can be, you'll truly appreciate what PageMill 3 can do for you. The built-in site management features will help you to avoid broken links and misplaced files.

How Is The Site Organized?

Earlier in this book, you learned how to plan the navigational structure of your Web site. In addition to considering how your Web site is organized from a navigational perspective, you must think about how to organize its file structure. The former will often dictate the latter.

When a site is small, all the pages can happily coexist in one directory. As it grows, however, things can quickly get out of hand. Your site may evolve to contain many *subsites,* or "sites within a site." When the level of complexity reaches a certain point, it will make good sense to reorganize your file structure so that each of the subsites has its own directory within the main site directory. Once the number of HTML and graphic files in one directory exceeds what you're comfortable wading through, this will rapidly become apparent.

If you carefully plan your site from the start, you can avoid much of the gut wrenching that accompanies rearranging your site on the fly. Manually changing all the internal URLs on a good-sized site can take eons. PageMill 3 saves your sanity and untold time with its automated link updates.

Where Do The Images Go?

In the simplest Web sites, you can toss all your image files in the same directory with your HTML pages. This methodology goes only so far, however. Once your site has grown past two dozen files or so, things can quickly get out of hand. You don't want to have to wade through long lists of intermingled files. For that reason, you would be wise to keep a separate directory (or directories) solely for images.

You may be able to get away with having one big image directory, or you may decide to break it up into smaller directories, based on subject matter or perhaps by subsite. It's up to you to decide the criteria. You also have complete control over what you name the directories; use whatever names suit your fancy.

One large (and not-so-large) site scenario might have you create a directory for common site graphics, along with separate directories contained in each of the subsite directories. This arrangement keeps the images with their subject matter and helps to trim down the size of the individual image directories. This way, you also can move complete directories around more easily should the need come to pass.

Maintaining Links

You can think of links as the chains that hold your unruly Web site together. Break a link and chaos will ensue. As shown in Figure 9.1, a site will "go 404," and return a "file not found" message when someone chooses a nonexistent file. Although getting such a message isn't a site-threatening event, it's an unpleasant experience for the visitor, at best. Good Webmasters strive to eliminate 404s from their sites.

A Web server will send back a 404 any time it can't find a specified file at a specific location. When a file actually is located on the server but

DON'T GO 404!

When visitors request nonexistent files, 404 errors are returned by the Web server. These errors are often the result of lackadaisical site maintenance. Some servers will include the actual error message number, whereas others will not.

Figure 9.1   Where did the page go? If the Web server can't find a file, it will return a message like this.

is not where it's supposed to be (or where the browser *thinks* it should be), 404s are returned. The server will look only in the location where the URL asks it to look. These 404 errors frequently appear when you've moved a file but haven't updated all its incoming links. Any time you move a file (or group of files) from one directory to another, you will have to update every occurrence of its URL within your site. Doing this task manually brings a whole new definition to the word *tedious*. You can be thankful that PageMill 3 turns link maintenance into a simple task.

Eliminating Orphan Files

Orphan files are Web site jetsam. These pages or graphics float unseen, just below the surface of your site and are not referenced by any other pages. Without any incoming links, a browser cannot find an orphan file because it doesn't know the file's URL.

Orphan files are created as your site evolves. You might have used a background GIF in an earlier version of a page, only to replace it with a different GIF later. Or perhaps you eliminated all links to a page, although you left the page untouched. Orphan files can be any type of unreferenced file, including the following:

- HTML pages

- GIF or JPEG graphics

- Sounds

- Movies

- Animations

- Image maps

The site management tools in PageMill 3 enable you to identify orphan files easily; in most cases, you'll want to eliminate the orphan files. Although they don't threaten the stability or navigational flow of your site, they take up unnecessary server space. Isolating orphan files without an automated site management application is a frustrating experience, however. It's no fun sitting down with a lengthy list of files on your site, trying to discern which files are live and which are not. Once again, PageMill 3 comes to the rescue, as it makes identifying orphan links easy.

Making A Case For Select Orphans

We can think of one good use for orphan files, however. You might want to have a "semi-secret" page, accessible only by typing in its specific address. You might distribute this URL to only a select group of people and for a particular reason, such as to distribute confidential information. This method is not secure, however, because a dedicated individual may be able to find the hidden files as easily as typing in obvious URL combinations. If you want your information to stay hidden, you should use password protection.

Site Management In PageMill 3

PageMill 3 delivers intuitive site management features. When you move or rename files, PageMill automatically maintains all the links within your Web site. How does it work? It's not magic; the program is basically running a search-and-replace routine each time you move or rename a file. PageMill looks for the old file name and location in each of the files in your Web site and replaces that information with the new file name and location.

Creating A New Site

PageMill creates new sites in a snap. Select Site|New to summon the New Site dialog box, as shown in Figure 9.2. Give the site a name, click on the Browse button, use the Open Site Folder to navigate to the new

DON'T LEAVE!

After you've started working with a Web site in the PageMill environment, you should make all the changes to the site within PageMill rather than on the desktop.

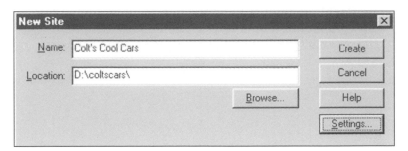

Figure 9.2 You can set up your site options when you first create a new site with the New Site dialog box.

site's root folder (directory), click on OK, and then click on Create. The new site will appear in the Site Overview and Site Detail windows. In the following sections, we'll take a look at how those windows work.

Site Overview

The Site Overview window displays the active Web site in a collapsible tree view. It shows the folders within the Web site, along with any Errors, Externals, and WWW Links. When you select a folder in the Site Overview window, the contents will be displayed in the Site Details window. The same holds true for Errors, Externals, and WWW Links. Clicking on the + (plus sign) markers will expand the tree. Clicking on the - (minus sign) markers will collapse the tree.

Site Details

The Site Details window lets you peer into and work with the individual directories. PageMill lets you look at this information in a number of ways. Selecting View|Detail allows you to choose from List, Links, or List and Links views, as shown in Figure 9.3. Selecting View|Links allows you to view the links All by Name, All by Type, or Pages Only.

List View

The List view (see Figure 9.4) provides file details on the Filename, Size, Type, Page Title, and Modified (date and time), along with the number of links In and Out of the file. Clicking on the respective header button will sort the active folder by that attribute. This feature comes in handy in a number of situations, such as when you want to see the most recently modified pages or perhaps the pages with the largest file sizes.

Let's go over the ins and outs of List View:

- If a file has a red "x" in its In column, there are no links into that file.

- If a file has a blue "-" in its Out column, there are no links out of that file.

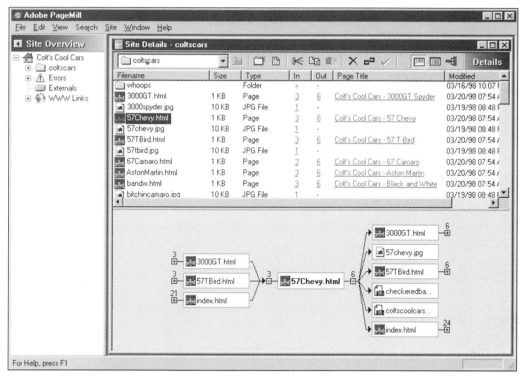

Figure 9.3 List and Links view provides the visual clues you need to assess the structure of your Web site.

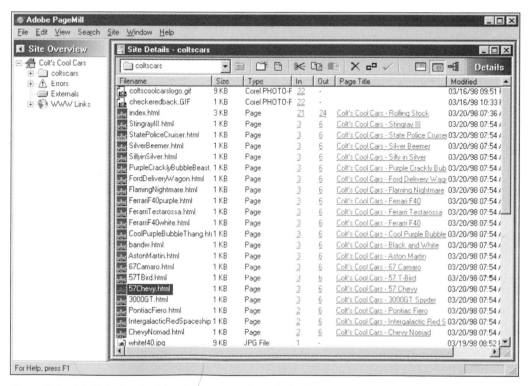

Figure 9.4 A full window List View lets you sort through the files.

- If a file has both a red "x" and a blue "-", it's an orphan file.

- Selecting a file's In or Out figure displays a menu of links into or out of the file.

- Selecting a linked file from the menu opens the file.

- Selecting a Page Title will open the respective page.

The button bar at the top of the Site Details window (and for the most part, you can get these same options by selecting Site|Site Selection) allow you to do the following (in order from left to right):

- Change folders
- Move up one level
- Create a new folder
- Create a new page
- Cut
- Copy
- Paste
- Delete
- Unlink
- Verify
- Toggle between List & Links, List, and Links views

Links View

The Links view displays the links between files in a visual manner. Active links are indicated with a black line. Broken links are indicated with a red line. Clicking on the "+" markers will expand the view, as shown in Figure 9.5. Clicking on the "-" markers will collapse the view.

Moving Files

The process of creating folders and moving files in PageMill's Site Details window feels much like working on the Macintosh desktop or in the Windows

Explorer. The most important difference is that when you move and rename files within PageMill's Site Details window, all the links within your Web site are instantaneously updated. Whether you're renaming or moving files, PageMill keeps a watchful eye and always asks before making a change, as demonstrated in Figure 9.6.

Verifying WWW Links

This next feature surely gets the nod as one of the coolest site management features in PageMill 3. To verify the external links in your Web site, first make sure that your computer has an open Internet connection. Then, select WWW links in the Site Overview window and select Site|Verify Remote URLs (or Site|Site Selection|Verify All Remote URLs). PageMill will go to work verifying the external links. You'll see the word "Verifying" at the lower right of the PageMill window. When the program is done verifying links, the link status will be shown in the Site Overview window:

- A red "x" denotes a broken link.
- A question mark denotes an unchecked link.
- A page icon denotes a valid link.

If a Web site comes up as a broken link, go back and try to reverify the link later in the day. Remember that Web servers can go offline. You can verify a single link by selecting Site|Site Selection|Verify This URL. If you've run the verification routine a couple of times, and the Web site is still missing, you'll have to go hunting. Problems often occur when you've targeted a specific page on a Web site; if the site's Webmaster has moved (or deleted) the page without leaving a forwarding page in its place, be prepared to spend some time crawling through the Web site.

Looking At Externals

Externals are local files (stored on a local or network disk, as opposed to being WWW links) that

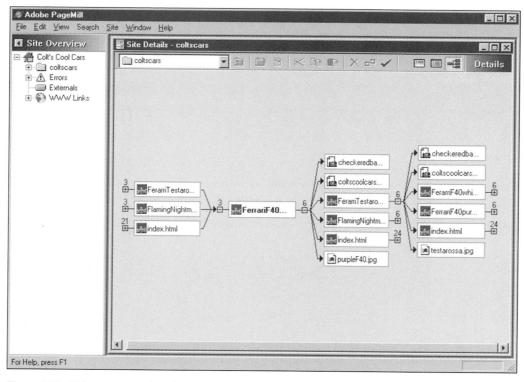

Figure 9.5 Links view provides a high level of feedback. You can see where your links are and if they're broken.

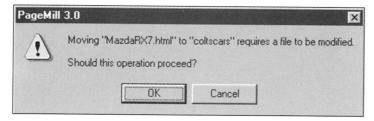

Figure 9.6 PageMill 3 watches for file name and location changes with diligence.

are linked to, but are not contained within, your Web site's folder. Folks often forget to move these files up to their Web sites because the files aren't stored with all the other files. This is the cause of many a broken link. PageMill 3 conveniently allows you to move these files into your site folder by choosing the Site|Selection|Gather This External or Site|Selection|Gather All Externals functions.

When the external files are gathered, they are placed into the Resources folder within your root folder, by default. If you've loaded a bunch of files into the Resources folder, you can always change the folder's name or move the files to the folders where they should *really* be located from within the Site Overview or Site Details window.

Fixing Errors

Select Errors in the Site Overview window (or from the Change Folder drop-down menu in the Site Details window) to find the potential errors in your Web site. Errors are basically just broken links. When you go error hunting, you should look for red. Red lines in the Site Details Links view, little red "x" marks in the Site Details List view's In column, and red "x" icons in WWW Links all denote broken links.

Fixing errors often consists of just finding the missing file and then correcting the broken link. If you need to change a URL on multiple pages, you can use PageMill's powerful search-and-replace function to make the change quickly on every occurrence within your Web site.

Using Search And Replace

PageMill's powerful site-wide search-and-replace utility can search on page content or link addresses. The Find dialog box, as shown in Figure 9.7, lets you search the entire site, a site selection, or an individual page. Selecting the Source Mode checkbox lets you search and replace directly on the HTML coding (rather than on the content as it appears in the Edit window).

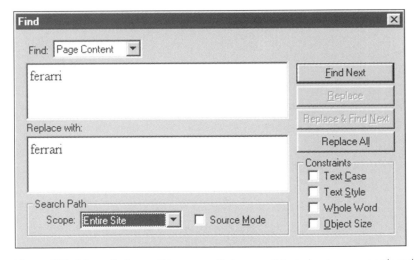

Figure 9.7 Misspelled something on multiple pages? Just plug in your search and replace strings; then, sit back and let PageMill do the hard work for you.

PROJECT 6 Rearranging A Web Site

Want to practice your Web site management skills? We've included "Colt's Cool Cars," a fun little Web site, included on the CD-ROM that accompanies this book. You'll find it in the CHAP-9 folder. Start by copying the directory to your computer's hard drive. Then, select Site|New to create a new Web site in PageMill.

Give PageMill's site management features a whirl. While connected to the Internet, verify the external links by selecting Site|Verify Remote URLs. Watch in awe as your computer does all the chump work. Then, try adding some subdirectories to the site, move some files around, and rename a file or two. PageMill will make all the changes to keep your links up-to-date.

Remember, you want to make all the file structure changes within the PageMill environment. If you change a filename or move a file in the Macintosh Finder or Windows Explorer, you're likely to end up with a bunch of broken links. If you're curious as to what happens when you make changes in the Finder or Explorer, go ahead and give it a try!

Uploading Your Site

In the bad old days, we had to upload our Web sites using FTP. PageMill 3 includes built-in site uploading capabilities (although you're always free to use an FTP program, if you so desire). To upload your Web site successfully, you'll need to know some details about the server and directory where your Web site is located, as well as your login and password.

Creating Site Settings

PageMill 3 accommodates folks who tend more than one Web site by allowing you to create profiles for each site. Select Site|Show Settings to edit, add, or delete a Web site. The Edit Site Settings dialog box, as shown in Figure 9.8, uses a four-tab interface. In many cases, you need never leave the *General* tab. Let's take a look at each of the options:

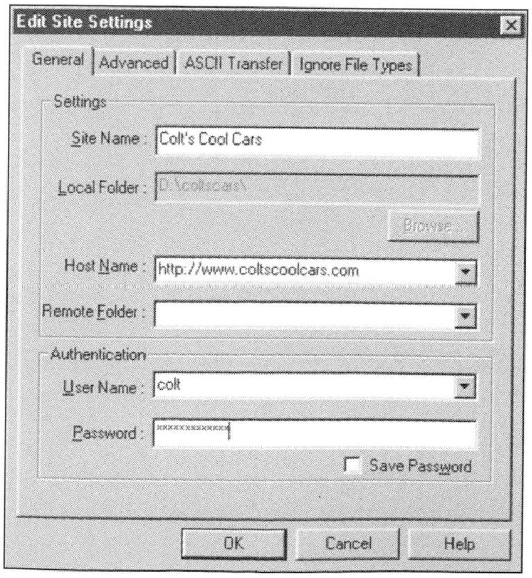

Figure 9.8 The Edit Site Settings dialog box must be configured for each Web site.

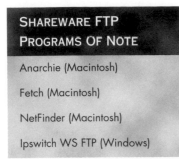

SHAREWARE FTP
PROGRAMS OF NOTE

Anarchie (Macintosh)

Fetch (Macintosh)

NetFinder (Macintosh)

Ipswitch WS FTP (Windows)

- *Site Name*—Give each Web site a descriptive moniker in this field.

- *Local Folder*—This field indicates the Web site's location on your local or network drive (not on the Web server).

- *Host Name*—This field indicates the Web server's name—for example, http://www.domainwhatever.com.

- *Remote Folder*—This field is used only when the Web site is in a subdirectory—for example, ~mydirectory.

- *User Name*—The name in this field must be authorized by the site administrator.

- *Password*—The password in this field must be authorized by the site administrator.

The *Advanced* tab allows you to tweak the Transfer, Connection, and Port Settings. Here, you specify whether PageMill always uploads files, whether it uploads only newer files, or whether it synchronizes the server and local sites. (You probably shouldn't have to fiddle with the Connection and Port Settings, unless your site administrator specifies that you change those settings.) The *ASCII Transfer* tab lets you tell PageMill which files (by file-name extension) to upload using ASCII file transfer. PageMill automatically transfers HTML, HTM, and TXT files using ASCII Transfer. The *Ignore File Types* tab lets you tell PageMill which files (by file-name extension) *not* to upload. This capability can come in handy if you happen to be storing original Photoshop (PSD) files within the local folder.

Getting Ready For Launch!

After you've entered all the Web site settings, and you've checked your site for errors, you're on the launch pad. Make sure your computer is online to the Internet, and then select Site|Upload. PageMill will open a connection to your Web server and begin uploading files, as shown in Figure 9.9.

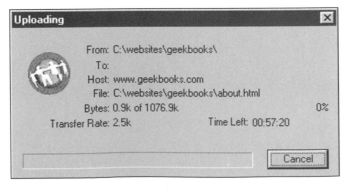

Figure 9.9 Watch that thermometer!

Rearranging Your Site: A Caveat

Once your site is live, you run a major risk by rearranging your file structure. If your site has been around for a while, its layout has been stored, analyzed, and disseminated in a number of ways. This process will take place outside your realm of control. These "runaway librarians" include the following:

- Search engines

- Print media citations

- Incoming links from other sites

- Individual (personal) browser bookmarks

Before you implement any site structure changes, you should consider how they will affect the ways that visitors are referred to the various URLs within your site. If you move a page from the URL where any of these sources expect to find the page, visitors will receive a "404-File Not Found" error when they try to access the URL. This is not a good thing! Let's take a look at how to deal with these important outside referrals.

What Happens With The Search Engines?

Left to their own devices, the search engines will find and catalog each and every linked page on your Web site. If you have pages that are

Figure 9.10 Don't forget to let your visitors know that you've moved.

WebTrends!

We've added a demo version of WebTrends (Windows) on this book's CD-ROM.

under password protection, the spiders won't catalog them, so you needn't worry about breaking those links. The only pages the spiders will catalog will be the pages that are open to all.

The search engines will actually help you in your efforts to rearrange your site. As the spiders revisit and recatalog your site, time will heal any wounds. They'll hit your pages, follow the new links, and do their jobs (you can hope) without a hiccup. Some search engines may appreciate notification when you make major changes. In any case, be sure to drop in linking pages in your key locations. Chapter 8 includes information on how to stay on top of the search engines.

How Should Print Media Citations Be Dealt With?

Everyone loves a mention in print. When a big magazine or book publishes your URL, you're likely to experience an increased hit rate. But when a publication prints a URL within your site rather than your "front door," the results can be indelible. After your URL is in print, it has been set in stone. If you move a page that's been cited in print, you'll infuriate your potential visitors if they can't get to the page.

Controlling the media is impossible. Instead, you have to keep a diligent watch on the pages that are drawing attention to your site. If you move a page, be sure to leave a linking page in its place for a certain period of time. If a publication prints the wrong URL (within your site), put a linking page (sending visitors to the correct page) at that address as soon as possible. And consider this situation an opportunity to contact the publication so that it can run a correction.

Incoming Links From Other Sites

If you've done your job well, pages within your Web site will make their way onto countless hot (and cool) lists. Although each and every one of these lists might not be huge and powerful, they're important to your Web site's success. You'll want to keep track of the referring URLs through some type of tracking program. Refer to Chapter 8, which mentions a number of popular Web server tracking packages.

Myrmidon!

We've added a demo version of Myrmidon on this book's CD-ROM.

After you've identified which Web sites have set up hotlinks to your pages, you can notify them if you make any changes to your site, such as the locations or names of your pages. This act is more than common courtesy. It's karma. The Webmasters should be grateful for your diligence in helping them avoid broken outgoing links. If you're linked back to them, they'll be more likely to return the favor when they're ready to rearrange their Web sites.

Individual Browser Bookmarks

Your visitors are likely to bookmark individual pages within your site rather than your front door. When you move or rename a page, and it just goes 404 on them, you're bound to tick them off. Unfortunately, you can't send email to everyone who has bookmarked your pages unless you've collected email addresses. Even so, sending out a note announcing a URL change might be considered bad netiquette. Once again, the best solution is to drop in some linking pages in key locations.

Converting Native Files To HTML

Want to save a ton of time producing text-laden Web pages? Get in gear with a program or two that support automated HTML conversion. Although HTML export features have crept into most of the mainstream applications—including word processors, spreadsheets, and page layout packages—you may often have to work with original source files from programs that do not support HTML export.

Terry Morse Software's Myrmidon

http://www.terrymorse.com/

Macintosh users have access to a wonderful HTML conversion resource in Terry Morse's Myrmidon. The program (which is included on this book's CD-ROM) takes a unique approach to the creation of HTML files. Myrmidon opens up huge possibilities by allowing you to create Web pages from any Macintosh program that can print text or graphics. Myrmidon is simply installed as a printer. Consequently, when you're ready to print, as shown in Figure 9.11, the (formerly Web-clueless) application thinks that it's sending a file to a printer. Myrmidon then gobbles up the stream of printer code that's sent down, chews on it for a while, and spits it back out as a Web page, complete with tables and inline images.

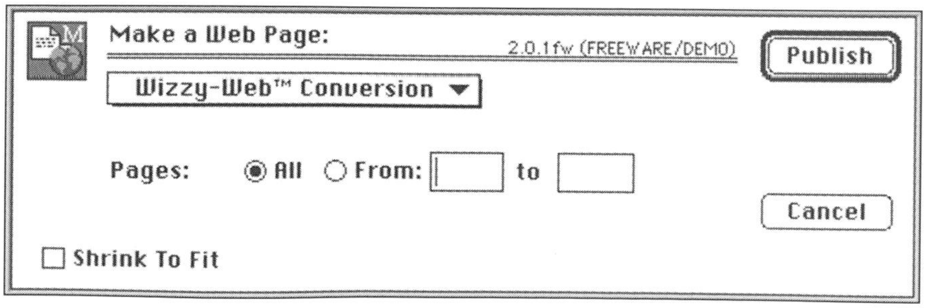

Figure 9.11 Myrmidon creates HTML documents with push-button ease.

Myrmidon is a very cool thing, indeed. The program lets you quickly format tables coming from almost any application. It promises to greatly speed up the process of converting legacy documents into Web pages, especially when you're working with files from older and custom Mac applications that lack HTML export capabilities. Myrmidon offers a world of utility for a modest fee (and just think what you can bill your clients).

InfoAccess HTML Transit

http://www.infoaccess.com/

InfoAccess HTML Transit is a powerful program for creating and maintaining Web sites based on existing documents. This Windows-based tool allows you to quickly convert your clients' documents into HTML formatted files, complete with navigation and table of contents. HTML Transit converts native format styles into HTML styles, in addition to automatically converting character styles, such as bold and italic. You have the option of using Wizards, as shown in Figure 9.12; these basic translations can be subsequently fine-tuned.

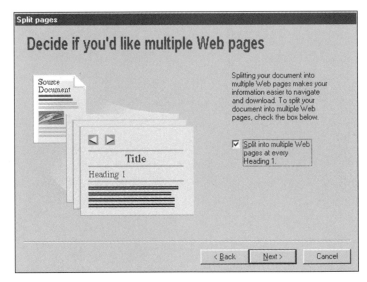

Figure 9.12 HTML Transit's Wizards ease the transition from native format into Web-ready pages. In this dialog box, you can choose to split pages at each Level One heading.

The program is ideal for creating intranet Web sites for corporate entities including human resources, training, and documentation organizations. HTML Transit can take an employee manual from word-processed text to finished Web site in a flash. And when the original word processing document is updated, it can be rapidly converted to Web pages. HTML Transit far exceeds the "export as HTML" capabilities built into the current wave of word processing programs.

HTML Transit converts documents from the following:

- Adobe FrameMaker (version 3.0 through 5.0)
- ASCII text
- Corel WordPerfect (versions 5.0 through 8.0)
- HTML
- Interleaf (versions 1.1 through 6.0)
- Lotus AmiPro (versions 1.1 through 3.1)
- Microsoft Excel (versions 7.0 and 8.0)
- Microsoft PowerPoint (versions 7.0 and 8.0)
- Microsoft Word (versions 3.0 through 8.0)
- Microsoft Write (3.x)
- Rich Text Format (RTF)

HTML Transit imports graphics from the following formats: BMP, CDR, CGM, DIB, DXF, EPS, GIF, HPGL, JPEG, MSP, PCC, PCX, PNG, PIC, RAS, TIFF, WMF, and WPG. The program exports files in GIF, JPEG, and PNG formats. The program's minimum system requirements are modest: a 486DX, with 16MB of RAM for Windows 95 or 32MB of RAM for Windows NT, 25MB of hard drive space for installation, and a CD-ROM. InfoAccess recommends at least a Pentium processor (100 MHz) and a 256-color display.

We've included the demo version of HTML Transit for Windows on this book's CD-ROM.

Converting QuarkXPress Pages

QuarkXPress is the most popular page layout package in the professional graphic arts community. As such, the program is used to create a staggeringly large number of printed pages. When the Web revolution began, Quark-based desktop publishers soon realized that they needed a convenient way to convert their existing print-oriented pages into Web pages. While Quark itself floundered around getting its Immedia multimedia/Web publishing program out the door, QuarkXTension

developers quickly moved in to fill the void. There are two Quark-to-HTML products of note, Extensis BeyondPress, and HexMax HexWeb XT.

Extensis BeyondPress
http://www.extensis.com

BeyondPress, the first QuarkXTension to support HTML export, was originally developed by Astrobyte LLC (way back in the dark ages of 1995). Extensis merged with Astrobyte in early 1998. BeyondPress uses a document content palette, which displays all the text and graphic elements contained within a document. You can pick and choose the elements and order in which you export to HTML. Text export functions offer a high level of versatility, as shown here:

- Special text characters (such as ampersands and copyright symbols) are converted to their HTML equivalents.
- QuarkXPress style sheets can be mapped to HTML styles.
- Tables and lists can be preserved, as can text color and alignment.
- Java, QuickTime, and GIF animations can be previewed within QuarkXPress.

BeyondPress offers a high degree of control over image export as well. Images are automatically converted to GIF or JPEG files, with support for interlaced GIF and progressive JPEG formats. Most importantly, the program will allow you to export any element (or group of elements), including text, as an anti-aliased image, with control over cropping, scaling, transparency, border width, and alternative text—all with the ability to index to either an optimal or custom palette.

The XTension offers more than just conversion capabilities, however. BeyondPress allows you to assign background textures as well as background, text, and link colors. Both client- and server-side image maps are supported as is Apple Events scripting. A GIF animation utility is provided as well.

HexMac HexWeb XT

http://www.hexmac.com

HexMac's HexWeb XT 2.5 provides the highest degree of flexibility for QuarkXPress-centric Web page designers. Although the company is based in Europe, its www.hexmac.com Web site offers products for sale to the American user base (the company has generated great interest in its support for the online newspaper market). HexWeb XT users include the *Detroit News*, the *Ottawa Citizen*, *Aftonbladet* (Sweden's largest evening newspaper), and *Kompas* (with a 500,000 circulation daily paper in Djakarta, Indonesia). HexWeb XT's features such as coordinated image and caption export, table conversion, article chaining, integrated FTP, and link checking make HexWeb XT well worth looking into.

Deciding Whether You Really Want To Hack Out HTML

At this point, we separate the wheat from the chaff, the men from the boys, and P.T. Barnum's proverbial suckers from their wallets. If you want to hack out HTML, you had better be committed to the task, lest you end up committed to someplace less comfortable. You've probably heard the warnings: HTML editing is not for the meek and timid. But you know what? If you really want to hack it out, you can do it! Hacking out HTML is really not rocket science.

One of the side benefits of PageMill is that it eases you into learning HTML. Although you might not want to get involved with the code, if you spend any significant amount of time creating pages, eventually you'll learn a good bit of HTML, if only through osmosis. Like it or not, HTML will creep into your consciousness. But don't worry; we're not going to get into any HTML specifics here. The bookshelves are stuffed with a wide range of books for that purpose. Instead, we'll recommend three power text tools (two for Macintosh and one for Windows).

Bare Bones BBEdit

http://www.barebones.com/

Bare Bones Software has been riding a wave of popularity, thanks to its hot-rod ASCII text editor, BBEdit. The stripped-down program has gained quite a high degree of regard in the Macintosh Web publishing

---

KEEP PAGEMILL FROM MESSING WITH YOUR CODE!

You can set up the all-important **<!--NO EDIT-->** tag as a NoteTab Pro Clipbook item. Insert the tags *before* your file enters the PageMill environment, and you can rest assured that PageMill won't fool around with your HTML or JavaScript code.

community and can help you to reach new levels of Web developer's nirvana. Although PageMill 3 includes an integrated text editor, it falls short of what's capable with a serious power tool. When used in combination with Adobe PageMill, BBEdit provides the extra punch that PageMill's text editor is lacking. Macintosh Web publishers, rejoice!

BBEdit's dexterity is most evident when performing intricate search-and-replace routines. The program allows you to perform multiple (batch) file search and replaces, which saves incredible amounts of time when you're changing repetitive Web page text such as copyright notices. With BBEdit's supercharged search-and-replace engine, you can target a directory full of files and swap a new chunk of text into every file that includes the matching pattern.

The search-and-replace engine provides the capability to save frequently performed searches as patterns, allowing you to recall the search terms with just a click. You can also use BBEdit's Grep function (named after a Unix utility, familiar only to serious geeks) to perform pattern matching, which further extends your search-and-replace possibilities by allowing you to swap out nonliteral text strings. Grep provides the ability to search for wildcard characters (such as any digit or line ending) as well as character strings.

In addition to serious search-and-replace functions (which are included in BBEdit Lite), the full version of BBEdit (available for just $79 to registered PageMill users) provides a host of other robust features, including support for scripting, drag and drop, FTP integration, spellchecking, integrated HTML editing tools, and single-keystroke insertion of glossary text.

NoteTab Pro

www.notetab.com

NoteTab Pro is a quintessential Windows text editor with a range of essential features. As its name implies, the program uses a unique tabbed interface that allows you to switch between open documents quickly. Integrated HTML tagging allows you to assign style tags and insert special characters with a double-click. This program can open files as large as 16MB, which makes it ideal for browsing through huge server log files. Files can be opened and saved in either DOS ASCII, Macintosh, or Unix format.

Essential utilities include automatic text-to-HTML conversion and HTML tag stripping, along with file-based search and replace. NoteTab

HTML GRINDER

We've added a demo version of HTML Grinder (Macintosh) on this book's CD-ROM.

Pro Clipbooks let you store and retrieve frequently used text strings. The Text Statistics tool doesn't just count the total number of characters and words, it also counts word frequency—just the ticket for checking on META tag keywords. And there are a host of features you might not expect to find in a text editor, including lists of common email acronyms and smiley faces, math and unit conversion utilities, and even a mortgage rate calculator.

With a highly customizable environment featuring more than 80 toolbar commands—along with the ability to create custom shortcuts—this pint-sized powerhouse will quickly become your text editor of choice. Once you've worked with NoteTab Pro, you'll never want to go back to the Windows Notepad again. At $9.95 for the full version, it's a must-have utility for Windows-based PageMillers.

The HTML Grinder

http://www.matterform.com

Matterform's HTML Grinder is a unique Web site maintenance tool. It goes one up on the built-in search-and-replace capabilities in PageMill 3 by providing a combination of control and convenience. The HTML Grinder is a drag-and-drop powerhouse. The program includes 15 plug-in modules, called "Wheels," that fall into five general categories. It also includes three specialized modules. Wheels can be saved with specific settings, in addition to being linked together to provide a highly automated Web page maintenance environment.

Here's a rundown on each of the Grinder wheels:

File Management Wheels

Eight Dot Three—Converts every file in your Web site to the eight-dot-three file-naming convention. Handles all file and image links. Invaluable when you're dealing with Windows systems that may truncate long file names.

Filename Fixer—Changes file names rather than contents. Comes in handy when you're changing all file names to lowercase.

Recreator—Provides the ability to change Macintosh file type and creator codes. This feature can come in handy when someone gives you an HTML file that was not created with PageMill.

Interface Creation Wheels

Auto Indexer—Builds an indexed list of anchored keywords, in one of 18 styles.

IS THERE A WINDOWS VERSION OF GRINDER?

Matterform is working on a Windows version, and it may be available by the time you read this chapter. Check the Web site at http://www.matterform.com/

Index Builder—Creates an indexed jumplist of pages, based on page titles. Lists can be numbered (ordered), bulleted (unordered), or plain. Provides control over line spacing (by inserting paragraph commands).

Scroller—Builds a jumplist, based on anchored heads, as shown in Figure 9.13. Provides multiple indents when you're indexing pages with standard <H1>, <H2>, <H3> headings and so on. Allows for "return to top" links.

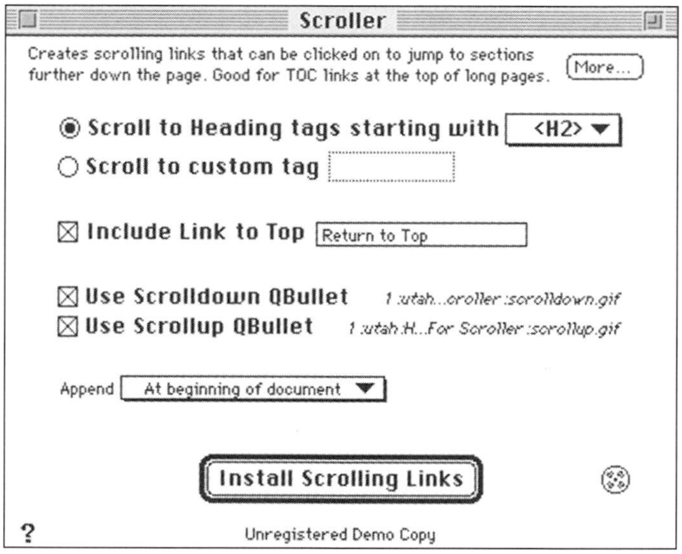

Figure 9.13 The Scroller wheel expedites table of contents creation.

Sequential Linker—Adds previous page/next page navigation into a group of pages, as shown in Figure 9.14. Allows for a table of contents page, if desired. Provides the ability to add text before, after, and between the links.

StretchList—Creates lists that provide the illusion of drop-down definitions.

Quick Coding Wheels

Altifier—Creates alternate tags for images, based on the image file name sans file extension.

Date Stamp—Inserts the last modified page date into pages (based on a file's System date), using either a short, long, or abbreviated format. Provides the ability to add text before or after the date stamp.

Page Labeler—Inserts the page title and/or URL into a page. Useful when you're printing Web pages for walkaway documentation.

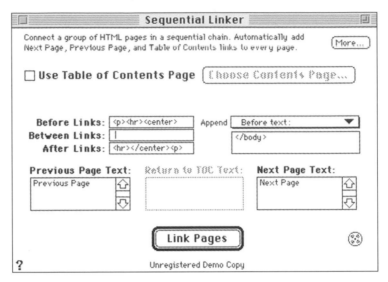

Figure 9.14 The Sequential Linker wheel lets you chain a series of pages together with navigational elements.

Search-And-Replace Wheels

Appender—Inserts text strings in one of four places in an HTML document: beginning of file, end of file, before text, or after text.

Find and Replace—Searches text strings up to 255 characters, replaces with a field as large as 30,000 characters. Case sensitivity is disabled in demo mode.

Glossary—Provides multiple search and replace capabilities in one pass.

Replace Tagged Text—Searches and replaces strings of text between two specific HTML tags.

Miscellaneous Wheels

AppleScript—Allows you to create powerful custom Grinder wheels, using AppleScript.

Code Police—Provides powerful style- and content-checking capabilities.

Color Calculator—Creates hexadecimal codes based on Color Picker selections. Redundant with the capabilities built into PageMill.

Matterform provides the Grinder program and the Find and Replace wheel at no charge. The other Grinder wheels will operate in a fully functional "try before you buy" mode for a while. Eventually, the wheels will stop working until you register the program. The HTML Grinder asks for a modest Mac; all you'll need is a 68030, System 7.0 or later, and 1500K free memory. That should cover just about any Macintosh used for Web site design and maintenance.

Moving On

Web site management does not have to be a painstaking, manual affair. With Adobe PageMill 3, you can keep your site neat and tidy without losing your mind. SiteMill keeps track of every link on your site without creating reams of paperwork or complicated schematics. If you manage a site consisting of more than just a few pages, you should seriously consider the upgrade. The peace of mind is well worth the cost of admission. Rearranging a Web site is not without its pitfalls. With due diligence, you can ensure that your visitors will find your site where they expect it to be.

Text-conversion and editing utilities are power tools that can help you get your job done faster and with less heartache. Choosing the appropriate tools means taking a close look at how your work flows now and how you plan on fine-tuning the flow in the future. The proper apparatus will enable you to produce pages in a highly automated manner, saving time and manpower. In the following chapters, we'll look at a how you can create a database-driven Web site.

BUILDING A WEB
STOREFRONT
10

In this chapter, you'll learn how easily you can build your own secure Web store by using ShopSite.

The World Wide Web is an entrepreneur's dream. Where else could you set up shop for just a few dollars a day? With an effective Web presence, a mom-and-pop business can compete in the same arena with a huge multinational corporation. Web stores are practical for both new and established companies. For the new venture, using a Web store is a way to enter the market without the huge startup costs associated with opening a real-world storefront. For the established company, it's a way to maximize existing investments in human resources and inventory.

Adobe has positioned PageMill 3 as a tool for the business masses. As part of that strategy, it has bundled Open Market's ShopSite Express (http://pagemill.shopsite.com/)—software that enables you to build a secure Web store easily, with the convenience of shopping baskets. Netizens have come to expect a certain level of professionalism when shopping online. With PageMill and ShopSite Express you can build a great place to shop without taking out a second mortgage.

Security is an essential part of successful Web commerce sites. For your store to be successful, your customers must have a level of comfort that their orders are placed in confidence. Secure Web sites use Secure Socket Layer (SSL) technology to *encrypt* information as it passes over the Internet. Encryption scrambles the information, making it downright impossible for would-be thieves to steal credit card (and other personal) information.

ShopSite Overview

Open Market's ShopSite Express software is completely server based. The software is available free of charge, but you must pay Web site hosting fees to the authorized ShopSite Express service provider. (It's important to note that Open Market does not host these sites and that Open Market does not charge for the software. It's all up to the hosting provider.) Your entire Web store can reside on the ShopSite Express server, or you can choose to keep your Web pages on another server and merely rely on the ShopSite Express server for the nitty-gritty. All the maintenance and day-to-day operations are handled through your Web browser, which allows for a completely cross-platform environment.

With ShopSite Express, you build your Web catalog pages as you would build any other Web page. This capability is an advantage over some catalog systems because standard HTML Web pages are easily indexed by the search engines. (In contrast, catalogs that are generated on the fly can be difficult to index.) Once the spiders begin to visit your Web

THE NAME GAME

ShopSite was originally developed by ICentral. Open Market acquired ICentral just weeks before the publication date of this book.

store, they'll index all your product pages. Potential customers will then be able to access specific product pages directly from the search engine results page.

After you've built your product pages, you'll populate the ShopSite Express products database (product name, price, and SKU) and configure your shopping basket tax and shipping information. The software delivers big store features, including unlimited simultaneous shoppers, automatic shipping and tax calculation, and order confirmation via email. In short, it provides all the stuff you need to get started.

The ShopSite Express package allows for a 25-item store. If your needs exceed that limit, Open Market offers two higher-end solutions: ShopSite Manager and ShopSite Pro. Both of these packages add the capacity for credit card authorization, direct media and database uploads, a media library manager, order database downloads, traffic statistics, Web page creation, and Web site management. ShopSite Pro also provides associate tracking, automatic product upsell, discount calculation, enhanced statistical information, global database editing, large database handling tools, site search, and other capabilities.

Through the kind cooperation of the folks at Open Market, we're going to take a peek behind the curtains and see how easy it is to build a Web store with ShopSite Express.

Building A ShopSite Store

Creating a ShopSite Express store is a breeze. In the following pages, we'll take a run through the steps necessary to open your doors to Web commerce. To get started with ShopSite Express, you'll need to sign up for a hosting plan. If your Web site doesn't exist yet, you might consider having the entire site hosted on the ShopSite Express server. (ShopSite is hosted by Best Internet, one of the largest Web hosting ISPs.) If you already have a Web site, you can just sign up for the ShopSite Express commerce capabilities.

After you establish your account, you'll log on to your Shop Site Express Back Office, as shown in Figure 10.1. From this main page, you'll access each of the aspects of your store. The first project you'll undertake is loading your products.

Adding Products

The Products page, as shown in Figure 10.2, lets you add products by specifying name, price, taxable status, weight, and SKU. Each product

HELP IS JUST A CLICK AWAY

ShopSite Express provides extensive online documentation via a link from the back office. There's also context-sensitive help for each page of the back office and explanations of most of the individual back office features.

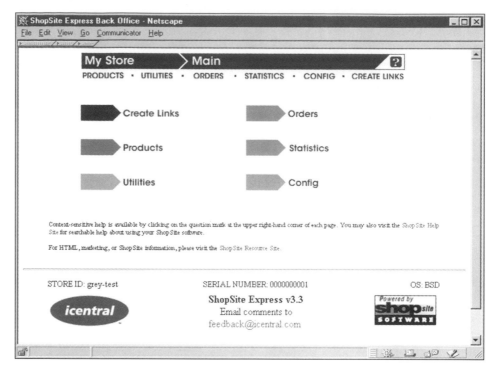

Figure 10.1 Get out your eyeshade and banker's lamp. This page is your new back office.

page can include distinct ordering options as well as a pull-down menu (for particulars such as size, color, and style information) and a text entry field. Click on the OK button to add the product to your catalog.

The Main Products page, as shown in Figure 10.3, lets you keep track of the products in your store. From this page, you can add new products (one at a time or in one fell swoop), edit existing product data, or delete products.

Configuring Your Store

The Main Configuration page, as shown in Figure 10.4, provides access to sales tax, payment types, order systems, language settings, shipping options, and technical settings pages. These pages will determine how much money you'll collect (and how you'll collect it), on top of the per-item fees to cover the costs of doing business online.

Sales Tax

What's the government's take? ShopSite Express provides entries for city, state, and local taxes, in addition to providing the capacity to add any new fees our friends in office might choose to levy on us. These taxes will be automatically calculated when your customers check out.

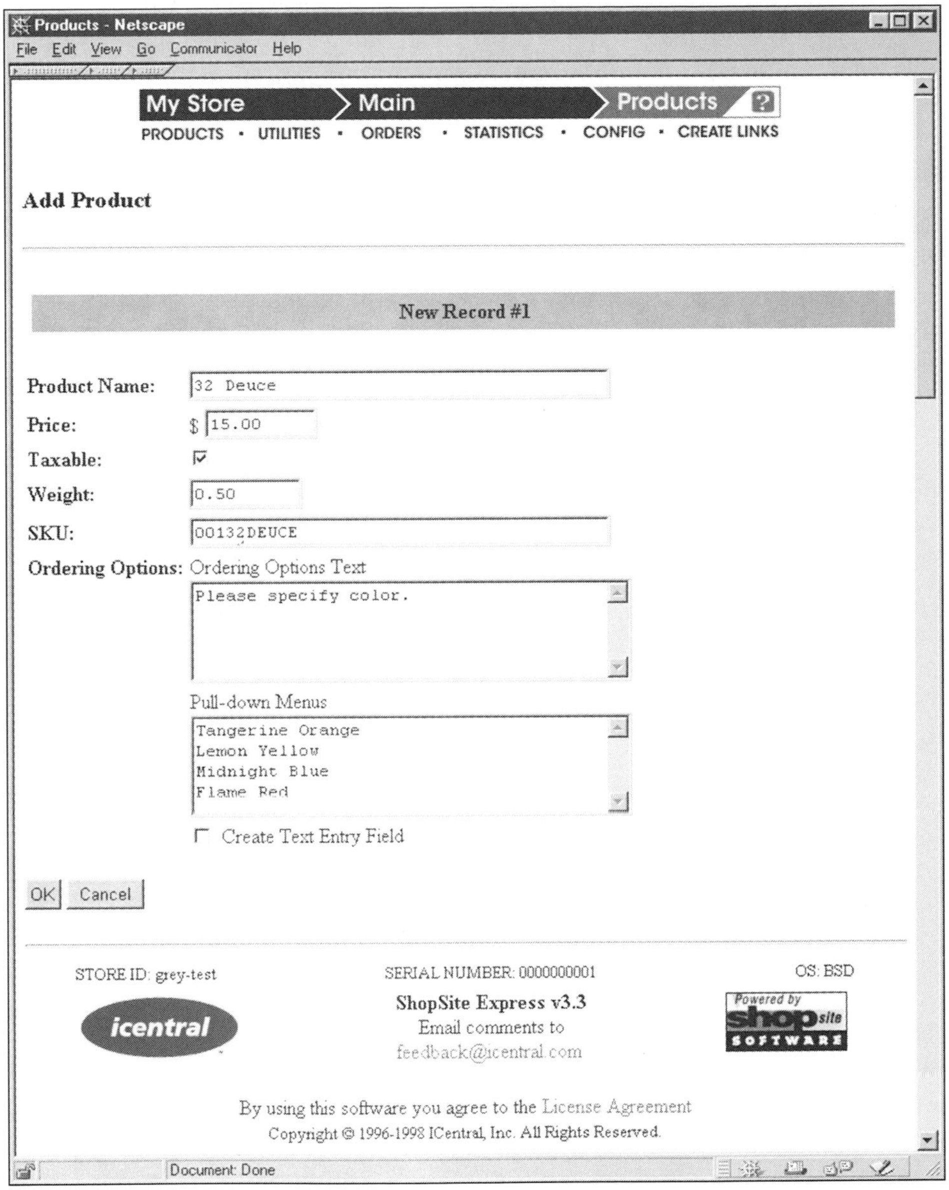

Figure 10.2 Adding products is a simple fill-in-the-blank procedure.

Payment Types

The Payment Types page, as shown in Figure 10.5, allows you to configure ShopSite Express to accept all your favorite credit cards (Visa,
MasterCard, Discover, and American Express) as well as purchase orders,
C.O.D., and checks. Of course, you'll have to be set up with a merchant
account at your bank to process the payments; ShopSite Express only lets
you accept the credit card information securely and store that information securely. It does not enable a merchant to authorize credit cards in
real time. That service is available in ShopSite Manager and Pro.

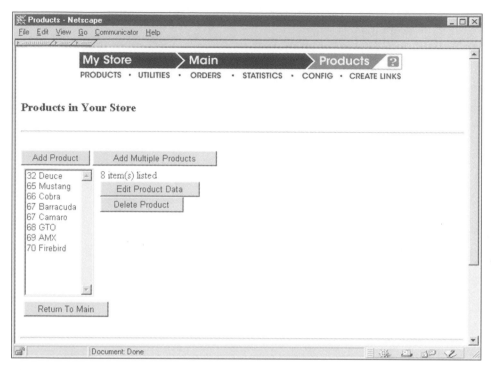

Figure 10.3 Looks like an interesting inventory, eh? Too bad these cars are just toys.

Order System

The Customize Ordering System page, as shown in Figure 10.6, provides complete control over the appearance of your shopping basket page, so you can apply your site's look and feel to the order form. You can select the Text, Background, Link, Visited Link, Active Link, and Table Shade colors from drop-down lists. You also can use a background image, if you want. You can find entry fields for the text at the top and bottom of the Shopping Basket page, along with an option to create an ordering instructions box. You should make sure that you add site-specific information; it's essential that your customers know they're still on your Web site.

Language Settings

You can change your general language settings and specific features, such as the shopping basket, receipts, billing, and shipping. Language, in this context, can mean either the specific phraseology or the actual language (English, French, Spanish, and so on). Providing any translations is your responsibility.

Shipping Options

You can find entry fields for the text at the top and bottom of the Shipping page, along with an option to create a customer comments box.

NEED REALTIME CREDIT CARD AUTHORIZATION?

ShopSite Express payment options are set to manual by default. If you want to have realtime credit card authorization, you'll need to upgrade to ShopSite Manager and have both a merchant bank and a credit card authorization service. Open Market provides the details at http://www.shopsite.com/help/payment.merchant.html.

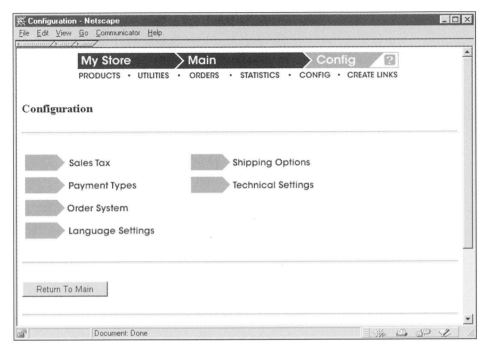

Figure 10.4   Now you're ready for the nitty-gritty.

You can modify both the "Thank You" page and email receipts that are returned to the customers after orders have been placed. Shipping can be configured by weight, currency, or flat charge.

Technical Settings

In all likelihood, there are only two technical settings that you'll ever need to change (unless you're dramatically altering your server). The first is the email address to which email notification of orders will be sent. The second is the "My store" link, which is specific to your site's URL.

Creating Links

After you've configured all the settings for your store and have entered your products, you'll need to create product links. The Create Links page, as shown in Figure 10.7, lets you select the products and build the links. You can build links for one product at a time or as a group. Links can be viewed as "buttons" (hyperlinked text) or as HTML code.

Figure 10.8 shows a sample button. To bring the links into your PageMill page, all you need to do is click and drag them from the ShopSite browser window into the PageMill window. (You'll need to drag the Order and Checkout buttons separately.) If you're working on a small monitor, things can be a bit tight; you probably should reduce the size of the browser window to fit everything on screen.

THINKING ABOUT A FRAMED ORDERING LAYOUT?

Framed Web ordering pages are at a disadvantage. The all-important secure symbol does not appear in the browser, even though the connection may be secure. If you're using a framed layout in your Web store, ShopSite offers three options. You can keep secure orders in a frame, bring the order screen to the top of the frames, or open the order screen in a new window.

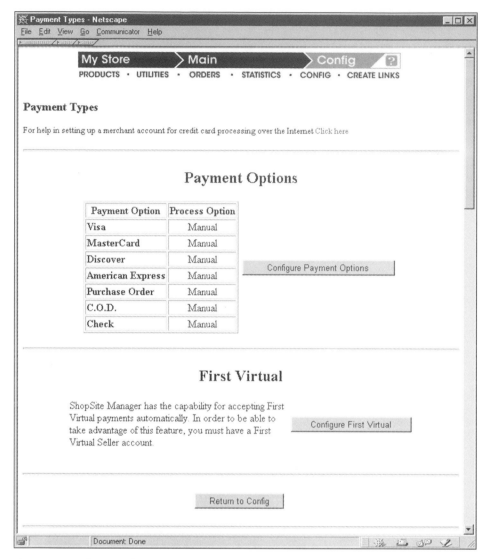

Figure 10.5 Show me the money!

If you're comfortable working in PageMill's HTML mode (or in an ASCII text editor), you can generate the HTML code for the button by using ShopSite, copy it, and then paste it into position within the HTML page. Figure 10.9 shows the HTML coding behind those magic buttons.

Placing A Test Order

As you begin to build your Web store—after you've entered the first few products—you should test the shopping experience. With your computer online, open a product page (that you built with PageMill) and try placing a test order. When you click on the Order button, you'll be taken to your Shopping Basket page. Figure 10.10 shows the default shopping basket, devoid of any serious modification. You can use the

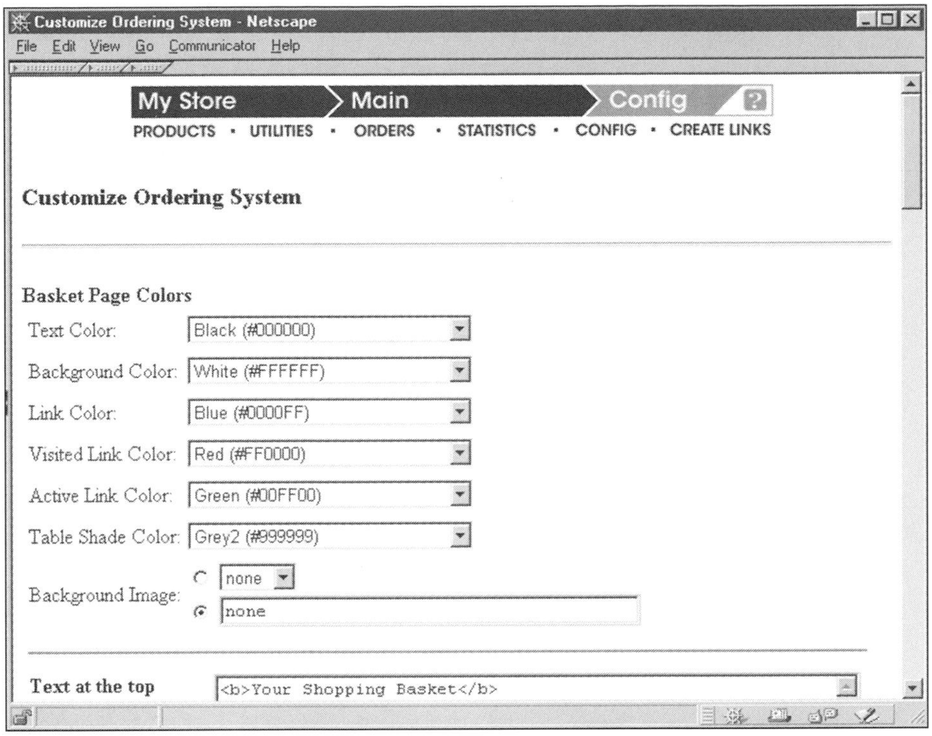

Figure 10.6 ShopSite Express provides a customizable shopping basket page.

Figure 10.7 Just pick the products that need links, and click on the appropriate view button.

Figure 10.8   Just drag and drop the "button" link into your PageMill page.

Figure 10.9   Okay, so it's not magic—it's a slick CGI.

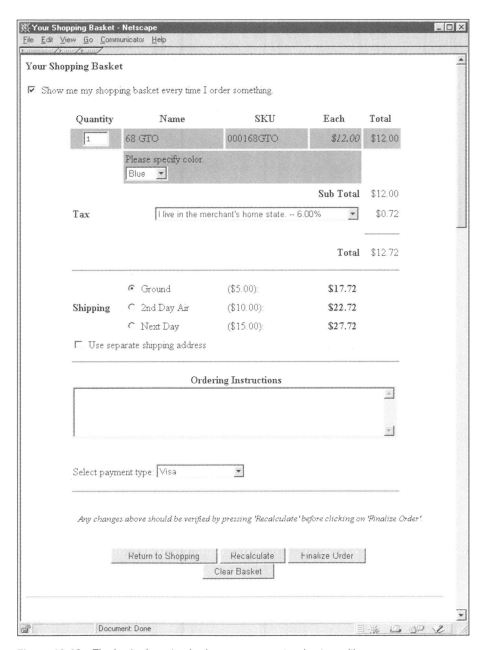

Figure 10.10 The basic shopping basket presents a crisp, business-like appearance.

Customize Ordering System page, as shown in Figure 10.6, to tweak the Shopping Basket page to your heart's content.

Customizing The Thank You Page

The all-important Thank You page is an essential part of your customers' experience. Customers need solid verification that they've placed orders. Figure 10.11 shows the default Thank You page. Take the time to customize the Thank You page to reflect your store's appearance.

Checking Your Orders

The beauty of a Web storefront is that it's up 24/7—twenty-four hours a day, seven days a week. Your customers can be shopping while you sleep, dine, or relax with your family. You can log in to your ShopSite back office at any time throughout the day or night to process your orders in a secure environment. When you check into your back office, you must enter a login name and password before you are presented with the encrypted orders. Figure 10.12 shows a sample order I placed from my fledgling Web storefront. (Note the little lock at the bottom-left corner of the Netscape Communicator window.)

After you have an order in hand, you can go to work. You can save the order to your local hard drive by selecting the save as feature from your browser or simply print the order on your desktop printer. In either case, you should make sure that you're working in a secure workspace. Thieves can steal those credit card numbers more easily from your garbage can than they can steal them over the Internet.

From this point on, you're working in a fairly conventional mail order environment. If the order has been placed with a credit card, you'll have to verify the account and transmit the information to your bank. Then, fill the order, pack it, and send it on its merry way. To further extend the warm fuzzies, you may want to follow up with email to your customers to inform them of their order status.

Moving On

You *can* set up shop on the World Wide Web. In this chapter, you learned that with the combination of Adobe PageMill 3 and Open Market ShopSite Express, you have all the tools you need to get started. A real, live Web storefront is only a day away. In the next chapter, we'll delve into the subjects of PageMill plug-ins and Acrobat PDF.

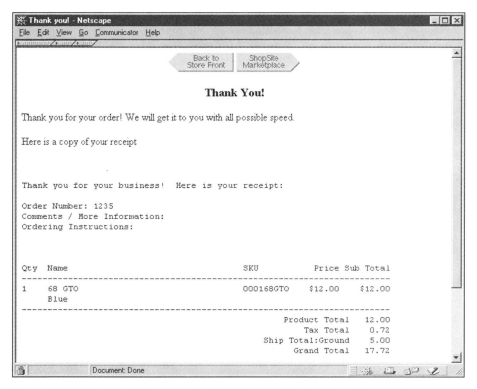

Figure 10.11 The Thank You page should deliver warm fuzzies along with a receipt.

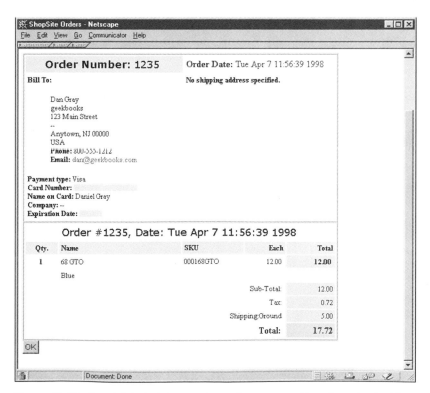

Figure 10.12 You didn't think I was going to leave my credit card number in this screen shot, now did you?

EXTENDING
PAGEMILL'S
FUNCTIONALITY

11

In this chapter, we'll cover PageMill plug-ins and Adobe Acrobat.

Throughout this book, I have provided information on scores of great Web-site creation resources, with a focus on tools that work with Adobe PageMill. This chapter delves into PageMill plug-ins and Adobe Acrobat—two important ways that Adobe has changed the manner in which we work. The addition of plug-ins is one of the most significant aspects of PageMill 3. You may be familiar with the concept of application plug-ins, which were first truly popularized by Adobe Photoshop. Exposing PageMill's Application Programming Interface (API) to plug-ins was a smart move, and follows suit with Adobe's legacy of plugged-in programs, which also include Acrobat, Illustrator, and PageMaker.

PageMill Plug-ins

When I first wrote the outline for this book, I looked forward to covering the topic of PageMill plug-ins. I'm completely sold on the concept of using plug-ins to extend a program's functionality. As a result of the process of writing my last book, *The Photoshop Plug-ins Book,* and my witness of the robust nature of the Adobe plug-in development community, I was convinced that when PageMill shipped, a number of third-party plug-ins would be announced, or might ship simultaneously. I expected to write about those great new PageMill plug-ins.

Unfortunately, this was not the case. PageMill shipped with nary a whisper from the development community. By the time you read this chapter, however, PageMill plug-ins should be hitting the market. Rest assured, I'll keep you abreast of PageMill plug-in developments on my Web site, www.geekbooks.com. After all, I watch Adobe plug-ins like some folks watch birds.

To write this section, I spent a good bit of time staring at the PageMill 3.0 Plug-in Development Guide. I'm not a programmer, even though I once held a job that had a Programmer/Analyst's job description (it's a long story). Nonetheless, I can spell out the basics of what PageMill plug-ins can do.

The PageMill API provides for five basic types of plug-ins: Creators, Global Filters, Inserters, Selection Filters, and NoEdit Selection Filters. Let's take a look at each type and dream about what plug-ins we might see for each.

Creators

Want to build a fill-in-the-blanks Web page creation wizard? Creator plug-ins can be used to create entire HTML documents, through a

GET THE PAGEMILL SDK!

Interested in creating your own plug-ins for Adobe PageMill? You'll either have to be a programmer or have some programming pals. You can find the Adobe PageMill System Developers Kit (SDK) at this address: ftp://ftp.adobe.com/ pub/adobe/devrelations/sdk/ pagemill/

simplified interface. Neophyte users can simply follow the instructions, fill in the fields, click on OK, and receive a fully formatted Web page, from **<HTML>** through **</HTML>**.

Some Creator plug-in possibilities include the following:

- Formatted Web page documentation, complete with header and footer information

- Automatic real estate or auto dealer listing Web pages

- Standardized employee Web pages

Global Filters

Need to attack entire HTML pages at once? Global Filters can look at and work with a complete HTML file, regardless of what's selected at the moment the plug-in is summoned.

Some Global Filter plug-in possibilities include the following:

- An integral META tagger

- Background sound control

- Table of contents (anchored list) generation, based on existing headings

- Text analyzer, including keyword counting

Inserters

Want to pop something into an HTML file at a specific spot? Inserters allow you to place HTML code into a document that already exists at the current insertion point.

Some Inserter plug-in possibilities include the following:

- JavaScript mouseover creation

- JavaScript menu creation

- Time and date stamping

- Header- or footer-based navigation

Selection Filters

Need to implement a change on a selected range of HTML? Selection Filters allow you to process only the HTML code that is selected at the moment the plug-in is summoned.

Some Selection Filter plug-in possibilities include the following:

- A "table-space remover" to take all the extra spaces and carriage returns out of PageMill-created tables. The table would be encased in **NOEDIT** tags when reinserted.

- An enhanced **<IMG SRC>** control box, complete with settings for horizontal and vertical space, as well as a LOWSRC image.

- An alphabetical line sorter.

- A simple page-width table builder.

- A thesaurus.

NoEdit Selection Filters

Want to work on the HTML within a NoEdit block? NoEdit Selection Filters let you make changes only within a selected NoEdit block.

Some NoEdit Selection Filter plug-in possibilities include the following:

- A JavaScript editor

- An enhanced table editor

- A protected HTML editor

Plug-ins can be applied to an entire Web site. This capability allows for fast site-wide changes. To get an even better idea of what might be possible with PageMill plug-ins, read the section on Matterform's HTML Grinder at the end of Chapter 9. HTML Grinder provides many of these capabilities today. We can only hope that Matterform will produce a PageMill plug-in version of HTML Grinder.

Next, let's take a look at what Adobe Acrobat can do for your Web site.

GEEKBOOKS PLUG-IN CENTRAL

Be sure to check http://www.
geekbooks.com for all the latest
PageMill plug-in developments.

Adobe Acrobat

The Adobe Acrobat Portable Document Format (PDF) provides a platform-independent means to exchange files between Macintosh, Windows, and Unix systems. As such, Adobe Acrobat is the most important development in the printing world since Adobe delivered PostScript in the mid-1980s. In short, if you need to put documents on your Web site that will be printed on your visitors' printers, your needs are best served by Adobe Acrobat.

With Acrobat PDF, the documents will print with fidelity. The layout will be intact, complete with fonts, images, and razor-sharp vector graphics. Printing HTML Web pages, on the other hand, relies on whatever fonts are on the visitors' computers, whereas graphics are limited to low-resolution 72 dpi bitmaps.

The Acrobat Reader can be installed as a Web browser plug-in. This way, your visitors can view Acrobat PDF files without launching the Acrobat Reader separately. So what kinds of documents are Acrobat PDF fodder? A good time to use PDF is when creating:

- Complex reports

- Business forms

- Scientific white papers

- Text with mathematical annotations

- Highly designed marketing material

- Product specification sheets

- Newsletter archives

- Documentation

Creating Adobe Acrobat PDF Files

Acrobat files can begin life in just about any program, from QuarkXPress to Microsoft Excel. Adobe PageMaker 6.5 can create Acrobat PDF files right out of the box. If you're not using PageMaker (or another program capable of creating PDF files directly), you'll need the full version of Adobe Acrobat to create PDFs. The full version of Acrobat will set you back a couple of hundred bucks, whereas the Acrobat Reader is distributed for free. Buying the full version is a small investment that can pay itself back many times over.

The full version of Adobe Acrobat comes with two tools, PDF Writer and Acrobat Distiller, which are used to create Acrobat PDF files.

PDF Writer

PDF Writer is installed in the same manner as a printer driver. When you're ready to create your PDF file, you target and print to PDF Writer as a virtual printer from within the application. This allows you to create PDF files in one step. PDF Writer is intended for the creation of basic PDF files on the fly.

Acrobat Distiller

Acrobat Distiller is a stand-alone application. Unlike PDF Writer, Acrobat Distiller requires a two-step process. First, the original application file is printed to a PostScript file. Then, the PostScript print file must be run through Acrobat Distiller to create the PDF file. Distiller is intended to handle all types of pages, from the simplest to the most complex. It can operate on a file by file basis, or in batch mode.

Implementing Adobe Acrobat In PageMill

To use Acrobat files in PageMill, you should have a copy of the Acrobat plug-in (or the ActiveX Control) installed in PageMill's Browser Plug-ins folder. The Windows Acrobat plug-in is named Nppdf32.dll. The Macintosh Acrobat plug-in is named PDFViewer.

You can implement Adobe Acrobat PDF files in PageMill in three different ways:

- *Linked*—Use this method when you want the PDF file to download as a file. Files downloaded using this method can also be automatically viewed in the external Acrobat Reader, if the browser is set up to use the Reader as a helper application. This method provides the lowest common denominator and is the safest bet for compatibility.

- *Embedded*—Use this method when you want to display a thumbnail version of the PDF file in a Web page. The browser must be configured with Acrobat.

ADOBE ACROBAT WEB RESOURCES

Here's a quick list of online Acrobat resources, from FAQs and Web zines through Acrobat plug-in developers:

- *Acrobat FAQs*—http://www.blueworld.com/acrobat.faq.fcgi

- *Acrobat Talk Mailing List*—http://www.blueworld.com/lists/Acrobat/

- *Adobe Systems*—http://www.adobe.com/prodindex/acrobat/main.html

- *Ambia*—http://www.ambia.com/

- *Emerge PDFZone*—http://www.pdfzone.com/

- *EnFocus*—http://www.enfocus.com/

- *Lantana*—http://lantanarips.com/

- *PurePDF*—http://www.purepdf.com/

- *xman software*—http://www.xman.com/

- *Embedded with ActiveX*—Use this method when you want an Acrobat file to display inside PageMill with the Acrobat ActiveX Reader controls. This method is slick but should be used only when you know that your audience will have the Acrobat ActiveX control installed in their browsers, such as in a controlled intranet setting.

Adobe Acrobat files have a .pdf extension. Begin by moving the Acrobat file into your Web site's root folder.

Linking A PDF File

To link the Acrobat file in the Web page, select Insert|Object|Acrobat File. In the Insert Object dialog box, select the Acrobat file and click on Link To. The name will appear as linked text on the page.

You can also drag and drop to link the PDF file to a graphic or range of text. Select the graphic or text, hold down the Alt key, and then drag the PDF file onto the selection.

Embedding A PDF Thumbnail

To embed the Acrobat file into the Web page, select Insert|Object|Acrobat File. In the Insert Object dialog box, select the Acrobat file and click on Place. The Acrobat Reader will launch (if it's not already running), and a thumbnail preview of the PDF file will appear in PageMill. With the thumbnail selected, you'll need to tweak the Inspector's Object tab. Enter "HREF" in the Name column and the PDF file name in the Value column.

Embedding A PDF File With ActiveX

To embed the Acrobat file into the Web page with ActiveX, select Insert|Object|ActiveX|Select File. In the Insert ActiveX dialog box, select the Acrobat file and click on Insert. The PDF file will appear in PageMill, complete with the Acrobat ActiveX controls. Use the Inspector's Object tab to change the height and width settings.

Moving On

Adobe's focus has long been on extending the functionality of its applications. Right out of the box, Adobe PageMill 3 is a wonderful Web site development tool. With an open interface, PageMill has grown into a customizable page creation engine. Third-party PageMill plugins have turned the program into an even more powerful means of Web site creation. Together with Adobe Acrobat, the world's best solution for cross-platform document delivery, PageMill delivers the goods.

In the appendix that follows, you'll find a host of online Web design resources.

CHECK PAGEMILL'S HELP FILE

PageMill 3's Help file contains an extensive section on using Acrobat files.

APPENDIX:
CD-ROM AND
ONLINE RESOURCES

This appendix has a simple mission: to help you find what you need, whether it's on the PageMill 3 CD-ROM or out on the Internet.

PageMill 3 CD-ROM Goodies

The Adobe PageMill 3 CD-ROM is packed full of goodies. We've pulled together a listing of the JavaScripts and Java applets so that you can quickly identify and locate the files you need without wasting time scouring the CD-ROM.

JavaScripts

The Goodies|JavaScript folder is filled with nifty JavaScripts, courtesy of The JavaScript Source. Here's a list of the JavaScripts organized by type, title, and file name. This is a fairly extensive collection.

Table B.1 Background Effects—Use these color changes and fades with caution.

Background Fade	js_game_bgfader.html
Blinker	js_bgeffect_blink.html
Color Table	js_bgeffect_colortable.html
Continuous Fader	js_bgeffect_cont-fader.html
Link Colors	js_bgeffect_linkcolors.html
Random Background	js_bgeffect_r-bg.html
Random Colors	js_bgeffect_r-colors.html
Random Images	js_bgeffect_r-images.html
Select List Changer	js_bgeffect_list.html
Themed Background Changer	js_bgeffect_themedfade.html

Table B.2 Buttons—Give your visitors pushbuttonitis.

Alert Button	js_button_alertbutton.html
Apologize E-Mail	js_button_apologizemail.html
Directional Buttons	js_button_directions.html
E-Mail Button	js_button_email.html
Pulldown Menu	js_button_gomenu.html
Random Link Generator	js_button_r-link.html
Subject E-Mail	js_button_subjectemail.html
Textarea Alert	js_button_textarea.html
Window Sizer	js_button_windowsizer.html
Your E-Mailer	js_button_emailer.html

Table B.3 Calculators—Crunch crunch crunch those numbers.

Advanced Calculator	js_calculator_advanced.html
Armor Penetration Calculator	js_calculator_armor.html
Atmosphere Calculator	js_calculator_atmosphere.html
Basic Calculator	js_calculator_basic.html
Body Calculator	js_calculator_body.html
Calorie Calculator	js_calculator_calories.html
Driving Distance Calculator	js_calculator_dist-ground.html
GPA Calculator	js_calculator_gpa.html
Human To Dog Years	js_calculator_dogyears.html
Interest Calculator	js_calculator_interest.html
Money Formatter	js_calculator_formatmoney.html
Multiply X By X	js_calculator_xbyx.html
Multiply X By X Calculator	js_calculator_xbyx.html
Radioactive Calculator	js_calculator_radioactive.html
Room Size Calculator	js_calculator_room.html
Scientific Calculator	js_calculator_scientific.html

Table B.4 Calendars—What day did you say that was?

Monthly: Day Hilited	js_calendar_m-dh.html
Monthly: Time - Day Hilited	js_calendar_m-t-dh.html
Monthly: Time - Time Entered - Day Hilited	js_calendar_mt-t-te-dh.html
Quarterly	js_calendar_quarter.html
Year	js_calendar_y.html
Yearly: Day Hilited	js_calendar_y-dh.html
Yearly: Day Links - Day Hilited	js_calendar_y-daylink-dh.html

Table B.5 Clocks—What time is it?

Clock Formats	js_clock_formats.html
Count Up & Down	js_clock_countup-down.html
Current Date	js_clock_currentdate.html
Current Date & Time	js_clock_datetime.html
Current Time	js_clock_basic.html
On/Off Clock	js_clock_on-off.html
Time Till 2000	js_clock_till2000.html

(continued on page 216)

Table B.5 Clocks *(continued from page 215)*.

| Time Till XXXX | js_clock_timetilltime.html |
| World Times | js_clock_worldtimes.html |

Table B.6 Cookies—Yum yum, eat 'em up!

Favorite Background Color	js_cookie_favoritebg.html
Name - Browser Info	js_cookie_n-browser.html
Name - Visits - Last Visit	js_cookie_n-v-lv-alert.html
Name - Visits - Message	js_cookie_v-msg.html
User Name	js_cookie_n.html
Visits	js_cookie_v.html

Table B.7 Equivalents—Throw out that book of conversions.

Acceleration Equivalents	js_equiv_acceleration.html
Area Equivalents	js_equiv_area.html
Energy Equivalents	js_equiv_energy.html
Length Equivalents	js_equiv_length.html
Mass Equivalents	js_equiv_mass.html
Metrology Equivalents	js_equiv_metrology.html
Pressure Equivalents	js_equiv_pressure.html
Programming Equivalents	js_equiv_programming.html
Velocity Equivalents	js_equiv_velocity.html

Table B.8 Forms—Extracting information from your visitors is more fun than pulling teeth.

Check E-Mail	js_form_check-email.html
Customized Window	js_form_openwindow.html
Date Validation	js_form_datevalidation.html
Form Validation	js_form_val-cookie.html
Guestbook Validation	js_form_val-guestbook.html
Information Validation	js_form_val-info.html
Initial Caps	js_form_caps.html
Items List	js_form_itemslist.html
Mail - Pick Subject	js_form_mail-picksub.html
Mailing List	js_form_mailinglist.html

(continued on page 217)

Table B.8 Forms *(continued from page 216).*

No Entry	js_form_noentry.html
No HTML	js_form_nohtml.html
Scratch Pad	js_form_scratchpad.html
Selection Validation	js_form_val-selection.html
Smut Engine	js_form_smutengine.html
Suggestions	js_form_suggestions.html
Validation	js_form_val.html

Table B.9 Games—What, you don't you have anything better to do?

Agecounter	js_game_agecounter.html
Background Fader	js_game_bgfader.html
Blackjack	js_game_blackjack.html
Buzzwords	js_game_buzzwords.html
CheckBoxes	js_game_checkboxes.html
Countdown	js_game_countdown.html
Countup	js_game_countup.html
Cows	js_game_cow.html
CurseBot	js_game_curse.html
Do the Feds Know You?	js_game_whereborn.html
Find The Spy	js_game_spy.html
Flipping Messages	js_game_flipper.html
Guess 1 - 100	js_game_guess-1-100.html
Guess-A-Number	js_game_guess-random.html
Hit The Dot	js_game_hitthedot.html
Insight Generator	js_game_insightgenerator.html
Magic 8 Ball	js_game_magic8.html
R-G-B Background Changer	js_game_bgchanger.html
Random Number	js_game_randomnumber.html
Reaction - Background	js_game_react-bg.html
Reaction - Button	js_game_react-button.html
Tic-Tac-Toe	js_game_tictactoe.html
Towers Of Hanoi	js_game_towersofhanoi.html
Who? What? Where?	js_game_question.html

Table B.10 Messages—Say what?

Alert	js_msg_alert.html
Alert & Confirm	js_msg_confirm-alert.html
Information Box	js_msg_infobox.html
Link Message	js_msg_link.html
Name Alert	js_msg_namealert.html
Name Write	js_msg_namewrite.html
Random Computer Puns	js_msg_rqt-comp.html
Random Life Quotes	js_msg_rqt-life.html
Random Murphy's Laws	js_msg_rqt-murphy.html
Random Puns	js_msg_rqt-puns.html
Random Quips	js_msg_rqt-funny.html
Random Sentence	js_msg_sentence.html
Time Message	js_msg_timemsg.html

Table B.11 Miscellaneous—A haberdashery of JavaScripts.

Born Which Day?	js_misc_born-weekday.html
Browser Check	js_misc_browser-check.html
Browser Details	js_misc_browser.html
Character Table	js_misc_charactertable.html
Daily Redirection	js_misc_dailyredirection.html
Directory	js_misc_directory.html
French Translator	js_misc_translator.html
HTML Builder	js_misc_htmlbuilder.html
Madlib - Caesar	js_misc_madlib-caesar.html
Madlib	js_misc_madlib-unknown.html
Midi Player	js_misc_midiplayer.html
onLoad / onUnload Alerts	js_misc_unloadalert.html
Plugins Alert	js_misc_checkplugins.html
Plugins Table	js_misc_checkmimes.html
Random Number Picker	js_misc_r-numbers.html
Refresh	js_misc_refresh.html
Search Engine	js_misc_search.html
Stopwatch	js_misc_stopwatch.html
User Quiz	js_misc_userquiz.html
Virus Scare	js_misc_virus.html

Table B.12 Navigational Scripts—You *can* get there from here.

Age Redirection	js_navig_ageredirect.html
Automatic Menu List	js_navig_menu-automatic.html
Menu List	js_navig_menu.html

Table B.13 Page Details—Build smart pages.

Break Frames	js_page_breakframes.html
Fake Page Counter	js_page_fakepagecounter.html
Last Modified	js_page_lastmodified.html
Page Born On Date	js_page_bornondate.html
Page Up For	js_page_puf_longdate.html
Page Viewed At	js_page_pageviewedat.html
Rotating Banners	js_page_rotatingbanners.html
Stamp - Date & Time	js_page_stamp-datetime.html
Time Entered	js_page_timeentered.html
Time On Page - Alert	js_page_top-alert.html
Time On Page - Clock	js_page_top-clock.html
Time On Page - Seconds	js_page_top-seconds.html

Table B.14 Password Protection—Can't use a CGI? Keep the door locked with these JavaScripts.

Cookie Protection	js_pass_cookie.html
Gatekeeper	js_pass_gatekeep.html
Password Prompt	js_pass_prompt.html
Three Tries	js_pass_tries-three.html

Table B.15 Scrolls—Perfect for the stock ticker on the Amalgamated Lint Corporation's home page.

Classic Scroll	js_scroll_classic.html
Editor	js_scroll_editor.html
Flasher	js_scroll_flasher.html
Textbox	js_scroll_textbox.html
Write And Slide	js_scroll_writeandslide.html

Table B.16 User Details—We know where you live, dude.

Browser Details	js_user_browser-details.html
Browser Name	js_user_browser-name.html
Browser Redirection	js_user_browser-entry.html
Browser Specific Entry	js_user_browser-entry.html
Browser Version	js_user_browser-version.html
History Length	js_user_historylength.html
IP Address	js_user_ipaddress.html
Plugins Alert	js_user_plugins-alert.html
Referrer	js_user_referrer.html
Screen Size	js_user_screendetails.html
User Plug-ins	js_user_plugins.html
Visitor Monitor	js_user_visitormonitor.html

Need more? You'll find a bunch of JavaScripts created by Michael P. Scholtis in the Goodies|JavaScript|stock folder.

Table B.17 Assorted Scripts—This collection adds more than 20 scripts to your repertoire.

Background Color Fade	bgcolorfade.html
Calculator	calculator.html
Equation Handler	calculator2.html
Calendar	calendar.html
Calendar (German)	calendar3.html
Confirmed Entry	checkedentry.html
Clock	clock.html
Confirm Dialog	confirmdialog.html
Don't Click Here	dontclik.html
Order Form	hyperform.html
JavaScript Test	jstest.html
Load Alert I	oadalert.html
NamePrompt	nameprompt.html
onmouseover	onmouseover.html
Pull Down Menu	pdmenu.html
Pull Down Menu (Version 4.0)	pdmenu4.html
Form Picture Button	picforbutton.html

(continued on page 221)

Table B.17 Assorted Scripts *(continued from page 220)*.

Rainbow Text	rainbow.html
Remote Window	remote.html
Remote Window 2	remote2.html
Scroll It (in Status Bar)	scrollit.html
Scrolling Text	ticker.html
Timers (Up and Down)	timer.html

Java Applets

Fabio Ciucci's special effect Java Applets can be found in the Goodies|Java folder. Each applet is stored in its own folder, along with supporting files.

Table B.18 Effects—Cool animation effects.

Anfy Banners	Banners.class, BannersMsg.class
Anfy Blobs	blob.class, blobs.class, Lware.class
Anfy Blur	anblur.class, Lware.class
Anfy Cfade	AnFade.class, Lware.class
Anfy Deform	Deform.class, Lware.class
Anfy Fire	fire.class, Lware.class
Anfy Flag	AnFlag.class, Lware.class
Anfy Fluid	fluid.class, Lware.class
Anfy Lens	AnLens.class, Lware.class
Anfy Life2d	life2d.class, Lware.class
Anfy Mandel	mandel.class, Lware.class
Anfy Plasma	Plasma3.class, Lware.class
Anfy Rotator	Rot2.class, Lware.class
Anfy Tmap Cube	TmapCube.class, Lware.class
Anfy Tunnel	tunnel.class, Lware.class
Anfy Voxel	voxel.class, Lware.class
Anfy Warp	warp.class, Lware.class
Anfy Water	AnWater.class, Lware.class
Anfy WormHole	wormhole.class, Lware.class

Internet Resources

JavaScript

Table B.19   JavaScripts Online—If you can't find what you need on the PageMill disk, these Web sites deliver the goods.

24 Hour Javascripts.com	http://www.javascripts.com/
Charity Kahn - BUILDER.COM	http://www.cnet.com/Content/Builder/Programming/Kahn/
developer.com JavaScript Directory	http://www.developer.com/directories/pages/
	dir.javascript.jsutil.ui.html
Doc JavaScript	http://webreference.internet.com/js/
JavaScript Source	http://javascriptsource.com/
JavaScript Tip of the Week Archive	http://www.webreference.com/javascript/
Matt's Script Archive	http://www.worldwidemart.com/scripts/
Netscape DevEdge Online Library	http://developer.netscape.com/library/examples/index.html
PageSplitter	http://www.pagesplitter.com/
Project Cool's JavaScript Developer Zone	http://www.projectcool.com/developer/javascript/
Ross Online	http://www.anweb.com/ross/
So You Want JavaScript?	http://neil.simplenet.com/javascript/
The JavasCrypt	http://www.geocities.com/~qarnos/
WebCoder.com	http://www.webcoder.com/index_real.html
Webmonkey JavaScript Tutorial	http://www.hotwired.com/webmonkey/98/03/index0a.html

Java

Table B.20   Java Online—Piping hot links to the best Java applets the Web has to offer.

100% Pure Java Applications	http://java.sun.com/100percent/latestlist.html
Applet Orchard	http://amadeus.ccs.queensu.ca/orchard/
AUSCOMP	http://www.auscomp.com/
Chris Cobb's "Obligatory" Applets	http://www.ccobb.org/
Cool Tool of the Day: Java	http://www.cooltool.com/java.html
EarthWeb's JARS.COM	http://www.jars.com/
electric butterfly online	http://www.ebutterfly.com/
Feeder - Scrolling Text	http://pw2.netcom.com/~sanjayd/java/scroller
	scroller_index.html
Formula Graphics	http://www.formulagraphics.com/
FreeCode	http://www.freecode.com/

(continued on page 223)

Table B.20 Java Online *(continued from page 222)*.

Gamelan	http://www.developer.com/directories/pages/dir.java.html/
Mainstay PageCharmer	http://www.mstay.com/target.html
Modern Minds	http://www.modernminds.com/
PictureWebPageBuilder	http://www.markwatson.com/
PineappleSoft	http://www.pineapplesoft.com/
SGI Cool Freeware Java Gallery	http://www.sgi.com/Fun/free/java-apps.html
TechWeb Tech Tools - Java Applets	http://www.techweb.com/tools/downloads/javaapp.html
The Coffee Grinder	http://www.trevorharmon.com/coffeegrinder/
The Java Boutique	http://javaboutique.internet.com/
Webmonkey: Java Collection	http://www.hotwired.com/webmonkey/java/
ZDNet Java Downloads	http://www.zdnet.com/pccomp/1001dl/html/category/webpub
	java.html

GIF Animation

Table B.21 GIF Animation Online—Check out these Web sites for thousands of animations, as well as great tools and tutorials.

Animagic	http://rtlsoft.com/animagic/
Animated Gif Artists Guild	http://www.agag.com/
Animation Zone	http://www.animationzone.com/
The Animation Factory	http://www.eclipsed.com/
GifBuilder	http://iawww.epfl.ch/Staff/Yves.Piguet/clip2gif-home/GifBuilder.html
Mars Hotel	http://www.themarshotel.com/
Warner Brothers Animation	http://www.wbanimation.com/
Web GraFX-FX	http://www.webgrafx-fx.com/

Graphics

Table B.22 Graphics Online—Gain access to scores of buttons, backgrounds, icons, and other cool graphics.

Andy's Art Attack	http://www.andyart.com
Background Generator	http://crystal.palace.net/~dprust/Applications/Bax/
Debbie's Background and Button Bonanza	http://www.grafxfactory.com/debbie/
Digit Mania	http://www.digitmania.holowww.com/
Gif Split	http://www.jbarchuk.com/gifsplit/
IconBAZAAR	http://www.iconbazaar.com/
ICONCITY	http://www.yoink.com/iconcity/

(continued on page 224)

Table B.22 Graphics Online *(continued from page 223)*.

i-us.com	http://www.i-us.com/
Online Logo Generator	http://www.cooltext.com/
ShoeString's PictureDicer	http://www.ziplink.net/~shoestring/dicer01.htm
StockObjects	http://www.stockobjects.com/
The Black Art of Preloading	http://www.webreview.com/97/10/17/feature/index.html
The Plug-in Head	http://pluginhead.i-us.com
The Plug-in Party	http://pluginparty.i-us.com
Zyris	http://www.zyris.com/

Shockwave

Table B.23 Shockwave Online—Get shocked!

Bezerk	http://www.bezerk.com/
Ezone Tremors	http://www.ezone.com/tremors/
Game Downer Shockwave Page	http://www.starcreations.com/gamedowner/ga-shock.htm
Headbone Zone	http://hbz.yahooligans.com/zone/shock_games.html
Intellimedia Bag 'o Tricks	http://www.intellimedia.com/bag/index.html
Macromedia ShockRave	http://www.shockrave.com/
Macromedia Shockwave Epicenter	http://www.macromedia.com/shockwave/
Macromedia Shockzone	http://www.macromedia.com/shockzone/
Mama's Shockwave Salon	http://www.eat.com/shockwave-salon/
Pop Rocket's Game Arena	http://www.poprocket.com/shockwave/
Shock-Bauble Showcase	http://www.adveract.com/abtboble.htm
The ShockeR List	http://www.shocker.com/shocker/

Sound And Music

Table B.24   Sound and Music Online —Does music calm a savage Web surfer?

Sound newsgroups	alt.binaries.sounds.cartoons
	alt.binaries.sounds.misc
	alt.binaries.sounds.midi
	alt.binaries.sounds.mods
	alt.binaries.sounds.movies
	alt.binaries.sounds.music
	alt.binaries.sounds.tv
	alt.binaries.sounds.utilities
Classical MIDI Archives	http://prs.net/midi.html
Digital Kitchen	http://www.dkitchen.com/
ifni MIDI archive	http://www.ifni.com/midi/
MIDI Farm	http://www.midifarm.com/files/
MIDI Jazz Network	http://miso.wwa.com/~blewis/
MIDIWORLD	http://midiworld.com/
Res Rocket	http://www.resrocket.com/
Sampleheads	http://www.sampleheads.com/
Sound Ring	http://www.nidlink.com/~ruger/ring.html
The Daily .WAV	http://www.dailywav.com/
The Ultra-Lounge	http://www.ultralounge.com/
Voice Crystal	http://www.voicecrystal.com/
Web Thumper's MIDI Page	http://www.webthumper.com/midi/
Woo-hoo! It's Homer!	http://home.eznet.net/~davlin/homer.htm

INDEX

A

Acrobat, 20, 210
    creating PDF files, 210
    Distiller, 211
    embedding a thumbnail, 212
    embedding with ActiveX, 212
    implementing in PageMill, 211
    linking a PDF file, 212
    PDF Writer, 211
ActiveX, 21, 136, 212
Address text format, 27
Adobe
    Acrobat, 20, 210
    FrameMaker, 182
    PageMaker, 24
    Photoshop, 56
    Photoshop LE, 49
    Premiere, 153
    SiteMill, 169
    Zapf Dingbats, 66
Afterburner utility, 146
Alignment, 40
    captions, 87
    graphics, 58
    tables, 80, 87
    text, 31
AltaVista, 153
Alternate Label, 57
Anarchie, 179
Anchors, 35
    frames, 101
    links, 44
Animations, 130
    buttons, 135
    client pulls, 130
    GIF89a, 131-35
    interactive vector, 146
    JavaScript, 139-43
    looped animations, 132
    QuickTime movies, 152
    server push, 129
    tips for using GIF89a files, 132
    Shockwave, 143-49

Apache HTTP Server, 15
Apple Personal Web Sharing, 15
AppleScript, 120
Applets, 21, 114. *See also* Java.
    buttons, 135
    creating with Interleaf Jamba, 136
    forms, 127
    list of builders, 138
ArchitextSpider (Excite), 153
ASCII transfer, 178
Assisted URL entry, 35
Astound Dynamite, 141
Astrobyte LLC, 184
Audience analysis, 3
Authorware, 146
Automated robots, 153

B

Background
    custom, 49
    full page images, 53
    frames, 98
    images, 49
    picking out, 53
    removing, 50
    seamless tiles, 53
    selecting color, 50
    setting, 50
    setting an image, 70
    speeding up loading, 54
    tables, 80
    tiling, 51
    Web sites, 54
Background images, 21, 49
    folders, 22
Banners, 135
Bare Bones Software, 185
Base
    font, 22
    target, 22
Bazaar Analyzer Pro, 164
BBEdit, 185
BeanMachine, 127, 138

Now the **best tools** for Windows and Macintosh multimedia are also the **best for JAVA!**

The Director of Your Dreams

Create interactive applications for delivery over the Web and on CD-ROM, hybrid CD, and DVD-ROM using the popular and powerful **DIRECTOR®6 MULTIMEDIA STUDIO™** and Macromedia® Shockwave™.

Develop interactive, animated sales and marketing presentations, informational kiosks, educational and entertainment titles, training tutorials, and promotional web games that keep your audience coming back for more.

Now the most powerful cross-platform multimedia tool is also the most powerful Java multimedia tool. Play back your Director files as Java applets with the new Director Export Xtra for Java.

Web Multimedia in a Flash

If you want to create winning animations or integrate existing graphics into your HTML web pages, you can do it all with Macromedia **FLASH 2**.

Use Flash to create animated, interactive advertising banners, navigation buttons, logos, technical illustrations, cartoons, and more. The compact Shockwave Flash player makes it a snap for everyone on the Web to view your creations. Flash files stream (play as they download), so your content immediately appears in Web browsers, even over slower modem connections.

Flash has always been the easiest way to create fast web animations for Windows and Macintosh. Now it's the easiest for Java, too, with the new Flash Player for Java.

For more information, visit http://www.macromedia.com/software/director or http://www.macromedia.com/software/flash.

To purchase, visit http://www.macromall.com or your favorite reseller or call 800 457 1774.

macromedia®

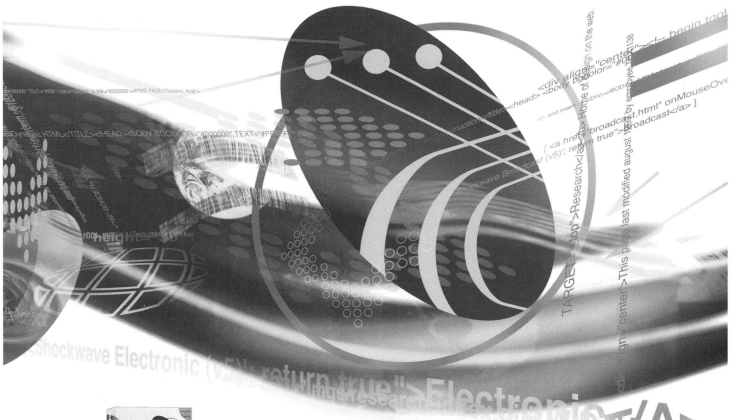

Discover the Design Tool of Your Dreams!

macromedia
DREAMWEAVER™
The Visual Tool for Professional Web Site Design

For the first time, you can take advantage of the productivity offered by a visual HTML development environment without giving up any control over source code.

Dreamweaver™ features error-free Roundtrip HTML™ between visual mode and source editors, absolute positioning, cascading style sheets, a Dynamic HTML animation timeline, an extensible JavaScript behavior library, drag-and-drop table and frame design, and a repeating elements library for managing sitewide changes.

Dreamweaver integrates with your favorite HTML editor, assuring code integrity, flexibility, and access. Only Dreamweaver provides simultaneous WYSIWYG and HTML source editing.

Now you can use HTML layers, an animation timeline, and a library of multimedia JavaScript behaviors to create multimedia content without scripting. You can even extend the user interface with your own JavaScript behaviors.

Site management features include style sheets, FTP for remote sites, file locking for collaborative development, and browser targeting reports.

Get all this in one professional package with Macromedia Dreamweaver!

For more information, visit **http://www.macromedia.com/ software/dreamweaver** or call **800 457 1774.**

macromedia®

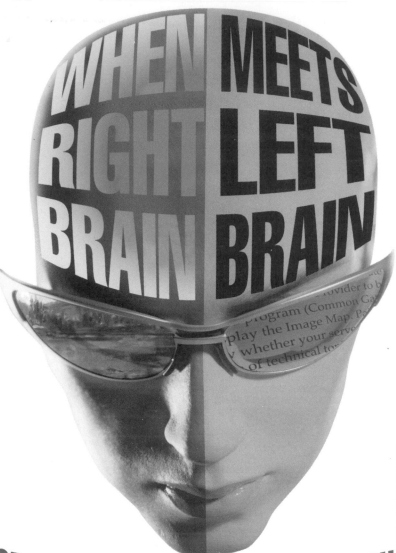

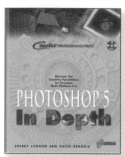

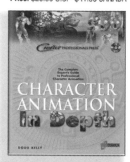